THE LIVELIHOOD
OF MAN

This is a volume in

STUDIES IN SOCIAL DISCONTINUITY

A complete list of titles in this series appears at the end of this volume.

THE LIVELIHOOD OF MAN

KARL POLANYI

Edited by

HARRY W. PEARSON

Bennington College
Bennington, Vermont

ACADEMIC PRESS New York San Francisco London 1977

A Subsidiary of Harcourt Brace Jovanovich, Publishers

ACADEMIC PRESS, INC.
111 Fifth Avenue, New York, New York 10003

United Kingdom Edition published by
ACADEMIC PRESS, INC. (LONDON) LTD.
24/28 Oval Road, London NW1

Library of Congress Cataloging in Publication Data

Polanyi, Karl, 1886–1964.
    The livelihood of man.

    (Studies in social discontinuity)
    Includes bibliographical references and index.
        1.   Economic history.   2.   Economics, Primitive.
3.   Economics.   I.   Pearson, Harry W.   II.   Title.
III.   Series.
HC31.P59   1977   330'.9   76-52734
ISBN 0—12—548150—0

For Charlie, George, and Rosemary
with whom it all began.

Contents

3 Forms of Integration and Supporting Structures

B. *Institutions*
The Emergence of Economic Transactions: From Tribal to Archaic Society

4 The Economy Embedded in Society

5 The Emergence of Economic Transactions

6 Equivalencies in Archaic Societies

7 The Economic Role of Justice, Law, and Freedom

The Catallactic Triad: Trade, Money, and Markets

Introduction

II TRADE, MARKETS, AND MONEY IN ANCIENT GREECE

11 The Hesiodic Age: Tribal Decay and Peasant Livelihood

12 Local Markets: The Political Economy of *Polis* and *Agora*

Karl Polanyi: Notes on His Life

If I were to evoke the image of Karl Polanyi in a single word, it would be one that was not infrequently in his mind—the *skandalon*, the block of offense, *der Stein des Anstosses*. For throughout his life he went counter to encrusted notions, relentlessly shaking people into some new awareness—as the fiery young orator in his days of the Galilei Circle;[1] in his apparent withdrawal in early manhood; in his novel approaches to the social sciences in the late decades of his life. "All his life a socialist," his daughter wrote about him in a memoir, "he was never associated with any political party. Nor did he participate in any political movement. Never doctrinaire, he many times cut across the main trends of debate within the socialist movements of Europe. Although not a Marxist, he was much less a Social Democrat. Although a humanist, he was eminently a realist. Although aware of the reality of society, and the constraints which this reality places upon the action, values, and ideas of all of us who inescapably live in society, his life was guided by an inner necessity to exercise

---

[1] The Galilei Circle, formed in 1908 with Polanyi as its first president, was made up of progressive students at the University of Budapest. Ilona Duczynska has on another occasion described its motif in these terms: "Let it be free in spirit, let it keep away from party politics, let it be dedicated, decent, let it appeal to the students who live in poverty in their thousands. Let it be a movement aiming to learn and to teach." Its mission: "To mobilize against clericalism, corruption, against the privileged, against bureaucracy—against that morass ever-present and pervasive in this semi-feudal country!"—Ed.

freedom of action and thought and never to give in to determinism or fatalism."[2]

I first met Karl Polanyi in November 1920, in Austria, where both he and I lived in exile. What I have written for another occasion[3] on his family chronicle, his childhood memories, the personalities of his parents, the moral impact which the Russian revolutionary emigration at the beginning of the century had on him in his early youth (through his fatherly friend Samuel Klatschko), all related to Polanyi's memories as they cropped up time and time again during our 40 years of marriage.

The Karl Polanyi of the Galilei Circle I had not known. Not merely on account of a ten years' age difference between us—rather, because there was a difference in the age. That newer age—mine—allowed no other argument than revolutionary action, nor did it use any other. Between the small group of activists to which I belonged in 1917–1919 and the group of the "former Galileists" there was no common ground.

Indeed, only in our declining years, in 1963 at Budapest, among Polanyi's contemporaries, was I, too, touched by some of that radiance of the Galilei Circle, reflected back over the half century.

More incisive still, for they provided a more vivid image of the young Polanyi as it remained imprinted on my mind, were the words of two of his close friends and fellow Galileists, Zsigmond Kende and Maurice Korach: "He had the makings of a prophet, and felt himself to be an anachronism. So he was, in 1911. But not in the years to come." Thus Kende.

"He was a genius, rhapsodic in his world of thought. He saw far into the future. He has foreseen problems of late emergence in the fields of sociology, of the theory of knowledge. He was not made for giving continuous, political lead. The moral impact he had on the young people was the essential thing—the honesty, veracity and candor. The young ones felt it. He was the fountainhead of the moral climate of the Galilei Circle. Never cold or superior—yet his argu-

[2] Karl Levitt: "Karl Polanyi and Co-Existence," Co-Existence: No. 2, 1964.

[3] Ilona Duczynska: Karl Polanyi (1886–1964)—A family chronicle and a short account of his life (in Hungarian).

ments had a cutting edge. He was the man for us, our hearts were with him." These were Korach's words.

In front of me I have a few sheets of paper, yellowed and crumbling, written over in Polanyi's bold hand, and preserved by the whims of chance, though not the beginning of the writing, nor its end. A mere chip off the block of offense.

> There was a time, when the godless, the atheists were called freethinkers. We have long since overcome that stage. Also among atheists there can be found plenty of narrow-minded, shiftless people, petty-bourgeois in their mentality, who should be regarded as anything rather than freethinkers—while the religious bent may make man fit for the most daring revolt of the spirit, and among those who died in the cause of free thought, the foremost place will ever be held by Jesus from the town of Nazareth.
>
> By freedom of the spirit we do not mean a denial of truth, nor of ethics, law or authority.
>
> On the contrary, we mean that freedom of the spirit will relentlessly seek truth, abide by the dictates of ethics, act according to the law and respect authority. Relentlessly and consistently. Not calling retreat before any consideration whatsoever, and rousing the human disposition out of its somnolence into ever alert watchfulness. Searching for truth behind and in the face of all and every kind of class-truth and race-truth; following the path of a pure ethic, despite the cut-and-dried precepts of the "moralists," and beyond those; taking its stand on the foundations of justice, even in defiance of the law, and bowing but to the authority of goodness and truth, turning against all phony authority that rests on debauched success and on the display of power.
>
> To search, then, for truth, and where the taboos of tradition bar the way, to act by the postulates of ethics, even if this is decried by the compromisers and opportunists as "super-idealism," as a show of "juvenileism," as "Donquixotery" or simply as being green and immature. To stand for justice, even against the law and to erect an altar to the authority of the heroes of goodness and truth on the ruins of the authority of conventions, cynicism, ignorance and the soul's torpidity.[4]

Continuous political leadership did not, and in fact could not emerge. Four decades later Polanyi wrote to his lifelong close friend Oscar Jászi a letter[5] which is perhaps the most revealing and most authentic document of the course of his life.

[4] Manuscript in Ilona Duczynska's possession.
[5] Karl Polanyi's letter to Oscar Jászi, 27th October, 1950, in Ilona Duczynska's possession.

In the ethical field the Galilei Circle was a creative success. Probably for the first time since 1848 did the student masses come to know of moral *engagement,* and did put it into practice in their personal lives. But politically my omission was past remedy . . . . It was due to the Galilei Circle's failing that there was not available in 1918 a generation, welded in one with the peasantry and with the national minorities in long-standing, stern battles. . . . Whose responsibility? Mine. I had been leading the Circle in an anti-political direction. Neither with the working class, nor with the peasantry, nor with the national minorities did I try to achieve, or even seek some unity based on action. . . . I have never been a politician, I had no talent that way, no interest even.

The letter was written in 1950, at a high point of Polanyi's teaching and research in the social sciences, in economic history. In retrospect he gives bitter judgment on the lack of realism he displayed in the preceding decades of his life "which in the theoretical as in the practical field condemned me to futility. From 1909 to 1935 I achieved nothing. I strained my powers in the futile directions of stark idealism, its soarings lost in the void."

In this overarching self-accusation the first intimations of developments in his later life-work—scattered, yet seminal—are necessarily lost to sight.

Such was the new turning towards socialism on a theoretical level in 1922, in the study "Sozialistische Rechnungslegung"[6] (Socialist Accountancy), at a time when bourgeois economists were assiduously proving the impossibility of socialist economic organization and of socialist accountancy and the counterarguments had nothing better to point to than the experiences of war communism in Soviet Russia. Needless to say, it drew fire from both sides;[7] its underlying considerations may not be without interest even today, or perhaps more particularly today.

Such, again, was, in the late 1920s, his sympathizing attitude towards socialism in the Soviet Union in its groping for solutions in

---

[6] Karl Polanyi, "Sozialistische Rechnungslegung," *Archiv für Sozialwissenschaft und Sozialpolitik,* Band 49, Heft 2, 1922.

[7] L. von Mises, "Neue Beitrage zum Problem der sozialistischen Wirtschafts rechnung," *Archiv für Sozialwissenschaft und Sozialpolitik,* Band 1, Heft 2. F. Weil, "Gildeneozialistische Rechnungslegung," *Archiv, op. cit.,* Band 52, Heft 1, 1924, K. Polanyi, "Die funktionelle Theorie der Gesellschaft und das Problem der sozialistischen Rechnungslegung, Eine Erwiderung." *Archiv, op. cit.,* Band 52, Heft 1, 1924.

the economic and theoretical field; such his deep solidarity with the proletariat of Vienna.

Political realism also made its appearance. He wrote to the editors of the Budapest *Láthatár (Horizon):*[8]

> You are right, belief in democracy is needed above all things. Today this is not enough. Take a leaf out of the reactionaries' book. They always go with the times. If democracy is true—and it is—do not balk at criticism. The mistakes of the past must be relentlessly shown up. And if its main mistake was to have been walking in the clouds, disdaining reality—then take bearings on reality. . . . An abstract idea of democracy which loftily disregarded the reality of class-structure, religion, war, violence, deserved the fate of being discounted by the realities.

In the same period, the late 1920s, Polanyi formulated for the first time his philosophical criticism of the contemporary religions as well as of contemporary socialism, in a manuscript "Ueber die Freiheit" (On Freedom)[9] which fell into oblivion. Here the transcending of the individual Christian ethic, the reality of society, society's final and inescapable nature ("die Unaufhebbarkeit der Gesellschaft"), and the awareness of this inescapability are given form—insights which were to become the cornerstones of Polanyi's future life-work and of his philosophy of life.

Emigration to England in the mid-1930s indeed brought a turning point in Polanyi's life. He found there a circle of kindred spirits and eminent scholars who combined their Christian outlook with an enthusiastic sympathy, one might say, an uncritical sympathy towards the Soviet Union. The outcome of their combined efforts was the symposium *Christianity and the Social Revolution.*[10]

But stronger in its shaping power than any intellectual influence was the trauma which is England. The meeting with full-fledged capitalism—of which we had imagined that we knew all that is worth knowing. But the houses which Engels had described were still

---

[8] Karl Polanyi, "Concerning the aims of Hungarian democracy" (in Hungarian), *A Láthatár,* March-April 1927.

[9] Manuscript in Ilona Duczynska's possession.

[10] Donald Kitchen and Karl Polanyi (eds.), *Christianity and the Social Revolution* (London, 1935; Left Book Club edition, 1937).

standing; people lived in them. Black hills of slag stood in the green
landscape of Wales, and from the depressed areas youngsters who
had never yet seen their parents employed drifted to London.

Adult education in the Tutorial Classes organized by the Workers' Educational Association and the Extramural Delegacies of the
Universities of Oxford and of London brought Polanyi into contact
with every stratum and shade of the British working class, in terms of
life and experience. He was teaching and he was learning. The
classes he held once a week each were in small towns and villages of
Kent and Sussex. There was plenty of opportunity to come to know
each other, especially as it was too late to return at night and the tutor
would find hospitality at the house of one or the other of his students.

Hand in hand with love for his students came to Polanyi the
hatred of the classical species of class society in its classical homeland. He was teaching economic history, the history of early
capitalism in England. And he collected the memories in which his
students, by way of oral tradition in their families, were richly
endowed. The memory of Blake's "dark, satanic mills" lived on
through the generations, and the British working class even after its
economic rise and in spite of it still bore the stigma of the crippling
event of its inception.

It is given to the best among men somewhere to let down the
roots of a sacred hate in the course of their lives. This happened to
Polanyi in England. At later stages, in the United States, it merely
grew in intensity. His hatred was directed against market society and
its effects, which divested man of his human shape.

"I was fifty years old" he wrote to Jászi,[11] "when circumstances
in England led me to studies in economic history. I earned my living
that way, as a teacher. For I was born to be one. I little thought then,
that yet another vocation was in store for me and that I was preparing
myself for it. Some three years later, apparently again under the
pressure of circumstances, I wrote a book,[12] once more trying to give
an interpretation of recent history . . . but this time I underpinned
my train of thought with a perspective in economic history."

The perspective of The Great Transformation, its outline, and,
above all, the experiences from which it stemmed, had been shaped

---

[11] Op. cit.
[12] Karl Polanyi, The Great Transformation (New York: Rinehart and Co., 1944).

by 1940. The book was published in New York in 1944, in London in 1945.

Polanyi, at a sociological congress in England, in 1946 formulated his theses in three points:

> 1. that economic determinism was predominantly a nineteenth century phenomenon, which has now ceased to operate in the greater part of the world; it was effective only under a market system, which is rapidly disappearing in Europe;
> 2. that the market system violently distorted our views on man and society;
> 3. that these distorted views are proving one of the main obstacles to the solution of the problems of our civilization. [13]

At the end of 1946 Polanyi was invited as a Visiting Professor of Economics to Columbia University to read the course in General Economic History.

"The real surprise," he continued in his letter to Jászi,[14] "came to me in the last four years. These four years were spent in the fever of one single uninterrupted work day. The outcome, whether I conclude my book or not, will be an interpretation of the economies of early societies, especially regarding trade, money and market phenomena, which will lay down the foundations for comparative economic history."

After Polanyi retired from his chair in 1953—at the age of 66—research work, with the active participation of his former students and colleagues, was carried on in organized fashion for another five years in the Interdisciplinary Project on the economic aspects of institutional growth. The result of their labors was published in 1957.[15]

The intensive study of eighteenth century Dahomey began at a very early stage, around 1949. It was given its final shape by Polanyi in the winter of 1962 under the title *Dahomey and the Slave Trade*. The book appeared posthumously.

In the later years of his life scholarly effort merged increasingly with the keenest feeling for, and insight into, the predicament of

---

[13] Karl Polanyi, "On belief in economic determinism." *The Sociological Review,* Vol. xxxix, Section One, 1947.

[14] *Op. cit.*

[15] Karl Polanyi, C. M. Arensberg, and H. W. Pearson (eds.), *Trade and Market in the Early Empires* (Glencoe, Ill.: Free Press and Falcon's Wing Press, 1957).

mankind. In a short article entitled "Marginal notes on the turning of
the tide towards socialism" (in Hungarian, written for a periodical
published in the Western world)—it remained unpublished, once
again a chip off the block of offense—he wrote:

> In Western Europe the intellectuals in some diffuse way think that
> the general cooling off of the heat inside the labor movement is an
> indication of socialism's waning topicality, and do not understand that
> it is the horror of atomic poisons, the revolt of the colored peoples, and
> the anarchy in world economics that is the measure of the new world-
> wide trend towards socialism, operating not in the realm of home
> policy, but in that of foreign policy the power of socialism becomes
> apparent in our days from fields of existence to which traditional politi-
> cal concerns are foreign. Out of the spheres of physical geography,
> demography, biology, astronomy emerge those situations and con-
> straints to which we must, and do look for answers coming from a
> planned economy, from a penetration of workers' democracy into pro-
> duction, and from a people's way of life that will consciously stand for
> the aim of mankind's survival.[16]

Even merely to suggest the main lines of Polanyi's researches in
the field of economic history and economic sociology would go
beyond the scope of these loose notes. But it would not be possible to
sketch the course of his life without touching on the fact that the
scholarly work of his later years and the consuming concern for
human destiny stemmed from one and the same root. He passion-
ately opposed an economic sociology that would attempt to foist
upon primitive and archaic economies the concepts of an economic
theory valid inside a market system and nowhere else. To do so, he
held, amounted to hampering the autochthonous development of
the world's nonmarket societies, thereby being instrumental to
neocolonialism and acting in its interests.

In his Columbia lectures Polanyi made *The changing place of
economies in societies* the theme of General Economic History, by
which he indicated from the start that, instead of the "outmoded
chronological accounts of general economic history" he wished to
develop his subject in the direction of economic sociology.

"If in the course of history the economy changes place within the
whole of society, then the question arises of necessity, from where to
where it is so changing its place," Polanyi said in his lecture given in

---

[16] Manuscript in Ilona Duczynska's possession.

1963 in Budapest. An economic history which is to search for the place occupied by the economy in society in a truly universal perspective cannot make use of a limited-scope economic sociology that is built entirely on the concept of "exchange," since

> The phenomenon of exchange is universal only in a market-society . . . . Socialism, for instance, today is in need precisely of that kind of widening of experiences and perspectives, which have a bearing on these areas where the frontiers of market-economy and market-less economy meet. Now, it would be capitalism seeing itself constrained to introduce elements of planning into its over-marketized realm, now, again, socialism would be considering enhancing its achievements in economic planning by the introduction of certain market elements. In the underdeveloped world, as well as among the new nations, market elements and non-market elements are contesting with each other. Socialism should all along take heed with the utmost open-mindedness of the sociologically modernized versions of economic history.[17]

His visit to Budapest, in 1963, a homecoming, in the knowledge of the deadly turn his illness was taking, was the fulfillment of his life: ". . . in the years of the crisis which is endangering all mankind, I have fully turned towards socialism, which is no longer merely the cause of the working class, but a matter of life and death for all humanity. In this no small part is due to my Hungarian homeland. My viewpoints now are wholly centered on my homeland, to which one whose youth was shaped by the Magyar fate owes all and everything," he wrote in his message to the new Hungary of young writers, poets, and scholars.[18]

The last decade of his life, the breathless scholarly work carried out in the small Canadian house on a woodlot above the river bend, the feel of life opening wide towards the world of man are perhaps most closely reflected in the fragment of a backwards-and-forwards looking letter Polanyi wrote in 1958 to the love of his early youth, Bé de Waard:

[17] Karl Polanyi, "Economic sociology in the United States," Lecture given at the Institute for Cultural Relations, Budapest, Oct. 9, 1963.
[18] Karl Polanyi, "Our Homeland's Duty" (in Hungarian), Kortárs, December 1963.

My life was a "world" life—I lived the life of the human world. But the world has seemed to have stopped living for decades, to catch up a century within a few years. This is how I am only now coming into my own, somewhere on the way I have lost thirty years or so—waiting for Godot—until things were at par again, the world in its course had caught up with me. Looking back, all this seems somehow funny—that martyrdom of isolation was no more than a *mirage*—in truth I was waiting only for myself. Now the dice are cast against us (against you, against me). One more decade—and I would stand vindicated in my lifetime. My work is for Asia, for Africa, for the new peoples. . . . The opposition which my world of thought has called forth at last, is a good sign. I should have loved to last and be in at the fight, but man is a mortal thing.[19]

Karl Polanyi died on the 23rd of April, 1964. He worked to the last evening of his life. Over his coffin lines by Attila József were spoken, lines written to the recondite God he was keeping hidden away, keeping out of all his matters.

> My God, I love you very dearly.
> Were you a newsboy selling sheets,
> I'd help you cry them out in the streets.

Ilona Ducyznska Polanyi
Pickering, Ontario
1970

[19] Karl Polanyi's letter to Bé de Waard, Jan. 6, 1958. Typescript fragment in Ilona Duczynska's possession.

Editor's Preface

It is presumptuous for anyone to edit and publish the unfinished works of another no longer present to protest. It may be out and out a mistake, for how can one put together the unfinished statements, or select from different versions of finished statements and say with assurance that they mean what the author ultimately wanted to say? In the case of Karl Polanyi's manuscripts published here, the doubts were multiplied because almost every one of them existed in several different versions, some mere fragments.

Nonetheless, at Polanyi's death there was the clear outline of a book to be entitled *The Livelihood of Man*. It had a table of contents, more than one version of a preface, an introduction, and Chapters 1 and 4 completed substantially as they appear in this book. Chapters 2, 3, and 8 also existed in different versions, which have been edited here to present the most complete statement on these questions from Polanyi's hand. In addition, there were several chapters on trade, money, and markets in ancient Greece (focusing mainly on Athens), and those most relevant to Polanyi's thesis have been included here as he intended them to appear in the book. The other chapters of the book he planned either had not been written or existed as but fragments of what he intended eventually to complete. There were, in addition, quite extensive lecture notes for the courses he taught at Columbia over the years 1947–1953, and the subject matter of many of these was the same as that to be covered by *The Livelihood of Man*. For the rest, there were a great many finished and unfinished papers, most of them in several different versions, but all bearing directly on the areas to be covered in the book. Parts of some of these had been put together for publication when an occasion offered, but none of these publications—not even those appearing in *Trade and Market in the Early Empires*—presented the range and the sequence that emerged from the manuscripts.

The first question, of course, was whether to publish at all. There is little doubt, I think, that Polanyi, even had he lived another ten years, would not have published *The Livelihood of Man;* he would not have been able to complete the enormous undertaking he had planned to his satisfaction. After several of us—former students who had become his closest associates—went over all of the manuscripts with that exceptional woman, his devoted wife, Ilona Polanyi, preparatory to depositing them in the special collections section of the Columbia University Library, we decided that it would be irresponsible not to offer this most complete version available of Polanyi's seminal views to the academic community, imperfect and incomplete as the result inevitably would be.

Mrs. Polanyi asked me to undertake the editing task, and it was my decision to attempt to bring the manuscripts together so as to follow as nearly as possible the outlined *Livelihood of Man.* The editing job has mainly been one of cutting and pasting and choosing among alternatives. Otherwise, I have only changed words or phrases in the interest of clarity, consistency, and continuity.

In Part I, Polanyi wrote with no footnotes, and I have supplied those I could find which seemed essential to the text. The footnotes in Part II were supplied mainly by Polanyi, but they required editing and checking as to source, publisher, and the like. In the references to ancient Greek sources, only the originals have been cited because it was not always clear which translation had been used, and Polanyi frequently did his own translation.

As he readily admitted, Polanyi was not an "expert scholar" in all the fields he surveyed, and the experts will surely find much to question and contend with in this book. (Twenty-one three by five file cabinets, crammed full of his notes from hundreds of sources, are nonetheless testimony to the extent and depth of his research over several years.) His principal aim, however, was to open the mind to new conceptions. I hope this book succeeds in that effort. It is Karl Polanyi, as truly as I knew him and can find him in the material I worked with over several years.

My gratitude for assistance in preparation of this manuscript must be expressed, first, to Ilona Polanyi. Her unfailing moral support and encouragement have provided sustaining sources of energy in a difficult task. Thanks must also be expressed for those whose devoted secretarial assistance have quite literally made the book possible: Isabel Sherwood, Margaret Michaelsen, and Laura Nowak. Lastly I owe a debt to this little college on a hill in southwestern Vermont. It has helped, within means, financially, but mostly, it has offered a congenial *place* to work.

Harry W. Pearson
Bennington College
1977

Editor's Introduction

"I should see the garden far better," said Alice to herself, "If I could get to the top of that hill: and here's a path that leads straight to it—at least, no, it doesn't do *that*—" (after going a few yards along the path, and turning several sharp corners), "but I suppose it will at last. But how curiously it twists! It's more like a corkscrew than a path! Well, *this* turn goes to the hill, I suppose—no, it doesn't. *This* goes straight back to the house!

"It's no use talking about it," Alice said, looking up at the house and pretending it was arguing with her. "I'm *not* going in again yet. I know I should have to get through the looking glass again—back into the old room—and there'd be an end of all my adventures!" (Lewis Carroll, *Through the Looking Glass*.)

The problem of locating the economy and analyzing its institutional structure in different societies seems to me not unlike that of Alice's persistent attempts to reach the top of the hill, the better to see the "Garden of Live Flowers." The hill is visible, but all the pathways belong to the Red Queen, the strongest piece on the board, and they all lead back to the familiar house and the other side of the looking glass whence she came.

The Red Queen is the economic theory of classical liberalism, of course, and the familiar house is the market economy of the modern West out of which that theory has developed. By and large, economists in this tradition are not interested in the question, "What is, or where is, the economy in different societies?" Most would probably be ready to extend to the economy the pragmatic view attributed to Jacob Viner regarding economics. If "economics is what economists do,"[1] then the economy is simply whatever economists study. An operational definition of this sort has its advantages. It allows the economist to get on with the problems of efficiency, stability of prices, and growth in the system he is most familiar with without having to keep defining and redefining his universe.

But today a growing legion of social scientists in all of the disciplines are questioning anew the reliability of the orthodox economist's theory in the analysis of economies past and present. Questions about the nature of the economic universe inevitably arise. The argument about the empirical relevance of economic theory goes back a long way, of course, and orthodoxy has had its ups and downs. By the 1950s, however—after the post-Keynesian "synthesis" and the rapid postwar economic recovery—liberal economic theory seemed clearly to have won the day. Its apparent success in policy at home, its hope of developing the "underdeveloped" abroad, plus the weight of a brilliant tradition and the beauty of its formal logic had regained for economic theory its regal position among the social sciences. Anyone who wanted to study the economy anywhere, past, present, or future, looked first to that discipline for his cues.

There were, of course, still the orthodoxies and heterodoxies of the left. But the socialist world was looking inward, and the general "cold war" atmosphere was not one for thinking much about fundamental problems anywhere. It was a time for building and reasserting the power and the truth of systems, and repressing the opposition.

In the late 1970s, we face a radically different situation. Questions and doubts are everywhere. The ever-increasing problems that contemporary economic theory has encountered since the high point of its confidence in the 1950s lead us back to the most fundamental questions about the economy and its functional relation to society. One need not any longer catalogue all the critical problems that policies based on conventional economic theory have failed to resolve

---

[1] See Kenneth Boulding, *Economic Analysis* (New York: Harper and Brothers, 1941), p. 3; and cf. Melville Herskovits, *The Economic Life of Primitive Peoples* (New York: Alfred Knopf, 1940), p. 29.

or even to confront. But it is important to emphasize that these problems are not only the traditional ones of employment, price levels, and growth in the economy, recalcitrant and enigmatic as these are in the 1970s. They are also the much more fundamental problems of the market economy's capacity to meet the generic needs of the society it is supposed to serve. Basic questions of the allocation of resources, and of the total effect of the economic system on the quality of our lives and habitat, are involved. It is the contemporary importance of this functional relation between economy and society, both in theory and policy, in Western and non-Western societies, in industrial as well as nonindustrial economies, that demands we return to a fundamental examination of what we mean and what we want when we speak of the economy and its role in society.

There is no better place to begin such an examination than with the work of Karl Polanyi. Most of Polanyi's writing appearing in this volume was actually done in the 1950s, against the prevailing mood. He was Adjunct Professor of General Economic History at Columbia University (1947–1953), and his writing was done in relation to his courses, the research projects he conceived, and the exhilarating interdisciplinary seminars he conducted. These last continued through the 1950s and brought students and established scholars from many places together for some of the most stimulating and memorable interchanges that any of us are likely ever to have enjoyed.

Polanyi was above all a teacher, and his radically different ideas expounded with boundless enthusiasm struck a responsive cord in the large number of his vaguely troubled and uncertain students at Columbia. Most of us were back from the war, heads still in the depression era, disenchanted with the empty dogmatism of the Marxist line, yet deeply skeptical of the happy facade which the new joining of Mammon and science seemed to offer in the "new economics" and the "end of ideology." It was the radically different quality and the depth of Polanyi's insights that pointed the way for so many students to a new understanding of the social reality behind the facade.

It is in the ferment of the 1970s, however, that his views on economy and society have found their time, stimulating worldwide interest and debate among social scientists seeking a fresh understanding of the transformation taking place during the last two decades between economy and polity, economy and society. Thus the reason for this posthumous volume, which attempts to give his principal concepts and views room to develop between two covers.

The question of "the changing place of the economy in society" was at the center of Polanyi's concern, and he pursued the question with a keen eye over the whole range of man's history. His method was that of the wide-ranging historical scholar, and although he painted with a very broad brush, he has caused a good many authorities in their field to rethink some important questions about the nature and organization of the economy in primitive, ancient, and modern societies and given us all some questions to ponder.

Polanyi's first theoretical concern was with the very meaning of the term, *economy*, and with the confusion resulting from compounding the economist's "formal" definition (derived from the logic of economically rational action) with the older and more common sense notion of the economy as the "substantive" material means-producing sphere in society.

This was not merely a semantic concern. It went to the heart of the problem met by all scholars who wish to study the economy anywhere, at any time in history. If one took his cues from the economic theory of Western liberalism, the question of just what and where economic institutions were—the economy's "place" in society—presented the investigator with an enigma. Here the economy was everywhere and nowhere. Essentially, pure economic theory deals with economizing, an aspect of human action. It thus identifies and logically formalizes a kind of purposive behavior, but that economic aspect of human action has no particular institutional home. As Frank Knight noted in 1958, when asked to write on the most important economic problem facing the United States, ". . . the question has no definite answer. Most problems involve some use of means, hence demand 'economizing,' avoiding waste and futility. Accordingly, economic problems form no distinct class, and any list would be largely arbitrary."[2]

The enigma is resolved for the economist by the rough coincidence between economizing behavior and the real institutional home of the economy in the modern West. The empirical reality, that

---

[2] Frank H. Knight, "On the Most Important Economic Problem," *Problems of United States Economic Development* (New York: Committee for Economic Development, 1958), Volume 1, p. 273.

economists in the Western liberal tradition study, is the system of markets, money, and prices which tends to make economizers of us all. But there are obvious dangers lurking here for all social scientists interested in the economy. If the social reality that economists in the liberal tradition actually study is taken to identify the economy in all societies, then all real economic activity everywhere will tend to be seen in the market image, and back we go through the looking glass.

Polanyi was, therefore, at pains to point out that the market-ordered institutional complex does not similarly identify the economy in all societies. Whether we look to the evidence from anthropology or history, it is clear that the competitive market–money–price complex, operating in its legal context of private property and free contract and its "economizing" cultural context, has either been absent or has played a subordinate role through most of man's history.

Polanyi's basic solution was to return to the notion of the economy as the material means-providing sphere and to examine the different institutional frameworks in which that sphere operated in different societies. Here, certainly, there is no enigma. Every society must somehow find the material means for its survival, and that activity is everywhere clear and evident, providing "substantive" evidence. The whole process will be organized differently in different societies, run on different motives, and use varying materials and technologies, but it will always be there, observable and capable of analysis as a set of identifiable activities with some shape, some unity, some stability, if not necessarily as a differentiated economic *system*.

Much has been written on both sides in the formalist–substantivist debate since the publication especially of Polanyi's chapter on "The Economy as Instituted Process" in *Trade and Market in the Early Empires*, in 1957. (That essay is reprinted here, considerably enlarged, as Chapters 2 and 3.) George Dalton largely kept the substantive point of view alive by republishing some of Polanyi's most salient pieces, and by many important contributions of his own. There seems little point in reviewing the whole debate here, but some issues still remain unclear, and it does seem important to attempt to clarify them. Certainly, no hope is held out of resolving the debate once and for all—only time will do that.

First, behind the debate there is the old question of the relevance and universality of formal economic theory. The debate goes back to the "empty boxes" claim of the German historical school, and has involved the American Institutionalists as well as many sociologists, anthropologists, and historians whose interest was in economic institutions and the social and cultural framework of substantive economic activity. Too often in the long history of the dispute over the empirical relevance of economic analysis, however, the question of the formal or logical validity of economics and its universality as a theory of economic rationality has been confused with the question of its relevance to the range of substantive problems which different social scientists confront in the analysis of economic institutions, their history and their functional interaction with society. The central issue in this debate is not the logical consistency of economic analysis, nor of the universality of economic rationality as an *aspect* of human behavior in all kinds of situations, from making love to fighting wars. The issue is whether, and to what extent, the discipline of formal economics and the whole panoply of its analytical arsenal provides a model of economic activity that unambiguously identifies the range of variables that interest social scientists when they direct their attention to the economy in different societies. In this debate it is not enough to prove that choosing and economizing are universal aspects of life, or that man shows foresight and acts rationally in the conduct of his affairs. It is necessary, if formal economics is to provide us with a general concept of the economy in society, that the operational definition of economizing (the maximal adaptation of scarce means to the achievement of graded ends) provide the universal *organizing* principles of the relations between men in the production and distribution of those material things that everyone recognizes as the substantial role of the economy in all societies. The gist of Polanyi's argument is simply that these conditions are not universally present in that generic sphere of activity in every society. And if it is that material sphere of human endeavor which interests us in any society, then the theory of the organization and development of the economy in this sense must be conceived independently of formal economics.

For Polanyi, then, it is not because of the scarcity of means that social order, sequence, rules of use, and of acquisition and disposition are inevitable exigencies of the economic process. It is rather because persons working on valued things, moving them and passing them from hand to hand must, regardless of the relative scarcity or abundance of the things, know the rules of authority, and the rights and obligations in regard to the productive use of persons and things, and the rules of distribution of things; the cadences of work; the measures of time, weight, and space without which chaos would result. These are problems of the social, cultural, and physical dimensions of the substantive economy, and cannot be understood simply in terms of the abstraction, economizing in the use of scarce means, or "avoiding waste and futility."

Polanyi demonstrates clearly in this book that in primitive and early historical societies the predominant technologies, the social arrangements, and the communication systems that order and integrate economic life do not yield situations wherein the human and natural elements of the economic process can be regarded by the participants in that process as generalized means or facilities adaptable to a variety of ends. The give and take relations between persons in regard to material things in these societies are typically embedded in a broad network of social and political commitments that do not allow the individual to maximize his "economic" advantage in these relationships. Even where markets, money, and prices do appear in these societies, Polanyi makes it clear that the social, cultural, and political integument does not create the kind of situation where inputs are measured against outputs, so that an economically optimum position for the individual, let alone the whole economy, might be determined, even in principle.

In his attack on the prevailing market system bias, Polanyi focused his attention primarily on trade, money, and markets, the institutions which he felt had been most seriously misunderstood in their history because of the myopic, modern Western view that they were naturally and inseparably linked in a chain of profit-making activities. In his attack, he drew most heavily on the work of Bücher, Toennies, Maine, Thurnwald, Malinowski, Weber, and Durkheim. His original achievement was to provide clear operational definitions of trade, money uses, and markets, the purposes they served, and the different kinds of social situations in which they functioned in the long history of man predating the advent of the market system in the West. Throughout, he analyzed the ways in which literal "exchanges" between persons could take place with and without markets, but, in any case, without the supposedly inevitable rule of the supply–demand–price mechanism.

He introduced the new concepts of operational devices and equivalencies, illustrating the way in which primitive and ancient economies could accomplish the complex tasks of measurement and establishing rates of exchange, without elaborate conceptual systems of weights and measures, and without the mysterious magic of prices created autonomously by the forces of supply and demand. He penetrated to the political and economic developmental significance of those ubiquitous cultural institutions of early society: treasure and prestige; and he traced the gradual "peeling off" of economic transactions from their societal context of status and power.

In thinking about Polanyi's work, however, one must always return to the fact that his broad historical investigation of trade, money, and markets was fitted into a larger conception and purpose. That larger conception was of a general theory of the economy in society, free of the overwhelming biases of the "market mentality" of our age. Thus, first of all, he was at pains to define the meaning, scope, and content of the material means-producing sphere generic to every society. He distinguished "locational" movements, those spatial "physical" movements essential to the man–nature aspects of the productive process, from "appropriational" movements which define the all-important boundary sphere between economy and society. These latter order the relations between men as they acquire and dispose of the regular inputs and outputs of the economic process. The material means, human agents, and technical knowledge that contribute to production must be moved or induced to move from their place in society, and the products of this activity returned to the members of society. This is the sphere in which are established the appropriational powers—the rights and obligations—which order the relations between men in the acquisition and disposition of valued things, and in the recruitment of the human agents of the economic process. Broadly, it might be thought of as the sphere of "property" relations, and, on the input side, at least one of the meanings attached to Marx's "relations of production."

The social organization of appropriational power is the key to any consideration of the economy as a social system. It locates the institutional matrix which orders man-to-man economic relations, and defines the place of the economy in society in the sense that it locates the societal source of the rights and obligations which sanction the movements of goods and persons into, through, and out of the economic process.

Polanyi has identified three general types of the social organization of economic activities under the heading "forms of integration." These are: "reciprocity, redistribution, and exchange." (A fourth sub-type, "householding," which might have characteristics of all the three main types, was identified to apply to the peasant household economy.) Although Polanyi does not explicitly say so, these refer to the appropriational sphere of the economy's social organization; that is, they identify typical patterns in the relations between men as they acquire and dispose of productive resources and the material means of want satisfaction. These types also serve to locate the economy in society in the sense that they identify, broadly, the kinds of institutional sanctions (social, political, economical) that fix the rights and obligations between persons in the economic process.

One typical form of the ordering of these appropriational movements was termed "reciprocity," though other terms such as mutuality or traditional might also have been employed. Each of these terms is apt in certain ways; none seems entirely adequate. In any case, the important thing is to describe clearly the situation. The central feature of this type of organization is that the sanctions, the validation, for goods and person movements into and out of the economy, and the productive uses of the material stuff of the substantive economic process are to be found in some part of the societal structure, like the kinship system, which has a function and a rationale that is not necessarily independent of, but goes beyond that of its role in ordering the relations between persons in the economic process. The family, or kinship system, is the prototype of this reciprocity situation, but it is also typical of relations between friends, neighbors, members of voluntary associations, peer groups, and the like. The central point here is that in reciprocity situations the goods and person movements and the sanctions regarding productive use of material resources derive from the behavioral requirements or expectations imposed by the particular kinship system, community, friendship circle, or association involved. The sanctions regarding such things as land use, inheritance, alienation of land, or other material means, and the movement of persons and things into and out of the economic process are here determined by the general expectations regarding behavior imposed by the prior existing or broader functioning social institution in question. Here, in other words, the universal questions of who is to do what, what means are to be used, how much is to be used and when, and to whom the productive results go in what amounts are questions that are decided by the behavioral norms of the particular social structure which rules in the given case.

The second term, "redistribution," is derived from the actual physical movement of goods into a central place from which they are redistributed. Prime examples of the redistributive economy are the vast bureaucratic empires of ancient Mesopotamia, Egypt, or the Incas of Peru. But it is essential to recognize that, as a type of organization, its distinctive feature is not the pattern of the physical movements of goods but of the rights and obligations that sanction the "between hands" movements of goods and persons into and out of the economy. The "centricity" of the redistributive pattern refers to the fact that the power to determine rights and obligations is located at an identifiable center, from which these are distributed through a matrix of formal rules and authority which order the movement of things between persons. The emergence of redistribution as a form of organization of the economy is, therefore, closely related to the emergence of the political order as a differentiated system in society.

The third pattern of organization is the transactional pattern of exchange. Its characteristic motive is rational self-interest. Its characteristic institution is the market, which is not to say that all markets fit the pattern. The self-regulating or "price-making" market of the modern West is the prototype of the exchange system. Here, as in the case of the other patterns of organization, the essential characteristic of exchange hinges on the manner in which appropriational rights and obligations are determined. The institutional medium of markets, money, and prices provides a self-contained mechanism through which rights are constituted, interests represented, and conflicts adjusted. The rights to acquire and dispose, while ultimately, and necessarily, sanctioned by the political order in the form of private property and free contract, are actually generated in the buying and selling activities that engage people in the market; interests are represented in markets open to all in possession of the necessary means; and conflicts resolved by the movement of prices. A distinctive feature of the exchange pattern is that it isolates the economic element (used here in the formal sense of economic rationality) in the essential give-and-take relations of the substantive economic process, the act of exchange always representing, in theory, a calculated gain to each individual involved.

Like each of the other two of Polanyi's "forms of integration," exchange is a principle of social organization which may, if the conditions are right, be extended to spheres of human activity other than the economy as it is defined here. Indeed, each of these three patterns identifies principles of social order that may apply to wide or dispersed areas of activity in any given society. The principles are easily identified and widely recognized as the inexplicit mutuality typical of the societal realm of face-to-face affective relationships, the rational control toward collective ends of formal rules and central authority, and the economically rational self-interest of exchange relations. Taken in this sense, they might be termed the social, the political, and the economical principles of order in society. Each has its typical mode of organization, its values, and its logic of operation. Our society, for example, is an exchange order because the market–money–price complex remains the primary mode of structuring the relations between persons, not only in the substantive economic sphere, but in and between most of the generic spheres of activity (such as sports, entertainment, art, communications, transportation, finance, and personal services) in that society. And other spheres (such as education, religion, politics, and the military) which, for the most part, are not directly structured through market relations, are deeply involved in and influenced by the dominant market exchange mode.

Polanyi's ultimate aim at this theoretical level was to create a substantive nonmarket economics which would, indeed, provide a general conceptual framework "for the whole range of earlier societies where patterns of integration other than exchange have been found to prevail."[3] That aim was never fully realized, but the groundwork was firmly laid, providing us with a conceptual framework to be developed which can apply to societies early and late, as Polanyi clearly intended.

Polanyi's scholarly aims were serious and compelling, and they continue to motivate scholars in many fields, but the deeper significance and the unifying theme of all of his work lies in the realm of social and political philosophy. Put most simply, his concern was

[3] See below.

that the market system of the modern West had usurped the generic functions and integrity of human society itself, making economic values supreme and turning both man and nature into commodities—all fodder for the "satanic mill" of the self-regulating market, as he put it in *The Great Transformation*. The driving force behind all of his historical work was the conviction that this had not always been so; that it had been possible to produce and distribute the livelihood of man while maintaining the integrity of society, and that premarket history offered many clues to the possibility of returning the mandate for man's fate to the variegated social, political, and cultural institutions of society. Thus did he challenge the liberal axiom that freedom and justice were inextricably tied to the market order. Thus did he also challenge economic determinism, one of the basic axioms of that other nineteenth-century orthodoxy, Marxism.

Much remains to be done. Polanyi's work presented here remains but a sketch of the massive undertaking he began. What I hope this book accomplishes is a more thorough, consistent, and complete view of his conceptual system, and of his role as a general economic historian than is anywhere available. With him, I also hope that it will lend some important insights to the problems of our time, problems which have hardly grown less urgent, nor have they been resolved, since his death in 1964.

For the gods have hidden the livelihood of men.

Hesiod, *Works and Days*

Preface

The purport of this work is to make universal economic history the starting point of a comprehensive reconsideration of the problem of human livelihood.[1]

Thus the initiative which was taken more than a decade ago in *The Great Transformation* is here to be followed up. *The Great Transformation* implied that in order to gain a more realistic view of the place occupied by the economy in human society, it is necessary that general economic history be reestablished on broad conceptual foundations.

More than five years of systematic inquiry, endowed by the Columbia Council for Research in the Social Sciences, were spent in that effort (1948–1952). That work was interrupted for several years while I was engaged, together with Professors C. M. Arensberg and H. W. Pearson, in editing *Trade and Market in the Early Empires* (1957), to which we also contributed various papers. The present work, entitled *The Livelihood of Man*, represents a return to the original effort.

On the theoretical level, an attempt is made to develop concepts of trade, money, and market institutions applicable to all types of societies. On the historical level, case studies are intended to bring to life our generalizations, by way of parallel and contrast. On the policy level, history should be made to yield answers to some of the burning moral and operational problems of our own age.

[1] This preface is taken from two different versions, one written in 1954 and the other not dated, but obviously written sometime after 1957. (Ed.)

What is the world of thought upon which we are inviting the reader to enter? And how are the facts, the arguments, and the perspectives to be presented?

I THEORY, HISTORY, AND POLICY

The use of the term "economic" is bedeviled by ambiguities. Economic theory has invested it with a time-bound connotation that renders it ineffective outside of the narrow confines of our market-dominated societies. Terms like supply, demand, and price should be replaced by wider terms such as resources, requirements, and equivalencies. The historian will then be able to compare the economic institutions of different periods and regions without running the danger of foisting upon the bare facts the market shape of things.

Once out of the rubber cell of self-defeating notions, we can come to grips with realities. In our market-organized economies, trade and money appear as mere functions of the market, which, of course, up to a point they are. Yet such an appearance, if generalized, must falsify the facts of the past. Foreign trade and some money uses are as old as mankind, while price-making markets are a comparatively recent innovation.

This particular insight may seem of limited scope, yet logically it must induce no less than a reappraisal of the time scale of Eurasian civilization. After the discovery, in 1902, of Hammurabi's Code of Laws, engraved on an obsidian stele, the all-out commercial character of Babylonian society was taken for granted. The high level of trading activities and the abundant use of money, for payment and as a "standard," was looked upon as evidence of commerce and flourishing markets. The origins of our commercial civilization now seemed to reach back to the very beginnings of recorded history. Yet trade and money uses, as we saw, need not imply markets and, as recent archaeological findings reveal, market places were actually absent in the whole area. Not Babylon, but rather Athens may have, in the future, to be credited with the possession of the first important city market. Already the historiography of market trade appears to be shifting, by no less than a millennium in time, and by several degrees of longitude in space.

The crucial policy slant comes home to us as the earlier millennia of human problems pass in review. What to our generation seem unique and fateful cross-roads—freedom versus bureaucracy, planning versus market methods—are then recognized as topical variants of recurrent human situations. The totally planned economy of Greek Egypt launched the first "world" market for grain in the Eastern Mediterranean. To harmonize the personal initiative of the trader with governmental direction of trade was an aim pursued by Assyrian rulers as early as the beginnings of the second millennium B.C. And not unsuccessfully either, judging by the ingenious devices by which their methods of colonial trading safeguarded the freedom of the individual trader. The so-called "Cappadocian" trading colony which we have here in mind lacked price-making markets and practiced a riskless type of business under fixed prices, the traders' profit being made on commission fees. Yet the safeguards of the rule of law and of the traders' personal liberty were striking. Similarly, ways were found to reconcile economic planning with the requirements of markets in communities as different as democratic Attica of the fifth century B.C. and the preliterate Negro Kingdom of Dahomey in West Africa, more than 2000 years later, where foreign commerce was still run by the trade organization of the royal palace while the economic life of village and kinship groups rested on local markets and genuine village autonomy.

Although in terms of livelihood our modern world may be even younger than we thought, the great problems of the human race— freedom and centralization, initiative and planning—certainly bear more lasting features than was believed to be possible.

Introduction

This work is an economic historian's contribution to world affairs in a period of perilous transformation. Its aim is simple: to enlarge our freedom of creative adjustment, and thereby improve our chances of survival, the problem of man's material livelihood should be subjected to total reconsideration.

No more than a beginning can be made in this book. An attempt will be made, however, to remove some deeply rooted misconceptions that underlie the social philosophy of our time concerning the place occupied by the economy in society. This effort will center on the study of trade, money, and market institutions so familiar to our age and yet, perhaps for that very reason, sources of a grievously incomplete understanding of the nature of the human economy.

If occasionally a personal note has intruded into the analysis of the cold facts, it is because the historian can no longer remain aloof from the needs of the age. True, by responding to their call he may introduce unwonted tensions into the traditional fabric of an academic discipline. Still, the perspective of the undertaking does not spring from an individually held view. The nature of the dangers cited can be gauged objectively, and the briefest survey of the present reveals some of the permanent factors in the oncoming period of history. Nevertheless, the approach to the task may well be deemed personal. Perforce there are subjective sources to the belief that even so academic and peripheral a figure as the student of economic history should be able to discover a definite use for himself in this secular process. That, for instance, he may help to disencumber our minds of obsolete notions and, to the extent to which he rightly discerns the ills of the age, he might even venture to offer a view of how to judge long-run policy problems.

The bare facts of the situation in which we find ourselves are, indeed, seen to be alike by many. About a generation ago, the demise of the system of world economy became apparent. After World War I, the international gold standard, world markets for commodities and raw materials, and the universal distribution of credits and investments were engulfed by changes, some sudden, some more gradual. At the same time, the political organization of the peoples of the planet started to disintegrate. The balance of power that had prevented major wars for a century ceased to work. New dictatorial forms of government arose and passed again. New organizations of the economy were tried, with varying success. Following World War II, the continents of Asia and North Africa became fluid at their borders. For a time, World War III seemed imminent. Despite the odds, however, the chances of life appear to be winning over the chances of death. But whatever the outcome, one conclusion can already be drawn with certainty: that further readjustments in the institutional setting of national and international life are inevitable. This may sound trite, for history never stands still. Actually, it is meant in this context to forecast changes affecting vital aspects of our collective existence even if, as now seems possible, no spectacular events like those of the decade from which we have just emerged break in upon us. For the crucial circumstance that needs to be emphasized, since it is easily overlooked, is precisely the obvious one that the contending political and ideological forces that have already entered the international scene will of necessity either clash destructively or harmonize constructively or, perhaps, both; yet such is the institutional nature of these forces that, even for nothing dramatic to happen, important step-by-step adaptation will have to occur. Of this we may be sure, therefore: that whatever else be in store, at least some degree of creative adjustment to these new permanent features of the human environment is inevitable. Mere coexistence, if it is to operate at all, logically requires as much.

But beyond the institutional devices that mere coexistence must involve, another kind of unspectacular change in the human world is possible, more comprehensive, in its undramatic way, than imagination has hitherto encompassed. Nuclear energy, once released, will never cease to haunt us. Those dominant concerns in which we have our being may alter their direction, changing from their present economic axis to one that may best be called the moral and political. No longer economic progress and welfare, but peace and freedom become man's supreme aims. Fear, that architect of power, is already quietly producing totalitarian tendencies of a magnitude hitherto unknown. For better or worse, the very framework of change is changing.

I. CHANGE AND ECONOMIC HISTORY

As for the hope of contributing his mite an economic historian may secretly nourish, it must be, as it were, esoteric. Indeed, to select the timeless question of man's livelihood and urge its reconsideration in the light of practical necessities must appear as a strange objective. The place occupied by various economies in different societies is a forbidding subject at best. Although an economy of some kind or other is essential to every society, it may be linked with the rest of that society in very different ways. Under the same technology, such far-reaching changes in economic organization may be encountered as transitions from capitalism to socialism. Again, the same organization of the economy seems compatible with sharp changes in the political system, e.g., when a market-organized society changes from a liberal democracy to fascism or vice versa. This phenomenon is all the more likely if change has been induced by an external force such as conquest, a common occurrence in world history. Under pressure from outside, or in the wake of acculturation, any major sphere of life—whether political, religious, or cultural, so it seems—may gain ascendancy over the other spheres and retain it over a stretch too long to be called merely temporary. Yet even though the economy may take only second or third place, it can never fail to complicate the issues in unforeseeable ways.

If, nevertheless, the unwieldy subject of the livelihood of man was elected for inquiry here, it was done in the conviction that it is not beyond the scope of intellectual effort to eliminate at least some of the most intractable biases under which the problem of the economy presents itself to the men of our century.

This belief, amounting almost to a personal engagement, stems from a compelling insight of many years' standing. It is my conviction that the largely unconscious weakness under which Western civilization labors springs precisely from the peculiar conditions under which it is shaping its economic fate. In all its singularity, this argument can be set out as follows.

Our social thinking, focused as it is on the economic sphere, is for that very reason ill equipped to deal with the economic requirements of this age of adjustment. A market-centered society such as ours must find it hard, if not impossible, justly to gauge the limitations of the significance of the economic. For once man's everyday activities have been organized through markets of various kinds, based on profit motives, determined by competitive attitudes, and governed by a utilitarian value scale, his society becomes an organism that is, in all essential regards, subservient to gainful purposes. Having thus absolutized the motive of economic gain in practice, he loses the capacity of mentally relativizing it again. His imagination is bounded by stultifying limits. The very word *economy* evokes in him not the picture of man's livelihood and the technology that helps to secure it, but recalls instead a set of particular motives, peculiar attitudes, and highly specific purposes, all of which he is used to calling *economic,* even though they are mere accessories to the actual economy, owing their existence to an ephemeral interplay of cultural traits. Not the permanent and abiding features of all human economies but the merely transitory and contingent ones appear to him as the essentials. He is bound to create difficulties for himself where otherwise there are none and stumble over easily avoided obstacles whose very existence is unknown to him. In his ignorance, he can grasp neither the true preconditions of survival nor the less obvious ways of attaining the possible. This obsolete market-mentality is, as I see it, the chief impediment to a realistic approach to the economic problems of the oncoming era.

On the face of it, such a proposition must appear almost self-contradictory. It may seem to imply that very overestimation of the importance of the economy against which it ostensibly wishes to forewarn. However, this is by no means the case. To assert that market-centered habits tend to be accompanied by a certain kind of economic rationale is entirely compatible with an outright rejection of the fallacious view of a timeless predominance of the economic factor in human affairs. The nineteenth century, which universalized the market, would naturally experience economic determinism in its daily life and incline to assume that such determinism was timeless and general. Its materialistic dogmatism in regard to men and society simply mirrored the institutions that happened to shape the environment. And to assert that such obsessive economy-centered notions, reflecting timebound conditions, must prove a hindrance to the solution of wider problems, including those of the adjustment of the economy to new social surroundings, is merely to point out the obvious.

It is, then, precisely on account of the disproportionate influence exerted by the market system on the society of our own personal experience that we must find it difficult to understand the limited and subordinate character of the economy as it presents itself outside such a system. But hence also the reasonable expectation that, once our deep seated bias has been recognized for what it is, it should not be beyond our capacity to rid ourselves of its deleterious effects. A wider knowledge of fact is the corrective to restrictive prejudice. To reduce to their true proportions the emergent questions of economic adjustment we must learn to see with the eyes of the historian.

Sloganized versions of history, however, would prove as fatal to our generation as a false map to a general on the eve of battle. First of all, world history is emphatically *not* economic history. The physical existence of a group, its safety of life and limb, the totality of its way of life transcend anything that can be reasonably presented as an economic interest. But to stress the opposite also has its danger. Whoever can offer economic solutions will always be at an advantage in the pure power game over one who cannot. Again, mere business practices, however fondly cherished, cannot present themselves as the only embodiments of such transcendent values as personality and freedom. This would be to substitute credit for creed, and fatefully to underestimate the impetus of a secular religion that happens not to put its faith in bank accounts. Nor should technological progress be made into an idol to which morality and human happiness are blindly sacrificed. Yet again, to elevate primitivism to a morality and seek shelter from the machine age in the Neolithic cave is a counsel of despair that ignores the irreversibility of progress.

Discordant generalizations such as these need not leave us in an agnostic mood. The varied, vivid experiences concerning man's livelihood will naturally carry false emphasis as their epigraph. Rather let us beware of the abstract generalizations in things economic that tend to obscure and oversimplify the intricacies of actual situations, for these actualities alone are our concern. Our task is to divest them of generalities and grasp them in their concrete aspect. No lengthy regression in time is needed to find the historical origin of our present entanglements.

The nineteenth century gave birth to two sets of events of a very different order of magnitude: the machine age, a development of millennial range; and the market system, an initial adjustment to that development.

In the machine age we see the beginning of one of those rare mutations that mark the lifetime of the human race in terms of which the history of man since the Old Stone Age counts no more than three periods: first, the Neolithic; second, the period of plough agriculture in which almost all history happened; third, the brand-new machine age. All along, technology provided the criterion. Neolithic man never passed much beyond the stage of food gathering and hoe agriculture. The growing of grain required a plough with a large beast to pull it; and its introduction started civilization some seven or eight thousand years ago. The use of machines powered by strength other than that of man or beast is of quite recent occurrence. It launched us on a new sea. By all counts, this new civilization that has already doubled the population of the globe should be expected to continue over a long period. It has come to stay. It is our fate. We must learn to live with it, if we are to live at all.

II. ECONOMICS AND THE MACHINE AGE

The fundamental fact is, then, that the machine created a new civilization. If plough agriculture is credited with giving rise to the first civilization, the machine gave rise to the second, the industrial. It spread over the planet, creating the perspective of the ages to come. Such an event transcends by far the economic field; only time will unfold its powers and perils and spell out its implications for the existence of man. Machine civilization has invested the frail frame of man with the effectiveness of lightning and earthquake; it has moved the center of his being from the internal to the external; it has added hitherto unknown dimensions to the scope, structure, and frequency of communication; it has changed the feel of our contacts with nature; and, more important than all else, it has created novel interpersonal relations reflecting forces, physical and mental, that still may cause the self-destruction of the human race.

The beginnings were unspectacular. At the end of the eighteenth century (a few rare spirits apart) no one suspected as yet that a new civilization was about to begin. Not many machines had yet been invented, and of those invented some, like the power loom, were still not in use. Nevertheless, by privilege of first sight a few recognized the signs and anticipated changes of unimaginable depth, subtlety, and pervasiveness. Some of their notions caused much merriment; yet, as we have since learned to see, not the tough realists but the childlike prophets were closer to the truth. Indeed, the grim questions of our day, as well as the hopes of centuries to come, are mere derivatives of that inconspicuous mechanical start.

Robert Owen was the first to perceive that a new world was engulfing the old. The machine would demand alterations in the details of everyday life, as in communal existence. He sensed not only the boon inherent in an explosive growth of the capacity to produce but also its potential to become an invidious gift unless the shock of a machine-made life was absorbed by new patterns of settlement and habitation, new sites of work, new relations between the sexes, new forms of relaxation and even attire—to all of which he devoted his attention. He advocated a root-and-branch reform of Christianity. Almost as an afterthought he referred to the economy, advocating a reformed currency and cooperative forms of economic life (no concept of capitalism yet existed). In France, Fourier's grotesque imagination engendered blueprints of *phalanstères* where the industrial division of labor would be geared, by virtue of psychological gadgets, to the spontaneity of men, women, and children. Saint-Simon proclaimed that his New Christianity would bring salvation to an "industrial society." Thus did the "utopian socialists" anticipate the menace of a cultural development which a century later became familiar to all the world as the fragmentation of man, the standardization of effort, the supremacy of mechanism over organism and of organization over spontaneity. Even the threat to personality and freedom was there from the start. By the close of the century, Henry Adams foretold the very date of the atom bomb.[1]

However, for a long time those early fears of what would follow in the wake of the machine remained latent. They were eclipsed by

[1] I believe the reference here is to a letter Adams wrote to Henry Osborn Taylor on January 17, 1905. In it he said, ". . . it will not need another century to tip thought upside down. . . . Explosives would then reach cosmic violence. Disintegration would overcome integration." See Harold Dean Cater, ed., *Henry Adams and His Friends* (New York: Houghton Mifflin, 1947), pp. 558–559.

the manifest changes in economic organization proper urgently required to allow play for the technological miracles of the day. Adam Smith had discovered the answer in the market. The factory system, which at first seemed to involve little more than some additional overseas trading stations of the usual kind, soon induced a process of institutional change of a very different magnitude. The outcome was the approximation of a self-regulating system of markets that revolutionized Western society in the early decades of the nineteenth century.

As we now know, this was only a first vigorous attempt at adjustment. Tremendously successful as the initiative proved, in spite of the bitter sufferings that it brought to a whole generation, the adaptation to the machine was neither complete nor final. The more comprehensive the market system became, the more it revealed its incapacity to satisfy the requirements of a stable society. Millions experienced recurrent unemployment and the employed suffered permanent uncertainty of tenure—scourges unknown to former societies—while continued dislocations provided a harassing accompaniment, all of which made the process of industrialization a burden almost too great to be borne. Socialist movements at home and a worldwide growth of tariffs on imports were manifestations of a societal tendency toward self-protection set in motion by the ravages of uncontrolled market forces.

Thus in our own days another phase of economic change set in. It followed logically from the earlier one, yet it pointed in a quite different direction. The breakdown of the most ambitious of all market institutions, the international gold standard, only half a century after its establishment ushered in the end of the market utopia. Roughly analogous economic reforms were now introduced under politically different regimes in all advanced countries of the West. Regular employment for all, regulated trading abroad, planned development of national resources at home were the postulates. Even in countries where the market system largely continued in the traditional way, there was a significant turn in the everyday motives of economic life. Social security and a more just taxation diluted the incentives of profit for the owner and fear of destitution for the worker, replacing them with the mixed motives of status, security of income, teamwork, and a creative role in industry.

The strains and stresses that accompany this second adaptation of the economy to the machine are strangely different from those of the technology that imperiled civilized life in the wake of the Industrial Revolution. If a century ago the inexorable working of interlinked markets for labor, land, and capital had to be countered so that the human shape of life could continue, the dangers now come from an unexpected quarter. They are, however, by no means less formidable. And the new threat forms as much a part of an industrial civilization as the unhealthy factory, the mushroom town, or the scientific cruelty of the poorhouse did in nineteenth-century England, its birthplace. But today the underlying concern is not for equality, justice, charity, and a humane life for the laborer, but rather for the freedom and survival of all. Industrial technology is showing itself wholly capable of generating suicidal tendencies that strike at the roots of liberty and life itself. Outside Europe there is fear of foreign domination and a determined insistence on independence and autarchy as means of controlling a process of industrialization that is universally both desired and dreaded. The apparent contradiction should not be surprising. Industrialism was an uneasy compromise between man and machine in which man lost out and the machine had its way. At the beginning of the nineteenth century, the market system may well have been the only means of employing expensive, elaborate machinery for the purposes of production. When machines were invented, neither the readiness and the capacity for risk bearing nor the knowledge of products and consumers was available except in that merchant class which for generations had been "putting-out" raw materials for finishing by home industry. The self-protection of society, partly by means of factory laws but mainly through the trade union movement, for a long time lagged far behind the impact of the machine. In the present spread of industrialization, the order is reversed. Asians, Latin Americans, and Africans have learned the lesson. The new economic organization puts the safety of society above the requirement of maximum technological efficiency. The emphasis has shifted from machine to man.

III. ECONOMY AND SOCIETY: TRADE, MONEY, AND MARKETS

So great a shift in the place of the economy in society must divest the economy of its traditional associations. Gain, competition, and utilitarian advantage are no longer the points of reference. The more familiar we are with the picture of the world as it presented itself in the nineteenth century, the less well will we be prepared for the realities of the twentieth. For an orientation in the emerging new conditions, a different map is required.

For an up-to-date frame of reference, a strategic point is required. The earlier and later maps contrast perhaps most sharply in the position assigned on them to the institutions of trade, money, and market. Under the dominance of the market, trade is no more than a function of the market, and money merely a means of facilitating trade, both appearing as adjuncts of the market. Actually, some forms of trade and various uses of money gain great importance in economic life independent of, and precedent to, markets; and even where market elements are present, they do not necessarily involve the existence of a supply–demand–price mechanism. Prices are originally set by tradition or authority, and their alternation, when it occurs, is again brought about by institutional, not by market methods. Contrary to all current assumptions, the origin of fluctuating prices, not of fixed prices, is the problem for the historian of antiquity.

The notion that individual acts of exchange were at the root of trade, money, and even of market institutions, is hardly tenable. Foreign trade, as a rule, preceded domestic trade, the exchange use of money originated in the foreign trade sphere, and organized markets were developed first in external trade; in all three cases, action was more of the collective than of the individual kind. In the light of these recognitions, it stands to question how, in the absence of price-making markets, trade, money, and market elements were integrated into the economy.

Such problems were left outside the scope of inquiry by the traditional assumption of the inseparable unity of trade, money, and markets. Where trade was seen, markets were assumed; and where money was in evidence, trade was assumed, and therefore markets. In point of fact, over the greater part of economic history trade, the various money uses, and market elements should be regarded as separate occurrences. But how does an economy function unless trade becomes market trade and money becomes exchange money? How, for instance, can money objects be in use for payment and other money objects be in use as a "standard" while no appreciable amount of exchange is carried on? Even more searching questions arise in regard to the large-scale functioning of trade and money in so-called primitive, marketless economies—questions which could, of course, not even have been formulated so long as the existence of such conditions was ignored, or their significance denied, in the name of a dogmatic notion of progress. We were thus apt to misjudge the general character of economic development in regard to both the sequence of facts and the facts themselves.

IV. DISCONTINUITIES AND CHANGE

It is mere prejudice to assume that in every development the smaller-sized specimen was necessarily anterior to the larger-sized. To postulate such a sequence in history is no more than an uncritical extension of the law of organic evolution. Trade over the longest distances generally preceded that over shorter distances, just as the farthest colonies were usually founded first, and vast empires arose earlier in history than smaller kingdoms. A similar mistake is to regard phenomena such as credit and finance as "late" developments only because, in the short perspective of the last few centuries, they happen to have come into prominence again following the emergence of the modern market system. This particular fallacy was epitomized in one of the more popular "stages" theories, which insisted upon the sequence, "natural economy, money economy, credit economy," as a supposed law of development. As a matter of fact, debts and obligations are primitive phenomena that antedate the existence of markets, and the storage economies of antiquity practised large-scale financial planning and accountancy long before the use of money as a means of exchange gained importance.

The predilection for continuity from which nineteenth-century historiography suffered often made us misread not only the sequence of the facts but also the facts themselves. The continuity taken to be implied in organic processes is only one mode of happening, alongside of which run the inherent discontinuities of development (the total process being a combination of the two). Besides continuous growth from small beginnings, there is also a very different pattern, that of discontinuous development from previously unconnected elements. The "field," in which such sudden change as the emergence of a new, complex whole occurs, is the social group under definite conditions. These discontinuities broadly determine both what ideas and concepts gain currency with the members of a group and at what rate. But once disseminated, these ideas and concepts permit change at an enormously accelerated rate, since the patterns of individual behavior can now simply fall into line with the new general pattern preformed by those ideas and concepts. Formerly unconnected elements of behavior thus link directly up in a new, complex whole, without any transition. In this light, the so-called idealistic and materialistic approaches to history appear not so much as opposites but rather as outcomes of two different phases in the total process. The idealist expresses, although in a mystificatory form, the fact that human thoughts and ideas play a decisive part in the emergence of institutions and the turns of history. The materialist stresses that objective factors condition the spread of those thoughts and ideas, which are not therefore, as the Hegelian idealists assumed, born of an abstract dialectic.

The history of mankind and the place of the economy in it, is not, as the evolutionists would have it, an account of unconscious growth and organic continuity. Such an approach would necessarily obscure some aspects of economic development vital to men in the present phase of transition. For the dogma of organic continuity must, in the last resort, weaken man's power of shaping his own history. Discounting the role of deliberate change in human institutions must enfeeble his reliance on the forces of the mind and spirit just as a mystic belief in the wisdom of unconscious growth must sap his confidence in his powers to reembody the ideals of justice, law, and freedom in his changing institutions.

The scholar's endeavor must be, first to give clarity and precision to our concepts, so that we be enabled to formulate the problems of livelihood in terms fitted as closely as possible to the actual features of the situation in which we operate; and second to widen the range of principles and policies at our disposal through a study of the shifting place of the economy in human society and the methods by which civilizations of the past successfully engineered their great transitions.

Accordingly, the theoretical task is to establish the study of man's livelihood on broad institutional and historical foundations. The method to be used is given by the interdependence of thought and experience. Terms and definitions constructed without reference to data are hollow, while a mere collecting of facts without a readjustment of our perspective is barren. To break this vicious circle, conceptual and empirical research must be carried forward *pari passu*. Our efforts shall be sustained by the awareness that there are no short cuts on this trail of inquiry.

To contribute to such an approach to the questions of the human economy is the aim of this book.

I

THE PLACE OF THE ECONOMY IN SOCIETY

A. Concepts and Theory

⊂≣ 1 ⊂≣

The Economistic Fallacy

Endeavors to attain a more realistic view of the general problem posed to our generation by man's livelihood meet from the outset with a formidable obstacle—an ingrained habit of thought peculiar to conditions of life under that type of economy the nineteenth century created throughout all industrialized societies. This mentality is personified in the marketing mind.

Our task in this chapter is to point out, in a preliminary way, the fallacies to which the marketing mind has given currency and, incidentally, to expound some of the reasons why these fallacies have influenced public thinking so pervasively.

First we will define the nature of this conceptual anachronism, then describe the institutional development from which it sprang, and enlarge on its influence on our whole moral and philosophic outlook. We will trace the reflections of this attitude of mind in the organized fields of knowledge, such as economic theory, economic history, anthropology, sociology, psychology, and epistemology, that make up the social sciences.

Such a survey should leave no doubt about the impact of economistic thinking on almost every aspect of the questions that confront us, notably the nature of economic institutions, policies, and principles as they are revealed in the forms of organization of livelihood in the past.

To sum up the central illusion of an age in terms of a logical error is rarely to the point; yet conceptually the economistic fallacy, in the nature of things, cannot be described otherwise. The logical error was of a common and harmless kind: a broad, generic phenomenon was somehow taken to be identical with a species with which we happen to be familiar. In such terms, the error was in equating the human economy in general with its market form (a mistake that may have been facilitated by the basic ambiguity of the term *economic,* to which we will return later). The fallacy itself is patent: the physical aspect of man's needs is part of the human condition; no society can exist that does not possess some kind of substantive economy. The supply–demand–price mechanism, on the other hand (which we popularly call the market), is a comparatively modern institution of specific structure, which is easy neither to establish nor to keep going. To narrow the sphere of the genus *economic* specifically to market phenomena is to eliminate the greatest part of man's history from the scene. On the other hand, to stretch the concept of the market until it embraces all economic phenomena is artificially to invest all things economic with the peculiar characteristics that accompany the phenomenon of the market. Inevitably, clarity of thought is impaired.

Realistic thinkers vainly spelled out the distinction between the economy in general and its market forms; time and again the distinction was obliterated by the economistic *Zeitgeist.* These thinkers emphasized the substantive meaning of *economic.* They identified the economy with industry rather than business; with technology rather than ceremonialism; with means of production rather than titles to property; with productive capital rather than finance; with capital goods rather than capital—in short, with the economic substance rather than its marketing form and terminology. But circumstances were stronger than logic, and overwhelming forces of history were at work to weld the disparate concepts into one.

I.   THE ECONOMY AND THE MARKET

The concept of the economy was born with the French physiocrats simultaneously with the emergence of the institution of the market as a supply–demand–price mechanism. The new phenomenon, never witnessed before, was an interdependence of fluctuating prices which directly affected multitudes of men. This nascent world of prices was the result of the comparatively recent spread of trade—

an institution much older than, and independent of, markets—into the articulations of everyday life.

Prices, of course, existed before, but in no way did they constitute a system of their own. Their sphere was, in the nature of things, restricted to trade and finance, since only merchants and bankers used money regularly, a much greater part of the economy being rural and practically tradeless—a thin trickle of goods in the vast, inert mass of neighborhood life on the manor and in the household. True, urban markets knew money and prices, but the rationale of controlling these prices was to keep them stable. Not their occasional fluctuation but their predominant stability made them an increasingly important factor in the determination of profits from trade, since these profits were derived from relatively stable price differentials between distant points rather than from anomalous price fluctuations in local markets.

But the mere infiltration of trade into everyday life need not of itself have created an economy, in the new and distinctive sense of the term, but for a number of further institutional developments. First among these stood the penetration of foreign trade into markets, gradually transforming them from strictly controlled local markets into price-making markets with more or less freely fluctuating prices. This was, in the course of time, followed by the revolutionary innovation of markets with fluctuating prices for the factors of production, labor and land. This change was the most radical of all in its nature and consequence. Yet not before it had proceeded for some time did the different prices, which now included wages, food prices, and rent, show any noticeable interdependence and thus produce the conditions that made men accept the presence of a hitherto unrecognized substantive reality. This emergent field of experience, however, was the economy, and its discovery—one of the emotional and intellectual experiences that formed our modern world—came to the Physiocrats as an illumination and constituted them a philosophical sect. Adam Smith learned from them of the "hidden hand," but he did not follow Quesnay on the path to mysticism. While his French master had noticed merely the interdependence of some revenues and their general dependence on corn prices, his greater pupil, living in the less feudal and more monetarized economy of England, was able to include wages and rent in the group of "prices" and thus, for the first time, glimpse a

vision of the wealth of nations as an integration of the varied manifestations of an underlying system of markets. Adam Smith became
the founder of political economy because he recognized, however
dimly, the tendency towards interdependence of these different
kinds of prices insofar as they resulted from competitive markets.

Although thus spelling out the economy in terms of the market
was originally nothing else than a common-sense way of relating
new concepts to new facts, it may be difficult for us to understand
why it took generations for the realization to occur that what Quesnay and Smith had really discovered was a field of phenomena
essentially independent of the market institution in which it manifested itself at the time. But neither Quesnay nor Smith aimed at the
establishment of the economy as a sphere of social existence that
transcends market, money, or price—and insofar as they did, they
failed in their aim. They reached not so much toward the universality
of the economy as toward the specificity of the market. Indeed, the
traditional unity of all human affairs that still informed their thinking
made them averse to the notion of a separate economic sphere in
society, although it did not prevent them from investing the
economy with the characteristics of the market. Adam Smith introduced business methods into the haunts of primeval man, projecting
his famous propensity to truck, barter, and exchange even to the
back yard of Paradise. Quesnay's approach to the economy was no
less catallactic. His was an economics of the *produit net,* a realistic
quantity in terms of the landlord's accountancy but a mere phantom
in the process between man and nature of which the economy is an
aspect. The alleged "surplus" whose creation he attributed to the soil
and the forces of nature was no more than a transference to the
"Order of Nature" of the disparity selling price is expected to show
against cost. Agriculture happened to occupy the center of the scene
because the revenues of the feudal ruling class were at issue, but
forever after the notion of surplus haunted the writings of classical
economists. The *produit net* was the parent of Marx's surplus value
and its derivatives. Thus was the economy impregnated with a
notion foreign to the total process of which it forms part, a process
that knows neither cost nor profit and is not a series of surplus-
producing actions. Nor are physiological and psychological forces
directed by the urge to secure a surplus over themselves. Neither the
lilies of the field, nor the birds in the air, nor men in pastures, fields,
or factories—tending cattle, raising crops, or releasing planes from a

conveyor belt—produce a surplus over their own existence. Labor, like leisure and repose, is a phase in the self-sufficient course of man through life. The construct of a surplus was merely the projection of the market pattern on a broad aspect of ˙that existence—the economy.[1]

If from the outset the logically fallacious identification of "economic phenomena" and "market phenomena" was understandable, it later became almost a practical requirement with the new society and its way of life which emerged from the throes of the Industrial Revolution. The supply–demand–price mechanism whose first appearance produced the prophetic concept of "economic law," grew swiftly into one of the most powerful forces ever to enter the human scene. Within a generation—say, 1815 to 1845, Harriet Martineau's "Thirty Years' Peace"—the price-making market, which previously existed only in samples in various ports of trade and stock exchanges, showed its staggering capacity for organizing human beings as if they were mere chunks of raw material and combining them, together with the surface of mother earth, which could now be freely marketed, into industrial units under the command of private persons mainly engaged in buying and selling for profit. Within an extremely brief period, the commodity fiction, as applied to labor and land, transformed the very substance of human society. Here was the identification of economy and market *in practice*. Man's ultimate dependence on nature and his fellows for the means of his survival was put under the control of that newfangled institutional creation of superlative power, the market, which developed overnight from lowly beginnings. This institutional gadget, which became the dominant force in the economy—now justly described as a *market economy*—then gave rise to yet another, even more extreme development, namely a whole society embedded in the mechanism of its own economy—*a market society*.

From this vantage point, it is not difficult to discern that what we have here called the economistic fallacy was an error mainly from the theoretical angle. For all practical purposes, the economy *did* now consist of markets, and the market *did* envelop society.

From this line of argument, it should also be clear that the

---

[1] See Harry W. Pearson, "The Economy Has No Surplus: Critique of a Theory of Development," in *Trade and Market in the Early Empires*, ed. K. Polanyi, C. Arensberg, and H. Pearson (Glencoe, Ill.: Free Press and Falcon's Wing Press, 1957).

significance of the economistic outlook lay precisely in its capacity for giving birth to a unity of motivations and valuations that would bring about in practice what it precognized as an ideal, namely the identity of market and society. For only if a way of life is organized in all relevant aspects, including pictures of the inner man and the nature of society—a philosophy of everyday life comprising criteria of common sense behavior, of reasonable risks, and of a workable morality—are we offered that compendium of theoretical and practical doctrines which alone can produce a society or, what amounts to the same thing, transform a given society within the lifetime of a generation or two. And such a transformation was achieved, for better or for worse, by the pioneers of economism. This is to say no less than that the marketing mind contained the seeds of a whole culture—with all its possibilities and limitations—and the picture of inner man and society induced by life in a market economy necessarily followed from the essential structure of a human community organized through the market.

II.   THE ECONOMISTIC TRANSFORMATION

This structure represented a violent break with the conditions that preceded it. What before was merely a thin spread of isolated markets was now transmuted into a self-regulating *system* of markets.

The crucial step was that labor and land were made into commodities; that is, they were treated *as if* they had been produced for sale. Of course, they were not actually commodities, since they were either not produced at all (like land) or, if so, not for sale (like labor).

Yet no more thoroughly effective fiction was ever devised. Because labor and land were freely bought and sold, the mechanism of the market was made to apply to them. There was now a supply of labor and demand for it; there was a supply of land and demand for it. Accordingly, there was a market price for the use of labor power, called wages, and a market price for the use of land, called rent. Labor and land were provided with markets of their own, similar to those of the proper commodities produced with their help.

The true scope of such a step can be gauged if we remember that labor is only another name for man, and land for nature. The commodity fiction handed over the fate of man and nature to the play of an automaton that ran in its own grooves and was governed by its own laws. This instrument of material welfare was controlled solely by the incentives of hunger and gain—or, more precisely, either fear of going without the necessities of life or the expectation of profit. So long as no propertyless person could satisfy his need for food without first selling his labor in the market and so long as no propertied person could be prevented from buying in the cheapest market and selling in the dearest, the blind mill would turn out ever increasing amounts of commodities for the benefit of the human race. Fear of starvation with the worker, lure of profit with the employer would keep the vast mechanism running.

Such an enforced utilitarian practice fatefully warped Western man's understanding of himself and his society.

As regards *man*, we were made to accept the view that his motives can be described as either "material" or "ideal" and that the incentives on which everyday life is organized necessarily spring from the material motives. It is easy to see that under such conditions the human world must indeed appear to be determined by material motives. If, for example, you single out whatever motive you please and organize production in such a manner as to make that motive the individual's incentive *to produce*, you will have induced a picture of man as altogether absorbed by that motive. Let the motive be religious, political, or esthetic; let it be pride, prejudice, love, or envy; and man will appear essentially religious, political, esthetic, proud, prejudiced, engrossed in love or envy. Other motives, in contrast, will appear distant and shadowy—ideal—since they cannot be relied upon to operate in the vital business of production. The motive selected will represent "real" man.

In fact, human beings will labor for a large variety of reasons so long as they form part of a definite social group. Monks traded for religious reasons, and monasteries became the largest trading establishments in Europe. The *kula* trade of the Trobriand Islanders, one of the most intricate barter arrangements known to man, is mainly an esthetic pursuit. Feudal economy depended largely on custom or tradition. With the Kwakiutl, the chief aim of industry seems to be to satisfy a point of honor. Under mercantile despotism, industry was often planned so as to serve power and glory. Accordingly, we tend to think of monks, Western Melanesians, villeins, the Kwakiutl, or seventeenth-century statesmen as ruled by religion, esthetics, custom, honor, or power politics, respectively. Nineteenth-century society was organized in such a fashion as to make hunger or gain alone into effective motives for the individual to participate in economic life. The resulting picture of man ruled only by materialistic incentives was entirely arbitrary.

As regards *society*, the kindred doctrine was propounded that its institutions were "determined" by the economic system. The market mechanism thereby created the delusion of economic determinism as a general law for all human society. Under a market economy, of course, this law holds good. Indeed, the working of the economic system here not only "influences" the rest of society but actually determines it—as in a triangle the sides not merely influence but determine the angles.

In the stratification of classes, supply and demand in the labor market were *identical* with the classes of workers and employers, respectively. The social class of capitalists, landowners, tenants, brokers, merchants, professionals, and so on was delimited by the respective markets for land, money, and capital and their uses, or for various services. The income of these social classes was fixed by the market, their rank and position by their income.

While social classes were directly determined, other institutions were indirectly affected by the market mechanism. State and government, marriage and the rearing of children, the organization of science and education or religion and the arts, the choice of profession, the forms of habitation, the shape of settlements, the very esthetics of private life—everything had either to comply with the utilitarian pattern or at least not interfere with the working of the market mechanism. But, since very few human activities can be carried on in the void (even a saint needing his pillar), the indirect effects of the market system came very near to determining the whole of society. It was almost impossible to avoid the erroneous conclusion that, as "economic" man was "real" man, so the economic system was "really" society.

III. ECONOMIC RATIONALISM

On the face of it, the economistic *Weltanschauung* may have seemed to contain in its twin postulates of rationalism and atomism all that was needed to lay the foundations of a market society. The operative term was rationalism. For what else could such a society be other than an agglomeration of human atoms behaving according to the rules of a definite kind of rationality? Rational action, as such, is the relating of ends to means; economic rationality, specifically, assumes means to be scarce. But human society involves more than that. What should be the end of man, and how should he choose his means? Economic rationalism, in the strict sense, has no answer to these questions, for they imply motivations and valuations of a moral and practical order that go beyond the logically irresistible, but otherwise empty, exhortation to be "economical." Thus hollowness was camouflaged by ambiguous philosophical colloquialism.

To maintain the unity of the facade, two further meanings of *rational* were brought in. With regard to the ends, a utilitarian value scale was postulated as rational; and with regard to the means, the testing scale for efficacy was applied by science. The first scale made rationality the antithesis of the esthetic, the ethical, or the philosophical; the second made it the antithesis of magic, superstition, or plain ignorance. In the first case, it is rational to prefer bread and butter to heroic ideals; in the second, it appears rational for a sick man to consult his doctor in preference to a crystal-ball gazer. Neither meaning of *rational* is relevant to the principle of rationalism, though per se one may be more valid than the other. While stark utilitarianism, with its pseudophilosophic balance of pain and pleasure, has lost its sway over the minds of the educated, the scientific value scale remains supreme within its limits. Thus utilitarianism, still the opiate of the commercialized masses, has been dethroned as an ethic, while scientific method justly holds its own.

Nevertheless, so long as *rational* is used, not as a fashionable term of praise but in the strict sense of pertaining to reason, the validation of the scientific test of means as rational is no less arbitrary then the attempted justification of utilitarian ends. To sum up: the economic variant of rationalism introduces the scarcity element into all means–ends relations; moreover it posits as rational, in regard to the ends and the means themselves, two different value scales that happen to be peculiarly adapted to market situations but otherwise have no universal claim to be called rational. In this way, the choice of ends and the choice of means are claimed to lie under the supreme authority of rationality. Economic rationalism appears to achieve both the systematic limitation of reason to scarcity situations and its systematic extension to all human ends and means, thus validating an economistic culture with all the appearances of irresistible logic.

The social philosophy erected on such foundations was as radical as it was fantastic. To atomize society and make every individual atom behave according to the principles of economic rationalism would, in a sense, place the whole of human existence, with all its depth and wealth, in the frame of reference of the market. This, of course, would not really do—individuals have personalities and society has a history. Personality thrives on experience and education; action implies passion and risk; life demands faith and belief; history is struggle and defeat, victory and redemption. To bridge the gap, economic rationalism introduced harmony and conflict as the *modi* of the individual's relations. The conflicts and alliances of such self-interested atoms, which formed nations and classes, now accounted for social and universal history.

No single author ever propounded the complete doctrine. Bentham still believed in government and was unsure of economics; Spencer anathemized state and government but knew only little of economics; and von Mises, an economist, lacked the encyclopedic knowledge of the other two. Among them they nevertheless created a myth that was the daydream of the educated multitude during the Hundred Years' Peace, from 1815 to World War I, and even after, up to Hitler's war. Intellectually, this myth represented the triumph of economic rationalism and, inevitably, an eclipse of political thought.

The economic rationalism of the nineteenth century was the direct descendant of the political rationalism of the eighteenth. It was as unrealistic as its predecessor, if not more so. As to the facts of history and the nature of political institutions, they were equally foreign to both brands of rationalism. The political utopians ignored the economy, while the utopians of the market took no note of politics. On balance, if the thinkers of the Enlightenment were notoriously unheedful of some of the economic facts, their nineteenth-century successors were totally blind to the sphere of state, nation, and power, to the point of doubting their existence.

IV. ECONOMIC SOLIPSISM

Such economic solipsism, as it might well be called, was indeed an outstanding feature of the market mentality. Economic action, it was deemed, was "natural" to men and was, therefore, self-explanatory. Men would barter unless they were prohibited to do so, and markets would thus come into being unless something was done to prevent it. Trade would begin to flow, as if induced by the force of gravity, and would create pools of goods, organized in markets, unless governments conspired to stop the flow and drain the pool. As barter quickened, money would make its appearance and all things would be drawn into the whirl of exchanges, unless some archaic moralists raised an outcry against lucre or unenlightened tyrants depreciated the currency.

This eclipse of political thinking was the intellectual deficiency of the age. It originated in the economic sphere, yet eventually it destroyed any objective approach to the economy itself, insofar as the economy possessed an institutional background other than a supply–demand–price mechanism. Economists felt so safe within the confines of such a purely theoretical market system that they only grudgingly conceded to nations more than a nuisance value. An English political writer of the 1910s was deemed to have clinched the case against the necessity for wars by proving that as a business proposition war did not pay; and in Geneva, the League of Nations to its last hour remained blind to the political facts that made the gold standard an anachronism. The discounting of politics spread from Cobden's and Bright's free-trading illusions to Spencer's fashionable sociology of "industrial vs. military systems." By the 1930s, almost nothing was left among the educated of the political culture of David Hume or Adam Smith.

The eclipse of politics had a most confusing effect on the moral aspects of the philosophy of history. Economics stepped into the vacuum, and a hypercritical attitude toward the moral vindication of political actions set in. This resulted in a radical discounting of all forces but the economic in the field of historiography. The marketing psychology, which regards only "material" motives as real, while relegating "ideal" motives to the limbo of ineffectuality, was extended not only to nonmarket societies but to all past history as well. Most of early history now appeared as a jumble of slogans about justice and law bandied about by pharaohs and god-kings for the sole purpose of misleading their helpless subjects who groveled under the knout. The whole attitude was self-contradictory. Why cajole a population of bondslaves? And if cajoling there must be, could it be done through promises that meant nothing to the cajoled? But if the promises meant something, justice and law must have been more than mere words. That a population of actual bond slaves need not be cajoled and that justice and freedom must have been recognized as valid ideals by all before they could be employed as a bait by the few, escaped the critical apparatus of a hypercritical public. Under the sway of modern mass-democracy, slogans became a kind of political organizing force that they could never have been in ancient Egypt or Babylon. On the other hand, justice and law, which were embodied in the institutional structure of earlier societies, had worn thin under the market organization of society. A man's property, his revenue and income, the price of his wares were now "just" only if they were formed in the market; and as to law, no law really mattered except that which referred to property and contract. The varied property institutions of the past and the substantive laws that made up the constitution of the ideal *polis* had now no substance to work upon.

Economic solipsism generated that unsubstantial concept of justice, law, and freedom in the name of which modern historiography refused all credence to the numberless ancient texts in which the establishment of righteousness, insistence on the law, the maintenance of a central economy without bureaucratic oppression was declared to be the aim of the ancient state.

The true condition of affairs is so different from what is congenial to the market mentality that it is not easy to convey in simple words. Actually, justice, law, and freedom, as institutionalized values, first make their appearance in the economic sphere as a result of state action. Under tribal conditions, solidarity is safeguarded by custom and tradition; economic life is embedded in the social and political organization of society; no economic transactions take place; and random acts of barter are discouraged as a peril to tribal solidarity. When territorial rule emerges, the god-king supplies that center of communal life of which the loosening of the clan threatens to deprive the group. At the same time, an enormous economic advance becomes possible, and is actually made, with the help of the state: economic transactions, formerly banned as gainful and antisocial are made gainless, and hence just and lawful, through the action of the god-king, who is the fount of justice. This justice is institutionalized in equivalencies, proclaimed in statutes, and practiced in tens of thousands of cases by those organs of palace and temple who handle the taxational and redistributive apparatus of the territorial state. The rule of law is institutionalized in economic life through the administrative provisions that regulate the behavior of guild members in their trade dealings. Freedom comes to them through law; there is no master whom they must obey; and, so long as they keep their oath to the godhead and their loyalty to the guild, they are free to act according to their business interests, responsible to no superior. Each of these steps towards man's introduction into a realm of justice, law, and freedom originally resulted from the organizing action of the state in the economic field. But such recognitions of the early role of the state were barred by economic solipsism. Thus did the mentality of the market hold sway. The absorption of the economy by marketing concepts was so complete that none of the social disciplines could escape its effects. Unwittingly, they were turned into strongholds of economistic modes of thought.

⊂ 2 ⊃

The Two Meanings of *Economic*

I. THE FORMAL AND SUBSTANTIVE DEFINITIONS

One simple recognition, from which all attempts at clarification of the place of the economy in society must start, is the fact that the term *economic,* as commonly used to describe a type of human activity, is a compound of two meanings. These have separate roots, independent of one another. It is not difficult to identify them, even though a number of broadly synonymous words are available for each. The first meaning, the formal, springs from the logical character of the means–ends relationship, as in *economizing* or *economical;* from this meaning springs the scarcity definition of *economic.* The second, the substantive meaning, points to the elemental fact that human beings, like all other living things, cannot exist for any length of time without a physical environment that sustains them; this is the origin of the substantive definition of *economic.* The two meanings, the formal and the substantive, have nothing in common.

The current concept of *economic* is, then, a compound of two meanings. While hardly anyone would seriously deny this fact, its implications for the social sciences (always excepting economics) are rarely touched upon. Whenever sociology, anthropology, or history deals with matters pertaining to human livelihood, the term *economic* is taken for granted. It is employed loosely, relying for a frame of reference now on its scarcity connotation, now on its substantive connotation, thus oscillating between two unrelated poles of meaning.

The substantive meaning stems, in brief, from man's patent dependence for his livelihood upon nature and his fellows. He survives by virtue of an institutionalized interaction between himself and his natural surroundings. That process is the economy, which supplies him with the means of satisfying his material wants. This phrase should not be taken to signify that the wants to be satisfied are exclusively bodily needs, such as food and shelter, however essential these be for his survival, for such a restriction would absurdly restrict the realm of the economy. The means, not the wants, are material. Whether the useful objects are required to avert starvation or are needed for educational, military, or religious purposes is irrelevant. So long as the wants depend for their fulfillment on material objects, the reference is economic. *Economic* here denotes nothing else than "bearing reference to the process of satisfying material wants." To study human livelihood is to study the economy in this substantive sense of the term, and this is the sense in which *economic* is used throughout this book.

The formal meaning has an entirely different origin. Stemming from the means–ends relationship, it is a universal whose referents are not restricted to any one field of human interest. Logical or mathematical terms of this sort are called *formal* in contrast to the specific areas to which they are applied. Such a meaning underlies the verb *maximizing,* more popularly *economizing* or—less technically, yet perhaps most precisely of all—"making the best of one's means."

A merger of two meanings into a unified concept is, of course, unexceptionable, so long as one remains conscious of the limitations of the concept thus constituted. To link the satisfaction of material wants with scarcity plus economizing and weld them into one concept may be both justified and reasonable under a market system, when and where it prevails. However, to accept the compound concept of "scarce material means and economizing" as a generally valid one must greatly increase the difficulty of dislodging the economistic fallacy from the strategic position it still holds in our thinking.

The reasons for this are obvious. The economistic fallacy, as we called it, consists in a tendency to equate the human economy with its market form. Accordingly, to eliminate this bias, a radical clarification of the meaning of the word *economic* is required. Again, this cannot be achieved unless all ambiguity is removed and the formal and the substantive meanings are separately established. Telescoping them into a term of common usage, as in the compound concept, must buttress the double meaning and render that fallacy almost impregnable.

How solidly the two meanings were joined can be inferred from the ironic fate of that most controversial of modern mythological figures—economic man. The postulates underlying this creation of scientific lore were contested on all conceivable grounds—psychological, moral, and methodological, yet the meaning of the attribute *economic* was never seriously doubted. Arguments clashed on the concept *man*, not on the term *economic*. No question was raised as to which of the two series of attributes the epithet was meant to convey—those of an entity of nature, dependent for its existence on the favor of environmental conditions as are plant and beast, or those of an entity of the mind, subject to the norm of maximum results at minimum expense, as are angels or devils, infants or philosophers, insofar as they are credited with reason. Rather, it was taken for granted that economic man, that authentic representative of nineteenth-century rationalism, dwelt in a world of discourse where brute existence and the principle of maximization were mystically compounded. Our hero was both attacked and defended as a symbol of an ideal–material unity which, *on those grounds*, would be upheld or discarded, as the case might be. At no time was the secular debate deflected to even a passing consideration of which of the two meanings of economic, the formal or the substantive, economic man was supposed to represent.

II. THE DISTINCTION IN NEOCLASSICAL ECONOMICS

Recognition of the twofold roots of the term economic is, of course, by no means new. It may be said that neoclassical economic theory was formed, in about 1870, out of the distinction between the scarcity and the substantive definitions of *economic*. Neoclassical economics was established on Carl Menger's premise (*Grundsätze* [*Principles*] 1871) that the appropriate concern of economics was the allocation of insufficient means to provide for man's livelihood. This was the first statement of the postulate of scarcity or maximization. As a succinct formulation of the logic of rational action with reference to the economy, this statement ranks high among the achievements of the human mind. Its importance was enhanced by a superb relevance

to the actual operation of market institutions which, because of their
maximizing effects in day-to-day activities, were by their very nature
amenable to such an approach.

Later, Menger wished to supplement his *Principles* so as not
to appear to ignore the primitive, archaic, or other early societies that
were beginning to be studied by the social sciences. Cultural anthropology revealed a variety of nongainful motivations that induced
man to take part in production; sociology refuted the myth of an
all-pervading utilitarian bias; ancient history told of high cultures of
great wealth that had no market systems. Menger himself seems to
have held that economizing attitudes are restricted to utilitarian
value scales in a sense that we should regard today as setting an
undue limitation on the logic of the ends–means relationship. This
may have been one of the reasons why he hesitated to embark on
theorizing about other than "advanced" countries, where such
value scales can be assumed.

Menger became anxious to limit the strict application of his
Principles to the modern exchange economy (*Verkehrswirtschaft*). He
refused to permit either a reprint or a translation of the first edition,
which he deemed in need of completion. He resigned his chair at the
University of Vienna in order to devote himself exclusively to that
task. After an effort of fifty years, during which he seems to have
again and again reverted to the task, he left a revised manuscript
behind him which was published posthumously in Vienna in 1923.
This second edition abounds with references to the distinction between the exchange or market economy for which the *Principles* was
designed, on the one hand and nonmarket or "backward"
economies, on the other. Menger uses several words to designate
those "backward" economies: *zuruckgeblieben, unzivilisiert, unent-
wickelt*.

The posthumous edition of the *Grundsätze* included four fully
completed new chapters. At least one of these is of prime theoretical
importance for the problems of definition and method that exercise
the minds of contemporary scholars in this field. As Menger
explained it, the economy has *two* "elemental directions," *one* of
which was the economizing direction stemming from the insufficiency of means, while the *other* was the "technoeconomic" direction, as he called it, derived from the physical requirements of
production regardless of the sufficiency or insufficiency of means:

I shall designate the two directions in which the human economy may point—the technical and the economizing—as elemental, for this reason. Although in the actual economy these two directions as presented in the two previous sections occur *as a rule* [my italics] together, and indeed *almost* [my italics] never found separately, they nevertheless spring from *essentially different and mutually independent sources* [Menger's italics]. In some fields of economic activity the two occur, in fact, separately, and in some not inconceivable types of economies either of them may in fact regularly appear without the other. . . . The two directions in which the human economy may point are not mutually dependent upon one another; both are primary and elemental. Their regular joint occurrence in the actual economy results merely from the circumstance that the causative factors that give rise to each of them *almost* [my italics] without exception happen to coincide.[1]

Menger's discussion of these elementary facts has, however, been forgotten. The posthumous edition, where the distinction between the two directions of the economy was made, has never been translated into English. No presentation of neoclassical economics (including Lionel Robbins' *Essay*, 1935)[2] deals with the "two directions." The London School of Economics edition of the *Principles* in its rare book series (1933) chose the first edition (1871). F. A. Hayek, in a preface to this "replica" edition, helped to remove the posthumous Menger from the consciousness of economists by passing over the manuscript as "fragmentary and disordered." "For the present, at any rate," Professor Hayek concluded, "The results of the work of Menger's later years must be regarded as lost." Some seventeen years later, when the *Principles*, with F. H. Knight's preface was translated into English (1950), the first edition—half the size of the second— was once more selected. Moreover, throughout the book, the translation rendered the term *wirtschaftend* (literally: engaged in economic activity) as *economizing*.[3] Yet, according to Menger himself, *econ-*

---

[1] Carl Menger, *Grundsätze der Volkswirtschaftslehre*, ed. Karl Menger (Vienna: 1923) p. 77.

[2] Lionel Robbins, *An Essay on the Nature and Significance of Economic Science*, 2nd edition (London: Macmillan and Co., 1935).

[3] Carl Menger, *Principles of Economics*, trans. and ed. James Dingwall and Bert F. Hoselitz, with an introduction by Frank H. Knight (Glencoe, Ill.: The Free Press, 1950). Cf. Karl Polanyi, "Carl Menger's Two Meanings of 'Economic,'" in *Studies in Economic Anthropology*, ed. G. Dalton (Washington, D.C.: American Anthropological Association, 1971).

omizing was the equivalent not of *wirtschaftend,* but of *sparend,* a term he expressly introduced in the posthumous edition in order to distinguish the allocation of insufficient means from another direction of the economy that does not necessarily imply insufficiency.

Because of the brilliant and formidable achievements of price theory opened up by Menger, the new *economizing* or formal meaning of economic became *the* meaning, and the more traditional, but seemingly pedestrian, meaning of *materiality,* which was not necessarily scarcity-bound, lost academic status and was eventually forgotten. Neoclassical economics was founded on the new meaning, while at the same time the old, material or substantive meaning faded from consciousness and lost its identity for economic thought.

III.   THE FALLACY OF RELATIVE CHOICE AND SCARCITY

The stress on theoretical analysis thus brought in its wake a complete disregard for the requirements of other economic disciplines, such as the sociology of economic institutions, primitive economics, or economic history, that were also engaged in the study of human livelihood. No sooner had the irreducible distinction between the two meanings been discovered than the substantive meaning was discarded in favor of the formal, thus producing the economic analysts' insistence, at least by implication, that all disciplines dealing with the economy have for their true subject not some aspect of the satisfaction, of material wants but the choices among the uses of scarce means. The compound concept was admitted on sufferance, on the assumption that its substantive ingredients could safely be forgotten, thus reducing the concept to the formal elements of choice and scarcity which alone were supposed to matter.

The difficulty of our task now becomes apparent. A clarification of the way the compound concept harbors two independent meanings is not enough, for as soon as we are within striking distance of that aim, showing the ambiguity of the compound concept so readily employed by layman and scholar alike, it turns out to be merely a screen for the scarcity definition, while the substantive aspect of the economy, on which we had wished to focus, is disdainfully relegated to oblivion.

Let us survey then the prima facie grounds on which a semantic monopoly of the term *economic* is so confidently claimed for the scarcity definition. An attempt to develop the substantive definition will follow. We will start from a formulation of the scarcity definition that is as broad as possible, yet sufficiently articulated in its applicability to be subjected to operational testing.

To make the best of one's means, which logically is the norm implied in the formal meaning of economic, refers to situations where *choice* is induced by an *insufficiency* of means, a condition of affairs which is justly described as a *scarcity* situation. The terms *choice, insufficiency* and *scarcity* as they occur in this context should be carefully viewed in their mutual relationship, for economic analysts' claims take on varied forms. We are told sometimes that economics has for its subject acts of choice, sometimes that choice involves insufficiency of means, at other times that insufficiency of means involves choice, at still other times that insufficient means are scarce means, and even that scarce means are economic ones.

Such assertions appear to establish the range of the formal meaning as comprising the economy in all its manifestations. For the economy, however instituted, would then consist of scarce means under conditions that induce acts of choice among the different uses of the insufficient means and, consequently, be capable of description in the formal terms of the scarcity definition. It could then be rightly claimed that the substantive definition of *economic* was superfluous, or at least of negligible importance, since all conceivable economies would fall under the scarcity definition. However, strictly speaking, none of these claims is valid.

To start with the broadest term, choice, it may occur whether means are sufficient or not. Moral choice is indicated by the intent of the agent to do what is right; such a crossroads of good and evil is the subject of ethics. A purely operational crossroads, on the other hand, would be this: a man, travelling along a road, reaches the foot of a mountain when two paths branch off, both leading by different ways to his destination. Assuming there is nothing to choose between them—same length, same amenities, same steepness—he is still called upon to decide upon either one or the other of the paths or else relinquish his aim altogether. At neither the moral nor the operational crossroads, it appears, is an insufficiency of means postulated. Indeed, ample means may make it rather more difficult, though no less necessary, to choose. If it is often awkward, sometimes even painful, to make a choice, this may be caused as much by an abundance of means as by their insufficiency.

Choice, then, does not necessarily imply insufficiency of means. But neither does insufficiency of means imply either choice or scarcity. To begin with the latter case: for a scarcity situation to arise, not only an insufficiency of means but also choice induced by that insufficiency must exist. Now, insufficiency of means does not induce choice unless at least two further conditions are given: more than one use for the means, otherwise there would be nothing to choose *from*; and more than one end, with an indication of which of them is preferred, otherwise there would be nothing to choose *by*. For a scarcity situation to arise, then, a number of conditions must be given, over and above the insufficiency of the means.

Yet—the point is vital—even if these conditions were satisfied, there would be still no more than an accidental connection between a scarcity situation and the economy. The rules of choice, as we saw, apply to all fields of means–ends relationships, factual and conventional, actual or imaginary. For means are anything that is serviceable, whether by virtue of natural qualities, like coal for heating, or by virtue of the conventional rules, like dollar bills to pay debts. It is also unimportant whether the grades of preference in regard to ends are based on technological, moral, scientific, superstitious, or purely arbitrary scales.

Thus the task of attaining the greatest satisfaction through the rational use of insufficient means is in no way restricted to the human economy. It is set whether a general is disposing his troops for battle, a chess player is scheming to sacrifice a pawn, a lawyer is marshalling evidence to defend a client, an artist is husbanding his effects, a believer is earmarking prayers and good works to attain the best grade of salvation in his reach, or, to come closer to the point, a thrifty housewife is planning the week's purchases. Whether troops, pawns, evidence, artistic highlights, pious acts, or week's pay, the insufficient means can be employed in different ways, but once used in one way, they cannot be employed in another; also the choosers have more than one end in view and are required to employ the means so as to attain those most preferred.

Examples could be multiplied indefinitely, but the more instances are adduced, the more apparent it becomes that scarcity situations exist in any number of fields, and that the formal meaning of *economic* bears in fact only an accidental reference to the substantive meaning. The "material" character of the want satisfaction is given whether there is maximizing or not; and maximizing is given whether the means and ends are material or not.

As to the rules of behavior, they are of equally universal validity. There are altogether two. The one, "Relate means to ends," covers the whole range of the logic of rational action. The second rule sums up formal economics, i.e., that part of the logic of rational action which is concerned with scarcity situations. It runs: "Allocate scarce means in such a way that no end with a lower order of rank on the preference scale is provided for while an end with a higher rank remains unprovided for." In plain English, "Do not act like a fool." Still, formal economics has for its content no more than exactly that.

Thus the two root meanings of *economic* are worlds apart; the formal meaning can in no way substitute for the substantive meaning. *Economical* or *economizing* refers to choice between the alternative uses of insufficient means. The substantive meaning, on the other hand, implies neither choice nor insufficiency. Man's livelihood may or may not involve the need for choice. Custom and tradition, as a rule, eliminate choice, and if choice there be, it need not be induced by the limiting effects of any "scarcity" of means. Some of the most important natural and social conditions of life, such as the availability of air and water or a loving mother's devotion to her infant, are not, as a rule, so limiting. The cogency at play in the one case, in the other differs as the power of syllogism differs from the force of gravitation. The laws of the first are those of nature, the laws of the other are those of the mind.

IV.   SCARCITY AND INSUFFICIENCY

But how then does formal economics apply to empirical situations at all? If means are not inherently insufficient, how can their insufficiency be tested? And, since "scarcity" was shown to be distinct from insufficiency of means, how in turn can the presence of scarcity be ascertained?

Means are insufficient if the following test is negative. Lay out the ends in a sequence and cover each of the ends in that sequence with a unit of the means; if the means are exhausted before the last end is reached, the means are insufficient. Should the performance of the test be inconvenient or physically impossible, "earmarking" will do—perform this same operation in thought and "allocate" each unit of the means to an end. If you run out of means before the last end is reached, the means are insufficient.

To speak in this instance of scarce means, instead of merely insufficient ones—a general practice today—lacks precision and only creates confusion. Means that have been found insufficient can be allocated only in the same way they would have been allocated if found sufficient, namely, to the given end. To call them scarce would imply that a choice had been induced by the insufficiency of the means, which is not so. To ignore this operational criterion is to lose the point of the definition of scarcity altogether—to create the illusion that there exists some distinctive way of allocating insufficient means, "a more economical one," so to speak. But insufficiency of means does not in itself create a scarcity situation. If you have not got enough, you must go without. For a choice to be set, the means, besides being insufficient, must also have an alternative use; and there must be more than one end, as well as a scale of preferences attached to them.

Each of these conditions—insufficiency of means, alternativity of means, multiplicity of ends, scales of preference—is subject to empirical testing. Whether in a given instance the term "scarce" applies to the means or not, is therefore a question of fact. It sets the limit to the applicability of the formal or scarcity definition of *economic* in any field—including the economy.

The current compound concept of economics, in fusing the satisfaction of material wants with scarcity, postulates no less than the insufficiency of all things material. The first pronouncement was that of Hobbes in the *Leviathan*. He deduced the need for absolute power in the state in order to prevent humans from tearing one another to pieces like a pack of famished wolves. Actually, his aim was to prevent religious wars through the strong arm of a secular government. Yet that metaphor may have reflected a world in which the medieval commonwealth was giving way to the forces released by the Commercial Revolution and predatory competition among the engrossing wealthy was devouring chunks of the communal village lands. A century later the market began to organize the economy in a framework that actually operated through scarcity situations, and Hume echoed the Hobbesian adage. An omnipresent necessity for choice arose from the insufficiency of the means universally employed—money. Whether the things money could buy were insufficient was not here being tested. Undeniably, given each individual's culturally determined needs and the scope of money, these means were insufficient to satisfy all needs. Actually, this situation was no more than an organizational feature of our economy.

Now, the universal belief that of no thing is there enough to go round was urged, sometimes as common-sense proposition about the limited nature of supply, sometimes as a philosophically reckless postulate of the unlimited nature of individual wants and needs. Yet in either case, while the statement claimed to be empirical, it was no more than a dogmatic assertion covering up an arbitrary definition and a specific historical circumstance. Once a human being was circumscribed as an "individual in the market," the proposition as we hinted, was easy to substantiate. Of his wants and needs, only those mattered that money could satisfy through the purchase of things offered in markets; the wants and needs themselves were restricted to those of isolated individuals. Therefore, by definition, no wants and needs other than those supplied in the market were to be recognized, and no person other than the individual in isolation was to be accepted as a human being. It is easy to see that what was being tested here was not the nature of human wants and needs but only the description of a market situation as a scarcity situation. In other words, since market situations do not, in principle, know wants and needs other than those expressed by individuals, and wants and needs are here restricted to things that can be supplied in a market, any discussion of the nature of human wants and needs in general was without substance. In terms of wants and needs, only utilitarian value scales of isolated individuals operating in markets were considered.

Once before we have encountered a famed discussion which, at closer view, revealed itself as a mere verbalization of undefined issues: Was economic man real man? But the meaning of *economic* was taken for granted, which excluded the possibility of any relevant answer.

Yet at the very dawn of formulated thought on the subject, Aristotle rejected the scarcity definition. Some of his argument, such as his views on the source of trading profits, seems misplaced or distorted by the context; at other points, as on slavery, his thinking is out of tune with present convictions. All the more astounding is his penetration of a problem which up to our days has baffled the mind.

Aristotle starts his *Politics* by denying that man's livelihood as

such raises a problem of scarcity. Solon's verse proclaimed falsely of
the urge for riches, "there is no limit set among men." On the
contrary, wrote Aristotle, the true riches of a household, or of a state,
are the necessities of life that can be stored and will keep. And they
are nothing more than means to an end, and like all means they are
intrinsically limited and determined by their ends. In the household, they are means to life; in the *polis*, they are means to the good
life. Human wants and needs are therefore not boundless, as Solon's
saying implied. This fallacy is Aristotle's main target. Do not animals, from their birth, find their natural sustenance waiting for them
in their environment? And do not men, too, find sustenance in their
mothers' milk and, eventually, in their environment, whether they
be hunters, herdsmen, or tillers of the soil? Even trade fits into this
natural pattern, so long as it is practiced as exchange in kind. No
need is considered natural save that for sustenance. Insofar as scarcity seems to spring "from the demand side," Aristotle puts this
down to a misconceived notion of the good life, twisted into a desire
for more and more physical goods and enjoyments. The elixir of the
good life—the thrill and elevation of day-long theater, mass jury
service, electioneering and holding office, and great festivals, but
also of battles and naval combats—can be neither hoarded nor physically possessed. True, the good life requires, "this is generally admitted," that the citizen have leisure in order to devote himself to the
service of the *polis*. As we saw, meeting this requirement entails in
part slavery and in part the payment of citizens for the performance
of their public duties (or otherwise not admitting artisans to citizenship at all). But, for yet another reason, the problem of scarcity does
not arise for Aristotle. The economy—in the first place a matter of the
domestic household—concerns the relationship of the *persons* who
make up such institutions as the household or other "natural " units
like the *polis*. His concept of the economy then, denotes an institutionalized process through which sustenance is ensured. He
could, therefore, put down the misconception of unlimited human
wants and needs to two circumstances: the first, the acquisition of
foodstuffs by commercial traders which thus linked the unlimited
activity of moneymaking to the otherwise limited requirements of
family and *polis*; the second, the misinterpretation of the good life in
the novel notion of a utilitarian accumulation of physical pleasure.
Given the right institutions, such as *oikos* and *polis*, and the traditional
understanding of the good life, Aristotle saw no room for the scarcity

factor in the human economy. He did not himself fail to connect this fact with the institutions of slavery and infanticide and his own violent aversion to the comforts of life. But for this realistic fact, his negation of scarcity might have been as dogmatic and as unfavorable to empirical research as the economic formalism of our time. As it is, the first of realist thinkers was also the first to recognize that an inquiry into the role of scarcity in the human economy presupposes an adherence to the substantive meaning of *economic*.[4]

V. THE SUBSTANTIVE ECONOMY: INTERACTION AND INSTITUTIONS

The claim of the scarcity definition to be the sole legitimate representative of the meaning of *economic* does not stand scrutiny. It leaves the sociologist, the anthropologist, the economic historian helpless in confronting the task of penetrating the economy of any time or place. For the accomplishment of that task, the social sciences must turn to the substantive meaning of economic.

The economy as an instituted process of interaction serving the satisfaction of material wants forms a vital part of every human community. Without an economy in this sense, no society could exist for any length of time.

The substantive economy must be understood as being constituted on two levels: one is the interaction between man and his surroundings; the other is the institutionalization of that process. In actuality, the two are inseparable; we will, however, treat of them separately.

Interaction accounts for the material result in terms of survival. It can be broken down into two kinds of changes, locational and appropriational, which may go together or not. The first consists in a change of place; the second in a change of "hands."

In a locational movement, as the term implies, things move spatially; in an appropriational movement either the person (or persons) at whose disposal things are, or the extent to which they have rights of disposal over them, changes. The locational movement is

4 Cf. M. I. Finley, "Aristotle and Economic Analysis," *Past and Present*, Number 47 (May 1970), pp. 3–25.

most clearly illustrated by transportation and production; the appropriational by transactions and dispositions.

Human beings play a prime part: they expend effort in labor; they themselves move about and they dispose of their possessions and activities in a process that eventually serves the end of their survival. Production represents what is perhaps the most spectacular economic feat, namely, the ordered advance of all material means towards the consumption stage of livelihood. Together the two kinds of movement complete the economy as a process.

Locational movements comprise hunts, expeditions and raids, hewing wood and drawing water, the international system of shipping, railroads, and air transportation. Carrying may, in early times, loom larger than production; and even later it plays a preponderant part in production itself. It has been asserted before that production can be reduced to locational movements of objects, large and small, from the biggest to the minutest particles of matter. The growth of grain from the seed is a movement of matter through space, as is the upsurge of skyscrapers in a boom. However, as we will see, the economic character of production is derived from the fact that the locational movement involves labor combined in a specific way with other goods. Of this later on.

Appropriation was turned into a broad factual term by Max Weber.[5] Its original meaning, that of legal acquisition of property, was extended to include de facto disposal over anything worth possessing, wholly or partly, whether physical object, right, prestige, or the mere chance of exploiting advantageous situations. Appropriational change may take place as between "hands," where "hand" denotes any person or group of persons capable of possessing. This forcibly brings out the shifts in the property sphere that accompany the interactional process. Things and persons pass partly or totally from one appropriational sphere to another. Management and administration, circulation of goods, distribution of income, tribute and taxation, all are equally fields of appropriation. That which changes "hands" need not be an object as a whole, it may be no more than its partial use.

Appropriational movements differ not only in regard to what is

---

[5] Max Weber, *Wirtschaft und Gesellschaft* (Tübingen: 1922), Chapter 1, part 10, p. 73 ff.; *The Theory of Social and Economic Organization*, trans. A. M. Henderson and Talcott Parsons, ed. Talcott Parsons (New York: The Free Press, 1947), p. 139 ff.

moved but also in the character of the movement. Transactional movements are two-sided and occur as between "hands"; dispositional movements are one-sided actions of a "hand" to which custom or law attaches definite legal effects. In the past, the distinction could be mostly related to the type of "hand" in question: private persons or firms were deemed to be making appropriational changes through transactions, while the public "hand" was credited with making dispositions. This distinction tends to be ignored in our day by corporations and governments alike. The state buys ånd sells, while private corporations administer and dispose.

   Combination of goods seems an odd term to employ for that part of the interaction commonly called production. Yet it is a basic fact of the substantive economy that things are useful because they serve a need either directly or indirectly through their combinations. This distinction between goods of a "lower" and a "higher" order, introduced by Carl Menger, is at the root of production.[6] Even in a state of general scarcity, no production ensues in the absence of goods of a "higher" order, foremostly labor. On the other hand, if "labor" is given, production will take place, whether labor is in abundance or not, so long as no goods of a "lower" order are available that can satisfy the needs. It is therefore misleading, as was made manifest in Menger's posthumous work, to attribute the phenomenon of production to some general scarcity of goods; rather, production stems from the difference between the goods of a "lower" order and those of a "higher" order—a technological faćt of the substantive economy. In this line of thought, the preeminence of labor as a factor of production is due to the circumstance that labor is the most general agent among all goods of the "higher order."

   On an interactional level then, the economy comprises man as a collector, grower, carrier, and maker of useful things, as well as nature as the silent obstructor and furtherer; also their interpenetration in a sequence of physical, chemical, physiological, psychological, and social events occurring from the smallest to the largest scale. The process is empirical, its parts are capable of operational definition and direct observation.

   Yet such a process has no separate existence. The thread of interaction may branch off, interlock, form a web; but whether the mesh of cause and effect is simple or complex, it can no more be

[6] Carl Menger, *Principles of Economics*, pp. 58–59.

physically detached from the ecological, technological, and societal tissue which forms its background than can the life process from the animal organism.

In order to achieve the manifold coherence of the actual economy, the bare process of interaction must acquire a further set of properties, without which the economy could hardly be said to exist. If the material survival of man were the result of a mere fleeting chain causation—possessing neither definite location in time or space (that is, unity and stability), nor permanent points of reference (that is, structure), nor definite modes of action in regard to the whole (that is, function), nor ways of being influenced by societal goals (that is, policy relevance)—it could never have attained the dignity and importance of the human economy. The properties of unity and stability, structure and function, history and policy accrue to the economy through its institutional vestment.

This lays down the foundation for the concept of the human economy as an institutionalized process of interaction which functions to provide material means in society.

ᴄᴈ 3 ᴄᴈ

Forms of Integration and Supporting Structures

I. INTRODUCTION

Of the various ways in which economies can be classified empirically, that one should be given preference which avoids prejudging the significant issues arising from the problem of the place occupied by the economy in the society as a whole. The issues which stand out are those involving the relations of the economic process to the political and cultural spheres of the society at large. To avoid prejudging these issues, it is suggested here that economies be grouped according to the form of integration dominant in each of them. Integration is present in the economic process to the extent that those movements of goods and persons which overcome the effect of space, time, and occupational differentials are institutionalized so as to create interdependence among the movements. Thus, for example, regional differences within a territory, the time span between sowing and harvesting, or the specialization of labor is overcome by whatever movements of the respective crops, manufactures, and labor make their distribution more effective. Forms of integration thus designate the institutionalized movements through which the elements of the economic process—from material resources and labor to the transportation, storage, and distribution of goods—are connected.

The main forms of integration in the human economy are, as we

find them, reciprocity, redistribution, and exchange. We are employing these terms descriptively, that is, as far as possible, without
suggesting any motivational or valuational association. This does not
mean, of course, that forms of integration do not differ precisely in
the manner in which, under each of them, the economy is related to
the political and cultural areas of the society. What matters here is
that our forms of integration are relatively independent of the aims
and character of the governments,as well as of the ideals and ways of
the cultures in question. A neutral attitude in regard to the moral and
philosophical implications of governmental policies and cultural values is, indeed, a requisite of any objective inquiry into the shifting
relations of the economic process to the political and cultural spheres
of the society as a whole. Unless our classification of empirical
economies is reasonably free of motivational and valuational associations, our conclusions might be vitiated by unwittingly assuming
what is supposedly deduced from the evidence.

One might think of the forms of integration as diagrams representing the patterns made by the movements of goods and persons in
the economy, whether these movements consist of changes in their
location, in their appropriation, or in both. As a form of integration,
reciprocity describes the movement of goods and services (or the
disposal over them) between corresponding points of a symmetrical
arrangement; redistribution stands for a movement towards a center
and out of it again, whether the objects are physically moved or only
the disposition over them is shifted; and exchange represents a
movement in a similar sense, but this time between any two dispersed or random points in the system. In a diagrammatic presentation, arrows connecting points that are symmetrically arranged in
regard to one or more axes might stand for reciprocity; redistribution
would require a star-shaped diagram, some arrows pointing towards
the center, others away from it; and exchange could be pictured as
arrows connecting random points, each directed both ways.

Clearly, such diagrams can serve no more than a formal purpose.
They explain neither how the movement they represent can happen
in society nor how that movement, once it occurs, brings about its
integrative effect. To have such effect, and indeed to come about at
all, such movement requires the presence of definite structures in
society.

It is important at this point to distinguish between forms of
integration, supporting structures, and personal attitudes. The diffi-

culty lies in the common usage of the terms *reciprocity, redistribution*, and *exchange*, which are often employed to denote different types of personal attitudes, as well as the forms of integration suggested here—two very different matters. The effective functioning of forms of integration depends upon the presence of definite institutional structures, and it has long been tempting for some to assume that such structures are the result of certain kinds of personal attitudes. Adam Smith's "propensity to truck, barter, and exchange" is perhaps the most famous example. It is not true, however, that individual acts and attitudes simply add up to create the institutional structures that support the forms of integration.

The supporting structures, their basic organization, and their validation spring from the societal sphere. In the case of redistribution, as will be readily seen, the movement cannot proceed without an established center from which the redistribution takes place. Redistribution is not an individual pattern of behavior at all; and even where started on a small scale, it would depend on the prior existence of a recognized center. With reciprocity and exchange, the position is essentially the same. They certainly also denote definite kinds of personal attitudes and actions, those of mutuality and barter; but diffuse individual acts of mutuality or barter lack the essentials of effectiveness and continuity on the societal plane. Neither reciprocity nor exchange is possible on that plane without the prior existence of a structure pattern which neither is nor can be the result of individual actions of mutuality or barter. As to reciprocity, it involves the presence of two or more symmetrically placed groups whose members can behave similarly toward one another in economic matters. Since such symmetry is not restricted to duality, the reciprocating groups, as such, need in no way result from attitudes of mutuality. As to exchange, random actions of barter between individuals, if they occur at all, are incapable of producing the integrating element of price. Here, as with reciprocity, the validating and organizing factor springs not from the individual but from the collective actions of persons in structured situations. Exchange, as a form of integration, is dependent on the presence of a market system, an institutional pattern which, contrary to common assumptions, does not originate in random actions of exchange.

In the writings of some authors whose interest lay in the direction of the sociology of economic institutions—notably Durkheim, Weber, and Pareto—attention was fixed, in general terms, on the societal preconditions for different types of individual action. Yet the first writer, to our knowledge, to note an empirical connection between personal attitudes of reciprocity and the independently given presence of symmetrical institutions was Richard Thurnwald, in 1916, in his study of the marriage system of the Banaro of New Guinea.[1] Bronislaw Malinowski recognized the importance of Thurnwald's remarks and predicted that, on close inspection, reciprocative situations in human society would always be found to rest on symmetrical forms of basic organization. His own description of the Trobriand family system and of the Kula trade made the point clear. From here it was only a step to generalize reciprocity into one of several forms of integration and, similarly, to generalize symmetry into one of several supporting structures. This was done by adding redistribution and exchange to the former category, and centricity and the market to the latter. These observations help make clear how and why individual personal attitudes so often fail to have societal effects in the absence of given societal conditions. Only in a symmetrically organized environment will reciprocative attitudes result in economic institutions of any importance; only where centers have been established beforehand can the cooperative attitude of individuals produce a redistributive economy; and only in the presence of markets instituted to that purpose will the bartering attitude of individuals result in prices that integrate the economic activities of the community.

II. RECIPROCITY AND SYMMETRY

To return to reciprocity, a group that decided to organize its relationships on that footing would, to effect its purpose, have to split up into symmetrical subgroups whose corresponding members could identify one another as such. Members of group A could then establish relationships of mutuality with their counterparts in group B, and vice versa; or three, four, or more groups may be symmetrical with regard to two or more axes, and the members of these groups need not reciprocate with one another but with the corresponding

[1] Richard Thurnwald, "Banaro Society: Social Organization and Kinship System of a Tribe in the Interior of New Guinea," *Memoirs of the American Anthropological Association*, Volume 3, Number 4, 1916.

members of third groups toward which they stand in analogous relations. A number of families, living in huts that form a circle, might then assist their right-hand neighbors and be assisted by their left-hand neighbors in an endless chain of reciprocity without any mutuality among them.

The best authenticated reciprocity system was described by Malinowski in regard to the Trobriand Islanders. A Trobriand man's responsibility is towards his sister's family, but he himself is not, on that account, assisted by his sister's husband. Rather, if he is married, his assistance comes from his own wife's brother—a member of a third, analogously placed family. Not only is subsistence farming based on reciprocal relations in the Trobriands, but the "fish and chips" arrangement between coastal and inland villages is also carried out on a reciprocity basis. The fish come at one time, the yams at another, and the exchange partners in this case are not groups of relatives but whole villages. The Kula, however, is by far the greatest institution of this type in the Trobriands. Here again partnership in exchange exists, but the acts of exchange are disjointed. Gift and countergift occur at different occasions, ceremonialized in such a way as to ban all notion of equivalency. Also, the trading of useful objects is not only separated from the Kula, but sharply contrasted to the Kula transactions.

Whatever the origin of man's feeling of satisfaction in experiencing an adequate reaction, the connotations of adequacy are very different depending on the situation to which they are referable. While our sense of justice seeks adequacy in terms of punishment and reward, reciprocal movements of goods require adequacy in terms of gift and countergift. Adequacy, in this case, means primarily that the right person at the right occasion should return the right kind of object. The right person is, of course, the symmetrically posited person. Indeed, but for such symmetry, the complex give-and-take involved in a system of reciprocity could not work. Adequate behavior is often that of equity and consideration, or at least a show of it—and not the *stricti juris* attitude of ancient law, as in Shylock's insistence on his pound of flesh. Hardly anywhere do we find the habit of reciprocal gifts accompanied by hard bargaining practices. Whatever the reason for the elasticity which gives preference to equity rather than stringency, it clearly tends to discourage the manifestations of economic self-interest in the give-and-take relations of reciprocity.

III. REDISTRIBUTION AND CENTRICITY

Redistribution obtains within a group to the extent that in the allocation of goods (including land and natural resources) they are collected in one hand and distributed by virtue of custom, law, or ad hoc central decision. In this way, the reuniting of divided labor is achieved. Sometimes the system amounts simply to storage-cum-redistribution, at other times the "collecting" is merely dispositional, i.e., there is a change in the rights of appropriation without any change in the actual location of the goods. Redistribution occurs for many reasons and on several levels, from the primitive hunting tribe to the vast storage systems of ancient Egypt, Sumeria, Babylon, or Peru. With a hunt, any other method of distribution would lead to disintegration of the horde or band; but, since only "division of labor" of the hunters can ensure results, the game or catch must then be distributed. In large territories, differences of soil and climate may make the reuniting of labor necessary; in other cases, it is caused by discrepancies in points of time, such as those between harvest and consumption.

Methods of collection in a redistributive system may differ widely, varying from a simple pooling of catch or game to elaborate methods of taxation in kind. The Trobriander chief had the privilege of polygyny. He might have forty wives, taken from the forty sub-clans of the island; and they ensured the purveyance of a large amount of produce to the chief's yam store from all the villages by the wives' brothers. Thus the chief exercised the political function of chiefdom on a basis derived from the marriage customs of the tribe, the link being the privilege of polygyny.

With some primitive peoples, public life is much more highly developed than with our latter-day societies of the West. Festivals, ceremonial food distribution, religious solemnities, mortuary feasts, visits of state, harvests, and other celebrations offer endless occasions for large-scale distribution of food and, sometimes, even of manufactured articles. An important function of the chief is collecting and giving away this wealth on such ceremonial occasions, which amounts to the redistribution of the produce collected and stored by him. It makes no difference whether the sanction for collection was kinship, feudal ties, political bonds, or forthright taxation, the result is always the same—storage-cum-redistribution. What, as in some native African kingdoms, may often appear to the

Western eye as despotic taxation or ruthless exploitation of subjects, is more often merely a phase in this redistributive process.

Redistribution—whether physical or merely dispositional—cannot take place unless there are channels through which the movement toward the center and the subsequent movement away from it can happen. Some degree of centricity is therefore imperative. Central organization is vital, not only politically but also economically. Among the Trobrianders, the incipient state is more a redistributing facility than an organ of defense or class rule.

The taxation system in modern states is but another form of redistribution. Such a redistribution of purchasing power may be valued for its own sake, i.e., for purposes demanded by social ideals, but the principle of integration is the same—collecting and redistributing from a center.

Redistribution may also apply to a group smaller than society, such as a household or manor. The best known instances of "householding" are the Central African kraal, the Northwest African Kasbas, the Hebrew patriarchal household, the Greek estate of Aristotle's time, the Roman *familia*, the medieval manor, or the typical peasant household the world over before the general marketing of its produce.

In ancient Greek as well as in Germanic, *householding* is the term used to denote catering for one's own group. *Oikonomia* in Greek is the etymon of the word economy; *Haushaltung* in German corresponds strictly to this. The principle of "provisioning one's self" remains the same whether the "self" thus cared for is a family, a city, or a manor. Traditionally it was thought to be the original form of economic life. Even Karl Bücher, who was the first to draw attention to the entirely different character of savage society, fell into the mistake of propounding the rule of the "individual hunt for food" as the preeconomic stage of human history.[2]

Householding, however, is by no means an early form of economic life. The notion that man began by looking after himself and his family must be discarded as erroneous. The further back in the history of human society we go, the less do we find man acting for his own personal benefit in economic matters, looking after his own personal interest. Only under a comparatively advanced form of

---

[2] Karl Bücher, *Die Entstehung der Volkswirtschaft*, Tübingen: 1893; *Industrial Evolution* (Toronto: University of Toronto Press, 1901), Ch. 3.

agricultural society does householding become practicable and then, it is true, fairly general. Before that, the widely spread institution of the "small family" is not economically institutionalized, except for some cooking of food.

IV.   EXCHANGE AND MARKETS

Exchange is a two-way movement of goods between persons oriented toward the gain ensuing for each from the resulting terms. In simpler terms, barter is the behavior of persons who exchange goods on the assumption that each makes the most of it. Higgling and haggling are of the essence here, since there is no other way each person can make sure he is gaining as much as possible from the bargain. Haggling, in this case, is not the result of some human frailty, but a behavior pattern logically required by the mechanism of the market.

It is usually not realized that random acts of barter would not, by themselves, produce prices unless a market pattern were in existence that made the bartering intent of the persons effective. In this sense, barter is very much like reciprocity and redistribution. The principle of behavior, in order to become effective, requires the presence of some institutional structure. The market pattern is never traceable to the mere desire of individuals to "truck, barter, and exchange." Its origins come from other directions, as we shall see.

V.   FORMS OF INTEGRATION AND STAGES OF DEVELOPMENT

Forms of integration do not represent necessary "stages of development." Several subordinate forms may be present alongside the dominant one, which may itself reoccur after a temporary eclipse. Tribal societies practice reciprocity and redistribution, while archaic societies are predominantly redistributive, though to some extent they also allow room for exchange. Reciprocity, which plays a dominant part in most tribal communities, survives as an important, although subordinate, trait in the redistributive archaic empires where foreign trade was still largely organized on the principle of reciprocity. Indeed, during an emergency it was introduced again on a large scale in the twentieth century, under the name of lend–lease, between societies in which marketing and exchange were otherwise dominant. Redistribution, the method in tribal and archaic society beside which exchange plays only a minor part, grew to great importance in the later Roman Empire and is actually gaining ground today in modern industrial states. Conversely, it would be a mistake rigidly to identify the dominance of exchange with the nineteenth-century economy of the West. More than once in the course of human history have markets played a significant part in integrating the economy, although never on a territorial scale, nor with a comprehensiveness even faintly comparable to that of the nineteenth-century West. However, here again a change is noticeable in the present century, during which a decline of competition and a recession of markets from their nineteenth-century peak has set in.

Nevertheless, a classification of economies according to the dominant forms of integration is illuminating. What historians are more-or-less traditionally wont to call "economic systems," i.e., empirical economies of a definite type, such as feudalism or capitalism, fall into this pattern. We need only fix our attention on the role of land and labor in society—the two elements on which the dominance of the forms of integration essentially depends. A tribal community is characterized by the integration of land and labor into the economy through ties of kinship. In feudal society, the ties of fealty determine the fate of land and of the labor that goes with it. In the floodwater empires, land was largely distributed (and sometimes redistributed) by temple or palace, as was labor, at least in its dependent form. The modern rise of the market to a ruling force in the economy can be traced by noting the extent to which land and food were mobilized through exchange and labor was turned into a commodity to be purchased in the market. This may help to explain the relevance of the (otherwise hardly tenable) grouping of economic systems into slavery, serfdom, and wage labor traditional with Marxism—distinctions that flow from the conviction that the character of the economy is, above all, set by the status of labor. Clearly, however, the integration of land into the economy should be regarded as hardly less vital.

B. *Institutions*

The Emergence of Economic Transactions:
From Tribal to Archaic Society

ᴄᴈ 4 ᴄᴈ

The Economy Embedded in Society

I. INTRODUCTION

It was characteristic of the economic system of the nineteenth century that it was institutionally distinct from the rest of society. In a market economy, the production and distribution of material goods is carried on through a self-regulating system of markets, governed by laws of its own, the so-called laws of supply and demand, motivated in the last resort by two simple incentives, fear of hunger and hope of gain. This institutional arrangement is thus separate from the noneconomic institutions of society: its kinship organization and its political and religious systems. Neither the blood tie, nor legal compulsion, nor religious obligation, nor fealty, nor magic created the sociologically defined situations that insured the participation of individuals in the system. They were, rather, the creation of institutions like private property in the means of production and the wage system operating on purely economic incentives.

With this state of affairs we are, of course, fairly conversant—livelihood is secured primarily by economic institutions that are activated through economic motives and governed by economic laws. Institutions, motives, and laws are specifically economic. The whole system can be imagined as working without the conscious intervention of human authority, state, or government. No motives other than those of preservation from hunger and of legitimate gain need be invoked, no legal requirement other than protection of property and enforcement of contract is necessary; yet, given the distribution of resources and purchasing power, as well as the individual scales of preferences, the result is assumed to be an optimum of want satisfaction. This is the case of "separateness" established in the nineteenth century. Now let us proceed to the less familiar alternative of "embeddedness" where we meet a number of questions that need clarification.

We will give a brief history of the problem, first in terms of status and contractus, then in the more recent terms of cultural anthropology.

II. STATUS AND CONTRACTUS

We begin with the discovery revealed by Sir Henry Sumner Maine in his *Ancient Law* (1861) that many institutions of modern society were built on contract, whereas ancient society rested on status. Status, which is set by birth—by position of and in the family—determines the rights and duties of the person, which, in turn, are derived from kinship (or adoption), totem, and other sources. This status system persists under feudalism and, with some qualifications, right up to the age of equal citizenship as established in the nineteenth century. It was gradually replaced by contractus, i.e., by rights and duties fixed through consensual transactions, or contracts. The facts themselves were first noted by Maine in his investigation of Roman law and developed in his work on village communities in East India, to whose nonmarket economies Marx also pointed.

Maine's influence on the continent was sustained by Ferdinand Toennies, a German sociologist whose conception was epitomized in the title of his work, *Community and Society (Gemeinschaft und Gesellschaft*, 1888). The terminology may appear at first confusing, but basically it is not. Community corresponded to "status society," society to "contract society."

Maine, Toennies, and Marx exerted a deep influence on Continental sociology through Max Weber, who consistently used the terms *Gemeinschaft* and *Gesellschaft* in the Toenniesian sense, *Gesellschaft* for contract-type society, *Gemeinschaft* for status-type society.

Between Maine and Toennies the emotional connotation of status or community, on the one hand, and contractus or society, on the other, were very different. Maine thought of the precontractus condition of mankind as the dark ages of tribalism; the introduction of the contract, he felt, emancipated the individual from bondage to the tribe. Toennies' sympathies, on the contrary, were rather with the warmth of the community against the impersonal business ties of society. He idealized "community" as a condition where human beings are linked together by the tissue of common experience, while 'society' was never far removed from the impersonality of the market and the "cash nexus," as Thomas Carlyle dubbed the relationship of persons connected only by market ties.

Toennies' ideal was the restoration of community—not, however, by returning to the preindustrial stage of society, but by advancing to a higher form of community that would follow upon our present civilization. He thought of it as a kind of cooperative phase of civilization that would retain the advantages of technological progress and individual freedom while restoring the wholeness of life. His position resembled, to some extent, that of Robert Owen or, among modern thinkers, that of Lewis Mumford. In Walt Whitman's *Democratic Vistas* (1871) one may discover prophetic analogies to this outlook.

Maine's and Toennies' insights into the evolution of human civilization have been broadly accepted by many scholars as keys to the history of modern society. However, for a long time no advance was made along the trails they blazed. Maine dealt with the subject as one of the history of law, including its communal forms surviving in the ancient villages of India. Toennies reconstructed the outlines of ancient and medieval civilization with the help of the "community–society" dichotomy. Neither of them attempted to apply the distinction to the actual history of economic institutions such as trade, money, and markets.

III. THE CONTRIBUTION OF ANTHROPOLOGY

The first important signs of theoretical development along these lines are found in the discoveries made in the contiguous field of anthropology by Franz Boas, Bronislaw Malinowski, and Richard Thurnwald. Their insights implied a critique of the so-called "economic man" of classical theory and led to the establishment of the discipline of primitive economics as a branch of cultural anthropology.

By a freak of history, during World War I, a trained anthropologist was marooned in his own "field." Bronislaw Malinowski was an Austrian subject, and thus technically an enemy alien, among the savages off the southwestern tip of New Guinea. For two years, the British authorities refused him permission to leave, and Malinowski ultimately returned from the Trobriand Islands with the material for "The Primitive Economics of the Trobriand Islanders" (1921), *The Argonauts of the Western Pacific* (1922), *Crime and Custom in Savage Society* (1926), *The Sexual Life of Savages* (1929), and *Coral Gardens and Their Magic* (1935). He died in the United States in 1942. His works have affected not only the study of anthropology but also the viewpoints and methods of economic history. Richard Thurnwald of Berlin, whose field was New Guinea, published his account of the Banaro in 1916 in the *American Anthropologist*. His influence was felt in the Anglo-Saxon world chiefly through its impact upon Malinowski. (Thurnwald himself, though praised as an anthropologist, was a pupil of Max Weber.)

Malinowski's account left the reader with the conviction that members of preliterate communities behaved, on the whole, understandably to us. Their seemingly exotic behavior could be explained in terms of institutions that stimulated motives different from those we usually act upon but not foreign to us in other ways. In regard to subsistence, there was a widespread practice of reciprocity, i.e., members of a group behaved toward members of another group as the members of that group, or a third group, were expected to behave, in turn, toward them. A man from a village subclan, for instance, provided his sister's family with garden produce, though the sister would usually dwell in her husband's village, sometimes at quite a distance from her brother's habitation—an arrangement that resulted in a great deal of uneconomical hiking on the part of a diligent brother. Of course, if the brother happened to be married, a similar service would be rendered to his family by his wife's brothers. Apart from this substantial contribution to matrilineal relatives' households, a system of reciprocal gifts and countergifts was generated that appealed to economic self-interest only indirectly, the controlling motives being noneconomic, e.g., pride in public recognition of civic virtues as a brother or gardener. The mechanism of reciprocity, effective in regard to the comparatively simple matter of food supplies, also accounted for the highly complex institution of the *Kula*, an esthetic variant of international trade. *Kula* transactions between inhabitants of the archipelago covered a number of years, dozens of miles of unsafe seas, and thousands of individual objects exchanged as gifts between individual partners living on distant islands. The whole institution acted to minimize rivalry and conflict and maximize the joy of giving and receiving gifts.

None of these facts recorded by Malinowski was especially new. Similar ones had been observed time and again in other spots. Although contrasting in tone and coloring with the *potlatch* of the Kwakiutl Indians, the *Kula* was no more peculiar than that hypersnobbistic display of wilful destruction, discovered and exhaustively described by the great American anthropologist, Franz Boas, in *The Social Organization of the Secret Societies of the Kwakiutl "Potlatch"* (1895).

Yet, Malinowski's brilliant attack on the concept of "economic man" that unconsciously underlay the traditional approach of ethnographers and anthropologists created, in primitive economics, a new branch of social anthropology of the greatest interest to economic historians.

The mystical "individualistic savage" was now dead and buried, as was his antipode, the "communistic savage." It appeared that not so much the mind as the institutions of the savage differed from our own. Even widespread communal ownership turned out, under the anthropologist's microscope, to be different from what it was supposed to be. Although land did indeed belong to the tribe or sib, a network of individual rights was also found to exist that deprived the term "communal property" of most of its content. Margaret Mead has described this as the man "belonging" to the piece of land rather than the land to the man. Behavior is ruled not so much by rights of disposal vested in individuals as by commitments of individuals to cultivate definite plots of land. To speak of either individual or communal property in land, where the very notion of property is inapplicable, appears hardly meaningful. Among the Trobrianders themselves, distributions happened largely through gifts and countergifts.

As a general conclusion, it can be stated that the production and distribution of material goods was embedded in social relations of a noneconomic kind. No institutionally separate economic system—no network of economic institutions—could be said to exist. Neither labor nor the disposal of objects nor their distribution was carried on for economic motives, i.e., for the sake of gain or payment or for fear of otherwise going hungry as an individual. If we take *economic system* to mean the aggregate of behavior traits inspired by the individual motives of hunger and gain, there was no economic system in existence at all. If, however, as we should, we take that term to comprise the behavior traits relating to the production and distribution of material goods—the only meaning relevant to economic history—then we find that while there was, of course, an economic system in being, it was not institutionally separate. In effect, it was simply a by-product of the working of other , noneconomic institutions.

We might understand such a state of affairs more easily if we concentrate on the role of basic social organization in channeling individual motives. In studying the kinship system of the Banaro of New Guinea, Richard Thurnwald found a complicated system of exchange marriage. No fewer than four different couples had to be united in marriage at the same occasion—each partner standing in a definite relationship to some other person of the reciprocating group. For such a system to work, grouping had to be already in existence, splitting the sib artificially into subsibs. To this purpose, the goblin-hall (or men's house) was habitually divided; those squatting on the right (*Bon*) and those squatting on the left (*Tan*) formed subsections for the purpose of the exchange marriage system. Thurnwald wrote:

> The symmetry in the arrangement of the ghost-hall is the expression of the principle of reciprocity—the principle of giving "like for like"— *retaliation* or *requital*. This seems to be the result of what is psychologically known as "adequate reaction," which is deeply rooted in man. In fact, this principle pervades the thinking of primitive peoples and often finds its expression in social organization.[1]

This remark was taken up by Malinowski in *Crime and Custom in Savage Society*. He suggested that symmetrical subdivisions in society, such as those Thurnwald had found in the goblin-hall, would be discovered to exist everywhere as the basis of reciprocity among savage peoples. Reciprocity, as a form of integration, and symmetri-

[1] Thurnwald, "Banaro Society."

cal organization went together. This may be the true explanation of the famous duality in social organization. Indeed, we may ask in regard to preliterate society—ignorant of bookkeeping—how could reciprocity be practiced over long stretches of time by large numbers of peoples in the most varied positions unless social organization met the need halfway by providing ready-made, symmetrical groups, members of which could behave towards one another similarly? The suggestion carried important implications for the study of social organization. It explains, among other things, the role of the intricate kinship relations often found in savage societies where they function as the bearers of social organization.

Since there is no separate economic organization and, instead, the economic system is embedded in social relations, there has to be an elaborate social organization to take care of such aspects of economic life as the division of labor, disposal of land, organization of work, inheritance, and so on. Kinship relations tend to be complicated because they have to provide the groundwork of a social organization that substitutes for a separate economic organization. (Incidentally, Thurnwald remarked that kinship relations tend to become simple as soon as separate political–economic organizations develop, since "there is no need for complicated kinship relations any more.")[2]

We have an institutionally separate economic system in our society, and an important integrating concept in our economy is that of an aggregate of interchangeable economic units. Hence the quantitative aspect of economic life. If we possess ten dollars, we do not as a rule think of them as ten individual dollars with separate names but as units that can be substituted one for another. Without such a quantitative concept, the notion of an economy is hardly meaningful.

It is important to recognize that such quantitative concepts are not generally applicable to primitive societies. The Trobriand economy, for example, is organized on a continuous give-and-take basis; yet there is no possibility of setting up a balance or using the concept of a fund. The multifarious "transactions" cannot be grouped from the economic point of view, i.e., the manner in which they affect the satisfaction of material wants. Although the economic significance of the "transactions" may be great, there is no way of assessing their importance quantitatively.

[2] Ibid.

To have shown this conclusively is another of the theoretical achievements of Malinowski. First, he listed the different kinds of economically significant give and take, from free gifts (as we would describe them) at the one extreme, to plain commercial barter (again, as we would describe it) at the other. Second, he grouped the sociologically defined relationships in which all of the different give-and-take relationships occur. He then related all the different types of gifts, payments, and transactions to those relationships.[3]

The category of "free gifts" Malinowski found to be altogether exceptional or, rather, anomalous. Charity is neither necessary nor encouraged, and the notion of gift is invariably associated with that of countergift. Consequently, even obviously "free" gifts are usually construed as countergifts for some service rendered by the recipient. Most important, he found that "the natives would undoubtedly not think of free gifts as forming one class, as being all of the same nature."[4] Clearly, such an attitude would make it impossible for an individual to form the notion of such gifts comprising an economic sphere of activity in the sense of maintaining or increasing a fund.

In the group of transactions where the gift must be returned in equivalent form, Malinowski encountered a surprising fact. Obviously, this is the group which, according to our notions, comes nearest to the exchange of equivalents and should be practically indistinguishable from trade. Far from it! Quite often the same object is exchanged back and forth between partners, thus depriving the transactions of any conceivable economic sense or meaning. Actually this simple device, equivalence, far from representing a step in the direction of economic rationality, becomes a safeguard against the intrusion of utilitarian elements into the transaction. The purpose of the exchange is to draw relationships closer and strengthen the ties between the partners. This purpose would obviously *not* be served by anything even approximating haggling over food between blood relatives.

Actual barter and trade among the Trobrianders is distinct from any other type of gift giving. Whereas in the ceremonial exchange of fish and yams a mutual sense of equivalence prevails between the two sides, in barter of fish for yams there is haggling. Such barter of

---

[3] Bronislaw Malinowski, *Argonauts of the Western Pacific* (New York: E. P. Dutton, 1961) p. 176 ff.

[4] Ibid., p. 178.

useful articles is characterized by the absence of ceremonial forms and special exchange partners. In regard to manufactured goods, barter is restricted to new objects, second-hand goods, which may have a personal value, being excluded.

In general, in all the forms of exchange excepting barter, the amounts and kinds of things given and taken in return are specifically related to the type of social relationship involved, whether that of family, clan, subclan, village community, district, or tribe. Each is distinct and separate in both terminology and native thought. Under such conditions, the aggregative concepts of fund or balance, of loss and gain, were obviously inapplicable.

The result of all these characteristics of primitive societies is the impossibility of organizing the economy, even in thought, as an entity distinct from the social relations in which its elements are embedded. There is, however, no need to organize it either, since the social relationships integrated in the noneconomic institutions of society automatically take care of the economic system. In tribal society the economic process is embedded in the kinship relations that formalize the situations out of which organized economic activities spring. What there is of production and distribution of goods, as well as organization of productive services, is therefore found instituted in terms of kinship. Various groups dispose of the grounds for hunting, fishing, trapping, and collecting and of pasture and arable land. Hoarding staples forms part of the corporate activities of the kin, whether engaged in hostilities or in ceremonial feasts. Treasure circulates by virtue of status or of religious or military requirements. Partial appropriation of the same physical units of land, trees, or timber to various strata of relatives fragmentizes the notion of property. Utilitarian needs often depend for their satisfaction not on the possession of things but rather on the claim to solicited services. In the absence of prices, acts of exchange lack the operational features essential to a quantitative approach; instead, the qualitative and prestige impact of the "valuables" steals the show. As a result, a man's practical orientation would be hampered rather than helped by an "economic" focus in a way of life that has its points of reference outside the economic sphere.

The solidarity of the tribe was thus cemented by an organization of the economy that acted to neutralize the disruptive effects of hunger and gain while exploiting to the full the socializing forces inherent in a common economic destiny. The social relations in which the economy was embedded sheltered the disposal over land and labor from the corrosive effects of antagonistic emotions. Thus the integration of man and nature into the economy was largely left to the working of the basic organization of society, which took care almost incidentally of the economic needs of the group, such as they were.

All this, of course, concerns only a subjective awareness of the economy. The objective process, as it actually unrolls, is given apart from any conceptual awareness on the part of the participants, for the causational sequence to which we owe the availability of the necessities of life is present no matter how men conceptualize their existence. The seasons bring around the harvest time with its strain and its relaxation; warlike trade has both the rhythm of preparation and foregathering and the concluding solemnity of the return of the venturers; all kinds of artifacts, whether canoes or ornaments, are produced and eventually used by various groups of persons; every day of the week, food is prepared at the family hearth. Yet, for all this, the unity and coherence of these economic activities may remain unconscious in the minds of the participants. For the accompanying series of interactions between men and their natural surroundings, whether centering on the physical moving of objects or on appropriational changes will, as a rule, carry meanings and reflect dependencies, of which the economic is only one. And even if the economic happens to stand out, there may be counteracting forces at work to prevent the institutionalized movements from forming a coherent whole. In effect, such counteracting forces are largely responsible for the absence of a concept of the economic in primitive society.

ᴄᴈ 5 ᴄᴈ

The Emergence of Economic Transactions

I. FROM TRIBAL TO ARCHAIC

For a study of the emergence of economic transactions, we may select that period of the story of man which starts with the tribal background of civilization and reaches to the archaic conditions so general at the outset of civilized society.

On the absolute scale, of course, different societies reached the civilized stage at different times, when clan ties began to loosen and the groups reached the threshold of history. But whether Far Eastern, Western European, Babylonian, or Mexican civilization is in question, a sharply drawn line separates the tribal and the archaic institutions of a society, whose continuity has otherwise been maintained.

The foremost obstacle to the study of the emergence of economic transactions in early times is the difficulty of identifying the economic process at all under conditions where neither its unity nor its coherence was safeguarded through any specifically economic institutions. Kin, state, magic, and religion are the outstanding noneconomic spheres to which the economic process is found attached in early society. These are also the originators of the status systems from which economic transactions eventually tend to "peel off."

It is the emergence of the state level that offers an explanation of the apparent gap separating archaic society from the tribal or clan level. War and trade—the activities that so frequently force clans or tribes to create a superior formation of power to serve as a roof over them—require means, in terms of men, cattle, and material, whose collection and manipulation induces movements in society that result in entirely novel institutions. But, however novel these may be on the institutional level, the actual land and people, the goods and the services, must have been present in the context of clan or tribe before they were repatterned in a more advanced form on the archaic level. At this stage of our argument, it must already appear likely that the manner in which land and labor were embedded in the noneconomic institutions of clan life exerted some influence on the form in which, subsequently, such institutions emerged under archaic conditions.

A brief comparison of tribal with archaic conditions will elucidate the nature of the problem. Essentially, it consists in the gradual emergence of the economic from its embeddedness in the tissue of society described in such general terms as "way of life," "status," or "goods of fortune." These terms do not yet leave room for the economic as a distinct aspect of the broader social unit. Out of this "way of life," however, a man's "occupation" (his economic role) tends to shade off. From comprehensive status transactions involving the appropriational movements of land, cattle, and slaves, so-called "economic" transactions become dissociated. From the distinguishable parts of the three "goods of fortune"—namely life, honor, and rank—the needs for safety of life and limb and for wealth rather than treasure eventually tend to separate. Essentially, the process happens on the institutional level. That is, unless economic activities differentiate from the general process of living; unless land can change hands apart from a change in the station of the person invested with it; unless honor is no longer identified with wealth nor wealth with honor; and unless neither of them is a mere corollary of the power that keeps a person alive where the wealthless and powerless are doomed for lack of ransom or means to pay a fine, the economic aspect of things cannot assert itself in its own colors.

In some archaic societies—though not in all—we find the new state of affairs developing. In one form or another, a new interest emerges centering on transactions of a new kind. Alongside of the status transactions practiced by the tribe, transactions that refer not so much to the status of men as to the importance of goods as such make their appearance. To adoption, marriage, emancipation, or indenture, transactions are added that concern solely the disposal over land or cattle. Although for a long time to come status transactions and economic transactions were linked too closely to be easily separated, the outcome of the development was not in doubt: the emergence of economic transactions proper would permit individuals to use more freely the economic means available in society and thereby to open up the possibility of an almost unlimited material advance throughout the community.

This was, as we hinted, not the only line of archaic progress. In the Sumerian city states and their enormously enlarged replica, the Pharaonic empire, economic transactions remained entirely subordinate. The economic achievements of the New Empire, and even those of Ptolemaic Egypt, were due primarily to a refinement of the methods by which a redistributive economy was run.

But Mesopotamia, in spite of its redistributive economy, did introduce transactional and dispositional methods of great economic significance. Superficially they resembled some of the market methods employed in the archaic city states of Greece. For in both marketless Babylon and the *agora* of Athens, although in very different ways, status transactions were supplemented by economic transactions.

How did this consequential development set in, and what determined its different direction in the East and in the West? This is the question.

II.   COMMUNAL SOLIDARITY IN ARCHAIC SOCIETIES

Of all the basic principles governing the development of early economic institutions, the need for the maintenance of communal solidarity deserves pride of place. Domestic and foreign relations are in stark contrast: solidarity here, enmity there, rule the day. "They" are the objects of hostility, depradation, and enslavement, "we" belong together and our communal life is governed by the principles of reciprocity, redistribution, and the exchange of equivalents.

The principles of "we" and "they" behavior meet and merge in many ways, but far from effacing the differences, this rather tends to emphasize them. Marriage and trade—the semipeaceful derivatives of raid and war—lead to a penetration of foreign usages into the "we" culture and, eventually, acculturation may ensue from such continuous intimate contacts. But domestic unity must be maintained all the more decisively in regard to the economy of the tribe. To this end, integrative methods are employed that shun contention and antagonism within the group and instead foster the arts of solidarity. Reciprocity shifts the emphasis from the utilitarian element of selfish advantage to the warmth of experience and gratification that flow from mutually honorific neighborhood contacts with those to whom we are joined in specific relations of objective status and personal intimacy. Redistribution strengthens internal communal ties by all the psychological means at men's disposal. Self-identification with power and authority; affection and admiration mixed with fear and reluctance towards the power at the center; vicarious enjoyment of the display of communal wealth; enjoyment of equal rights of status and standing; participation in a variety of celebrations linked to the "funneling" and "syphoning" of festive food—all these invigorate the societal emotions and bind the community closer.

All this is inimical to an atmosphere in which economic transactions thrive. Tribal solidarity and embeddedness of the economy rely on relationships of the gift and countergift type, as well as on the practice of allowing perishable victuals to accumulate at a center and the reverse practice of allowing the hoarded produce to flow out again to the members. Solidarity in the economic field is thus maintained through institutions that ensure noncontentious dealings with food. As a logical result, a quasi taboo emerges, similar to those governing the breach of sex laws or the defiance of the authority of chief and priest, those embodiments of the protective and redistributive functions in society. This taboo enjoins gainful transactions in regard to food. Since the very existence of the community depends on the unremitting action of extreme forces toward solidarity, buttressed by ritual, magic, and religious sanctions, no random behavior contrary to this supreme directive on survival can be countenanced. This would be so, even if a strong pressure of economic self-interest did make its appearance, which is doubtful. Once the prize of status and recognition is set on them, pride, honor, and vanity are at least as efficacious in directing man's selfishness as are gainful economic motives.

For this reason, it becomes all the more important to explain why, in some archaic societies, economic transactions do make their appearance. To this the economistic mind had a ready answer: as soon as the superstitions of magic had sufficiently faded to permit enlightened thoughts to enter the field, the hold of tribal taboos was loosened, and man's natural acquisitive instincts asserted themselves. The individual, released from the shackles of irrational fears, followed the path of natural self-interest, and started out on gainful barter. Ricardo's deer and beaver tell the rest of the story.[1] The philosophers of the cash nexus did not stop to ask the obvious question. What, then, prevented this emotionally atomized community from dissolving into its component particles?

The answer to the question of how economic transactions emerged must be dominated by the consideration that neither tribal solidarity nor its redistributive mechanism disappeared in archaic society. On the contrary, it was from these selfsame sources that the new civilizations derived their superlative staying power. The religious sanctions, so vital to territorial government in both early Assyria and Hammurabi's Babylonia, coupled in each case with a further increase of redistributive activities over those of the tribal stage, should suffice to prove this conclusively.

The true explanation lies in a diametrically opposite direction from that suggested by the economic rationalism of the nineteenth century: exchange, the most precarious of human ties, spread into the economy when it could be made to serve the validation of the community. In effect, economic transactions became possible when they could be made gainless. The peril to solidarity involved in making selfish gain at the expense of the food of one's brother had first to be removed by eliminating the invidious element inherent in such exchanges. This was achieved through the declaration of equivalencies in the name of the representative of the godhead itself. Exchange behavior was made legitimate by establishing the equivalence of that which was to be exchanged. The quality of the Mesopotamian states, by virtue of which they were enabled to achieve this, was honored by men ever after through the recognition of the state as the fount of justice.

An entirely different resolution of the conflict between communal solidarity and the antisocial perils of economic transactions was achieved by the development, in the small city states such as Athens and (partly) Israel, of the peasant type. Hesiod's curse on the

[1] David Ricardo, *The Principles of Political Economy and Taxation* (London: J. M. Dent & Sons Ltd., 1911), p. 6.

"Iron Age" and Amos's outcry against the marketers of foodstuffs introduce us to civilizations that permit gainful transactions in the means of man's livelihood. Soon these transactions were to be made openly in the marketplace. Herodotus focused his monumental study of the war between Europe and Asia on the clash of two ways of life: freedom and mobility of the marketplace against blind obedience in a marketless empire of justice. And yet the Athenian *agora* did not know freedom of the market in the modern sense, and the city state continued to practice all the prerogatives of the tribal body over its members. Nonetheless, the principle of gainful exchange between members of the community had been admitted, and a safeguard against discord removed from their ranks. All too often, a disruption of the *polis* into the city of the rich and the city of the poor was thereby induced and perpetuated. Also, the confines of the neighborhood market set narrow limits to the expansion of the state. The Greek *polis* of the mother country, which owed so much of its radiant and invigorating freedom to the early use of small coins in a popular food market, never succeeded in overcoming either the territorial limitation inherent in the *agora* or the disruptive class struggle that appeared to be its accompaniment.[2]

This all too rough sketch of the ways in which economic transactions entered the social fabric of early societies nevertheless indicates some of the very different avenues of their political and economic development. Archaic economic institutions evolved everywhere from the embedded economies of the tribal stage, and this development was never unrelated to the transcendent requirements of social solidarity.

---

[2] Cf. Karl Polanyi, "On the Comparative Treatment of Economic Institutions in Antiquity with Illustrations from Athens, Mycenae, and Alalakh," in *City Invincible: A Symposium on Urbanization and Cultural Development in the Ancient Near East*, ed. C. H. Kraeling and R. M. Adams (Chicago: University of Chicago Press, 1960), pp. 333–340.

☙ 6 ☙

Equivalencies in Archaic Societies

It is a peculiar fact that, of the different ways of distributing food, the working of redistribution from a center, or reciprocity action between members of the community, should be fairly well known to us while the beginnings of the exchange methods that form our everyday life are still obscure. Paradoxically enough, this situation stems mainly from our exchange and marketing bias, for exchange appeared "natural" and therefore in no need of explanation and the supposedly universal institution of the market seemed to account for the omnipresence of exchange. Since 1776, our alleged propensity to truck, barter, and exchange was looked upon as the complete explanation of exchange behavior. It was more than a century later that Karl Bücher noted that, far from being of a trucking disposition, primitive man was strongly averse to acts of barter. Moreover, we may add, his native aversion to the exchange of foodstuffs was eventually overcome not so much in favor of the market habit, as our forefathers thought, but rather by virtue of that quite different set of institutions we have here referred to as equivalencies.

Equivalents as such are merely devices by which quantitative relations are set up between goods of different kinds, like a measure of corn and a jar of wine (one to one), or big and small cattle (one to ten). The usual rendering of such relations as "price" is misleading since, as hinted above, it tends to restrict the concept of equivalency to market exchange. Actually, the scope of equivalencies was by no means limited to situations of market exchange. Indeed, on these simple devices hinged a series of institutions that channeled the movements of staple foods and similar objects in early society.

An operational definition of equivalency would have to center on the fact that the term indicates the number of units of one kind of object which, when substituted for a number of units of another kind, leaves the result unaffected with respect to a definite operation such as reciprocating, redistributing, or exchanging.

When a gift is reciprocated, the adequate countergift is, as a rule, indicated in conventional terms: an inland village's vegetables reciprocated with fish from a village near the sea; male bride-price goods with female dowry goods; the commoner's modest gift with the chieftain's richer countergift; or, on the contrary, the subject's feudal dues with a slight recognition from the prince.

I. SUBSTITUTIVE EQUIVALENCIES

In the redistributive process, equivalencies play no less vital a part. Whether goods are being collected by the center or redistributed by it, whether the objects are classified as taxes or feudal dues or maybe even as voluntary gifts, it is frequently inevitable that one kind of goods should be substituted for another.

From the Old World, we will list a series of cases of substitutive equivalencies. Given an economy in kind, the relevant principle will everywhere be found to be identical. Whether taxes are defrayed, rations are claimed, or a singular vow of temple bondage is redeemed (Lev. 27), the items of large-scale staple finance are balanced, debts are cleared, or an exchange system of goods is arranged between central government and citizens. In all these cases, there is a need for reckoning with goods of different kinds, replacing one by the other or, as the saying goes, "adding up apples and pears." Established ratios are the only possible device for these operations.

Taxation systems in the irrigational empires of the Ancient Near East, for instance, provide for payment of a fixed amount per unit of land, whether actual payment is made in barley, oil, wine, or wool; correspondingly, claim for rations, whether of workers or soldiers, should provide for choice among the various kinds of necessaries such as barley, oil, wine, and wool. In regard to taxes, any rigid insistence on payment in definite produce would be impractical in the absence of markets and money; similarly, in regard to rations, the total absence of choice would also often be impractical. The central administration itself is largely indifferent to these choices since they will cancel out among the various regions of the country. Hence, at the basis of state finance we find a system of equivalencies that allows for the complexities of taxation with tithing, along with the fixing of rations by means of a point system.

An administrative exchange of goods between farmers and palace was practiced in Babylonia, for example. From a document concerning cancellation of debts under Hammurabi it appears that farmers were free to list surplus produce they wished to exchange against palace goods. These goods might be assumed to be either foreign imports or tax goods from other regions or even manufactures of the palace. Inevitably, much uncertainty attached to the transaction before it could be carried into effect. The total value of the goods offered by the farmer and of those received in exchange from the palace would eventually have to be equal. The palace might not be in possession of enough of the goods desired in exchange (the latter should always be assumed to be of the approved kind and quality). To the mediating official would fall the intricate task of adjusting the palace goods to the goods desired by the farmer (the various officials presumably pooling their information before deciding on the proportions in which the farmer's wish, if possible, could be satisfied). All in all then, when there was such exchange between the government and farmers, substitution between the items on either side's lists was regulated through equivalencies. On both sides, "apples and pears" would have to be added up before totals could be equated.

Trading in kind was also much indebted to substitutive equivalencies for calculating the remuneration of the traders and for the clearing method of payment between traders. Profits made on turnover were reckoned on totals of the equivalents, irrespective of the specific staples involved. In the absence of such equivalencies, obligations could not have been registered with the accounting authorities—whether traders' guild or palace treasury or perhaps (in some cases, like slave sales) the palace officials—thus enabling the creditor to enforce his claims through a clearing process that charged the debtor's account. Payment through clearing was regularly practised in metropolitan and in Cappadocian trade. This might explain how large numbers of arbitration awards, setting out the sums the defendant was beholden to pay the successful plaintiff, seem to have been self-executing. Though no executive organs are in evidence, there is not a single clear case on record in which the claimant complained of not receiving from the debtor the sum awarded to him.[1]

Neither the riskless methods of trading nor the clearing practices of payment produced in such marketless economies are understandable without reference to substitutive equivalencies validated by custom or law.

II. RATIONS

The importance of rationing for economies in kind is amply confirmed by the Sumerian and Babylonian tablets that set out the amounts of barley due to persons of varying ages and the feed of domestic animals. The operation of rationing presents a combination of the quality and quantity of provisions mirrored in the double aspect of the word "necessaries." These may mean both the kinds of foodstuffs needed for survival and the amounts of them actually required to sustain life. It is in this sense that Aristotle refers to the compulsory exchange of necessaries still practiced by some "barbarian" peoples in his time.[2]

The same meaning inheres in the term for bread ration used in the Lord's Prayer, "give us our daily bread." Old Testament references in Luke 11:3 and Matthew 6:11 indicate a definite amount of bread is meant, namely a normal loaf (*ton arton*), no less and no more. Proverbs 30:7–9 runs "7. Two [things] have I required of thee; deny [them] not before I die; 8. Remove far from me vanity and lies; give me neither poverty nor riches; feed me with food convenient for me; 9. Lest I be full, and deny thee and say, Who is the Lord? or lest I be poor, and steal, and take the name of my God [in vain]." The archaic meaning of *convenient*. (O.E.D.) is given as "suitable, becoming, appropriate." Luther's translation reads *"mein bescheiden Theil Speise."*

---

[1] Karl Polanyi, "Marketless Trading in Hammurabis' Time," in *Trade and Market in the Early Empires,* ed. K. Polanyi, C. M. Arensberg and H. W. Pearson (Glencoe, Ill.: Free Press and Falcon's Wing Press, 1957), pp. 12–26.

[2] Aristotle, *Politics,* Book I, Chapter 9.

Again, *bescheiden* here means *portion*. The Schlachter translation has *"mein zugemessenes Brot."* Operationally, a weighed-out portion is meant. (Cf. Lev. 26:26 below.) Schlachter's *Zugemessen* is the term employed by Schwenzner for *Nig. Ba: "Ba:* ration, portion."[3] The "Zadokite Document," contemporaneous with the Dead Sea Scriptures, refers to rations.[4] Chronologically, it falls between Leviticus and the New Testament. A much later Talmud prayer has, "the necessary food."

Famine rations are designated in the Old Testament as weighed out, but "not satisfying" in amount, in Jehovah's curse (Lev. 26:26): "And when I have broken the staff of your bread, ten women shall bake your bread in one oven, and they shall deliver you your bread again by weight, and ye shall eat and not be satisfied." And Elias Bickerman has shown the Hebrew slave in Ptolamaic Egypt was entitled to a ration.[5] Further research is clearly indicated, but the concept of ration seems to have held operational significance.

This meaning of ration, the amount limited in both quantity and quality, appears to belong to man as a basic economic right in archaic society.

Justice was ensured throughout the community as long as payments or obligations, claims or rations were discharged in the terms of the alternatives spelt out in the equivalency. Under another, no less important aspect of redistribution, equivalencies made budgeting and planning possible, together with the checks and controls necessary for their efficacious performance. The equivalency here served less as a standard of value (to employ the modern term) than as a means of "accountancy."

III. EXCHANGE EQUIVALENCIES

Once exchange becomes frequent, equivalencies clearly can play the role of prices if there is indirect exchange by way of money. But the range of equivalencies is then by no means limited to goods such as foodstuffs, precious metals, or raw materials. Any dealing in the

---

[3] Walter Schwenzner, *Das geschäftliche Leben in Alten Babylonien* (Leipzig: J. C. Hinrichs, 1916).

[4] *The Dead Sea Scriptures,* trans. and ed. Theodor H. Gaster (Garden City, N.Y.: Doubleday, 1956), p. 83.

[5] Elias Bickermann, *Die Makkabäer* (Berlin: Schocken Verlag, 1935).

sphere of the substantive economy that involved what we would regard as a transaction stood under the law of equivalence. Only equivalents were exchangeable, whether the notion referred to land or labor, goods or money, or any combination of these; whether it involved ownership or use only, or even conditional items such as surpluses still to be achieved.

To be more specific (adding a modern translation in brackets), equivalencies are on record concerning goods (prices); services (wages); use of money or other fungibles over time (interest); the use of a boat plus boatman (hire); the use of land or house (rent); and others. Equivalencies in the Mesopotamian world comprised in this way almost all dealings, such as the sale and rent of land, houses, men, and cattle, as well as boats, not excluding transactions in regard to fungibles such as silver, barley, oil, wine, bricks, copper, and lead. In striking contrast to modern notions, no distinction was made among the different sources of revenue such as wages, rent, interest, and profit. The one condition of the validity of transactions or disposals was that they involve no exploitation on either side, that they be just by maintaining equivalence.

Exchange equivalencies are of special importance for the independent peasant farmer: they help to tide him over in an emergency whether the neighbor is bound to lend him the "necessaries" he needs or to exchange them against the equivalent (Deut. 15:7–8).

Aristotle's argument on "natural trade" in his *Politics,* for example, rests on the premise that, like other forms of exchange, trade stems from the requirements of self-sufficiency. Pristine self-sufficiency is impaired when the family increases in numbers and its members are compelled to settle apart. The individual families which formerly "used in common the goods they held in common" are now forced to a mutual sharing of their surpluses. The resulting exchange—a purely operational outcome of the sharing—then restores their self-sufficiency. Natural trade is such a gainless exchange. In support of his argument, Aristotle appeals to the following contemporary facts:

> Some barbarians still practice such exchange, for they are expected to give in exchange the necessaries of life, as much as is actually needed, but certainly no more, for example wine for corn, handing over the one and taking the other in return, and so with every one of the staples of the sort. The practice of barter of this manner and type was not, there-

fore, contrary to nature, nor was it a branch of the act of wealth getting, for it was instituted for the restoring of man's natural self-sufficiency.[6]

In case of a crop failure or other emergency, a householder could thus count on his neighbor to supply him with a minimum of the necessaries, though no more. The transaction is incumbent on the latter 1. in regard to all the basic staples, 2. to the amount necessary in the circumstances, but definitely no more, 3. against an equivalent amount of other staples, and 4. with the exclusion of credit. For the householder who happens to possess the needed goods, exchange within these limits is compulsory. However, should the householder who is in need possess no sufficient staples to give in return as an equivalent, then he or his family will have to "work off" their debt (Neh. 5:5).

The Old Testament laws on the subject had a more articulated background. They decree a preferential treatment on behalf of members of the tribe in need. Again, the rule is 1. assistance in kind 2. to the extent needed and no more, 3. the amounts being credited ("lent"), 4. a considerate and humane handling of the debtor, and 5. a strict prohibition of any advantage derived from loaning. There is here no compulsory exchange, but an injunction of a short-term lending of the minimum amount. As a rule, a pledge is required. In case of default, it appears, the pledge is forfeit; alternatively, the debtor (or his children) are bound over to "work off" the debt.

Equivalents are rarely mentioned in the Old Testament. Nevertheless, their presence must be assumed, since otherwise doubt about the amount owed would arise, of which there is no sign, and the stringent prohibition of all forms of interest or gain would be out of place.

The Aristotelian reference to some contemporary "barbarians" differs, as we see, from the Old Testament obligation in its explicit insistence on a transaction *in rem* (exclusion of credit). However, a striking similarity appears between the Israelites and those "barbarians" insofar as the "necessary" staples, whether exchanged or lent, bear the connotation of "necessaries" both in regard to quality *and* to quantity. In modern terms, something like *rations* is meant. According to Bickerman, as referred to above, the Hebrew use of *peras* in the Tebtunis documents (46 A.D.) signifies ration or food allow-

---

[6] Aristotle, *Politics*, Book I, Chapter 9 (K.P.'s translation).

ance (e.g., "*homologia trophimou doulikou,*" to be understood as an agreement re slave rations). Westermann, in the posthumous version of his "Slavery" article in *Pauly-Wissowa,* concludes that in Ptolemaic Egypt, and possibly also in Rome, the slave had a claim to a *ration* ("*as much* of the necessaries *as are needed* to maintain life"). "Necessaries" thus often implied a restricted amount. Rations combined with equivalencies may have provided a flexible quantitative instrument of the archaic substantive economy in general.

The Mishnah is imbued with the Old Testament abhorrence of profit or advantage, derived from any transaction between members of the tribe. Its prescriptions show an obsession with the moral peril of profiteering, even if involuntarily or inadvertently. Equivalents are here deliberately employed as a safeguard against this danger.

IV. THE SOCIOLOGY OF EQUIVALENCIES

We now come to the manner in which equivalencies were established and formulated. In primitive society, the equivalency—the *Uta* of the Tikopia, for example—is mostly a matter of custom and tradition.[7] A definite shell may be exchanged for pigs; the equivalency is satisfied so long as the string of shells reaches from the pig's snout to the tip of his tail. In the laws of Eshnunna, unit measures of oil and wine are equated to other unit measures. In Hammurabi's Code, the equivalent "cost" of a boatman's hire is set out. In the Central Sudanese capital of Kuka, equivalencies of strings of cowrie and Maria Theresa dollars were proclaimed every Wednesday in the market place.

But the problem of origins is even broader than that. It includes the types of transactions that assume equivalency and the manner in which the equivalency is institutionalized. In Nuzi society of the fifteenth century B.C., one of the chief transactions, designated as *ditennutu,* may be described as the free exchange of the *use* of land, persons, cattle, money, vehicles, or other goods, against any of these goods, on the assumption that the use to the two parties can be regarded as equal. Ownership is not transferred; use alone is.

---

[7] Cf. Richard Thurnwald, *Economics in Primitive Communities* (New York: Oxford University Press, 1932), p. 252 ff.; Marcel Mauss, *The Gift,* trans. Ian Cunnison (New York: W. W. Norton, 1967), p. 8 ff.

Neither party is supposed to make a profit. In principle, the exchange, since it refers to use only, is limited in time. Clearly the uses comprised in *ditennutu* would, in modern terms, be described as usufruct, tenancy, renting, labor service, interest, or profit. But these distinctions are here ignored. The one vital condition of validity is the absence of gain made at another's expense. Admittedly, it is more precise to say that it implies equal profit or gain to both parties than that it excludes gain altogether, but the principle here is all important. The *ditennutu,* which antedates the Mishnah by a millenium, contains the clearest indication we possess of the meaning of the casuistry contained in that law book on the prohibition of interest taking by Jew from Jew.

What concerns us here is the reference of *ditennutu* to gain or profit. The very fact that the use of labor power, the use of a boatman together with his boat; the use of land, house, or cattle, as well as the use of money, is comprised in *ditennutu* proves that securing revenue was one of the "uses" of the goods given or received in *ditennutu.* Thus *ditennutu* "equalizes" not only the subjective gain to both parties implied in all voluntary exchange but also the "objective" gain, as reckoned by methods of accountancy; the gain of both parties is legitimate, since it is just; and just it is, since it forms an equivalency.

The implications of this archaic thought are of crucial significance for understanding the early development of the institution of the "just price"—the precursor of price.

Equivalencies between the units of different goods were meant to express proportions that both resulted from the conditions existing in that society and contributed to the maintenance of those conditions. The "justice" expressed in the equivalency is a reflection of the "justness" of the society it mirrors. How could this be otherwise, once the status rewards and standards of life that obtain in the society were necessarily reflected in the equivalencies? Consequently, what we are wont to call gain, profit, wages, rent, or other revenue, must be comprised in the equivalency, if those revenues are required to maintain existing social relations and values. This was the *rationale* of the "just price" as postulated by the schoolmen. Far from being the expression of a pious hope or of an uplifted thought irrelevant to "economic realities," as the orthodox economic classics tended to believe, the just price was an equivalency, the actual amount of which was determined either by municipal authority or by the actions of the guildsmen in the market, but in either case according to determinants relevant to the concrete social situation. The guildsmen who refused to sell below a price that would endanger the standard of his colleagues, and equally refused to accept a price that would secure for him a revenue higher than that approved by his colleagues, cooperated to create the "just price" as effectively as the municipal authority that could be called upon to fix the price directly in order to uphold these very principles.

V. EQUIVALENCIES AND MARKETS

We have briefly presented under the name of "equivalencies" a vital feature of some of the ancient economies. We will now remark on their presumable affect on the development of patterns of exchange, mainly markets and exchange-money.

The exchange use of money—and only this use of money is here in question—would hardly be necessary under conditions where transactions can rely on the help of equivalents. The use of money as a standard, on the other hand, is made many times more effective by the device of equivalents. With the help of equivalents, mutual offers can be added up and thus equated; the remaining difference may then be paid in cash.

The effect of a widespread use of equivalents on the development of markets is ambiguous. While equivalents might seem to favor set-price markets, administrative forms of trade might be even more facilitated and obviate markets altogether. The function of the modern price-making market, with its fluctuating prices that respond directly to movements in supply and demand, could, of course, not arise, since its function consists primarily in the formation of the prices. All that can be said with assurance is that the operation of trade and money in complex societies that possessed no markets would hardly be understandable in the absence of established equivalencies. In effect, the breakdown of equivalencies where they have been known to exist may, in some cases, have induced a development towards price-making markets. It should be stressed, however, that in the absence of adequate factual data, such considerations must remain largely speculative.

☞ 7 ☜

The Economic Role of Justice, Law, and Freedom

Inside primitive society, transactions in regard to food are shunned as antisocial because they disrupt community solidarity. But while other taboos (such as those regarding sex, for example) are explicit, the ban on gainful manipulations of food is implicit in the very constitution of tribal society.

In archaic society, the ban on food and other transactions begins to lift, thus opening the way for one of the most notable advances in the history of human livelihood. Exchange of goods and services—whether sale–purchase, renting–hiring, or loaning–borrowing—permits a flexibility in the elements of the economy that causes a sharp rise in their usefulness in production and consumption alike. This significant change comes about with the dissolution of tribal society mainly in two ways: either by a limited and strictly controlled acceptance of certain kinds of transactions, or by eliminating the principle of gain from such transactions. The first is typical of some small peasant societies, e.g., Hesiodic Greece or parts of Israel in the time of Amos, the other is the method followed by the irrigational empires of Babylonia and Assyria. While the peasant society is thus put on the road to the formation of markets, the irrigational empire strikes out on a different path of no lesser consequence to the future of mankind. For it is out of this development that justice, law, and individual freedom, as creations of the state, first achieved a decisive role in the history of the human economy.

The economic role of justice in archaic empires consists in removing the tribal ban on transactions by eliminating the stigma of gain, with its disruptive implications. An economic force is thereby released which multiplies manyfold the productivity of labor in a flood-controlled agriculture. The proclamation of equivalencies is one of the main functions of the archaic king. Such a declaration provides a semireligious sanction for transactions that conforms to the "rate" or "proportion" approved by the appointee of the deity. From the early Assyrian trade colonies, the laws of Eshnunna and the Code of Hammurabi, down to the Mishna and the Babylonian Talmud of some 2500 years later; indeed, up to the time of Thomas Aquinas, if not considerably longer, the just price remained the only rate at which transactions were deemed legitimate.

But the irrigational empire achieved even more than that. While sanctioning gainless transactions and initiating an avenue for internal improvement, especially in agriculture, it avoided any development toward markets and opened up instead a nontransactional line of economic dealings, which we have termed dispositional. It is made possible by setting up rules of law, along the lines of which trading activities are expected to run. In effect, by far the greater part of trade flowed in such dispositional channels, while a much smaller part continued to proceed on transactional lines. Numerous devices ensured that no merging of the two should ensue.

Both equivalencies, which made gainless transactions possible, and rules of law, which organized riskless dispositions into a trading system, were a result of the dominance of redistributive forms of integration. But these did not operate in the ways of tyrannical administrative bureaucracy, as assumed by historians in the past. The absence, or at least the very subordinate role, of markets did not imply ponderous administrative methods tightly held in the hands of a central bureaucracy. On the contrary, gainless transactions and regulated dispositions, as legitimized by law, opened up, as we have seen, a sphere of personal freedom formerly unknown in the economic life of man.

The Catallactic Triad:
Trade, Money, and Markets

Introduction

The whole area of trade, money, and market institutions is beclouded by a methodological mist. The sociologist, the anthropologist, and the economic historian often find it difficult to ascertain the meaning and, even more so, to judge the appropriateness of the catallactic terms offered by the economist. These terms, in fact, are often worse than useless to them. Here we wish to offer three propositions on trade, money, and markets to be discussed in detail in the following three chapters.

I. SEPARATE ORIGINS OF TRADE, MONEY, AND MARKETS

From Aristotle to Karl Marx, economic specialization, or increasing division of labor, was traditionally identified with the development of trade, money, and markets. These institutions seemed to be merely different aspects of the process of economic growth. Trade appeared as the movement of goods in the market, and money as the means of exchange which facilitated that movement. Such a view can no longer be upheld in the light of present findings. As we have already suggested in the introduction, some forms of trade and various money uses gain great importance in economic life, independent of and precedent to markets. Even where market elements are present, they do not necessarily involve the existence of a supply–demand price mechanism. Prices (equivalencies) are originally

set by tradition or authority, and their change, if it occurs, is brought
about by such institutional means, not by market methods. For the
student of antiquity, fluctuating prices, not fixed prices, are the
problem. All this involves a recasting of our views of the early
organization of trade, the role of trading personnel, the characteristics of the various types of markets, the methods of carrying on
large-scale trade on conventional terms or prices, the function of
brokerage in early society, the institutional origins of the different
money uses, the role of changing weights and measures in stabiliz-
ing relative prices, the part played by treasure and stored staples in
the functioning of the monetary system under archaic conditions,
and other matters concerning the early forms of economic life.

II. SEPARATE EXTERNAL AND INTERNAL
       DEVELOPMENT

Max Weber, in his epochal work on the origins of some
economic institutions, suggested that foreign trade preceded domestic trade, that the exchange use of money originated in the foreign
sphere, and that organized markets were developed first in external
trade. Richard Thurnwald followed this up with supporting facts
drawn from the economic life of primitive communities. It can now
be stated with some assurance that the priority of the external over
the internal development of trade, money, and markets is a
phenomenon of general validity. Along these lines of research, a
number of facts have been ascertained such as the sharp separation
of the external and internal markets in Athens, in Persian towns of
the seventeenth century A.D., and in Dahoman towns of the
eighteenth and nineteenth centuries; the widely spread role of
brokerage in linking internal and external markets; administrative
methods of trading "ports of trade" from antiquity to modern times;
the use of a corn-export monopoly in Ptolemaic Egypt as a means of
establishing a "world corn market" in the eastern Mediterranean; the
role of internal and external currencies in fourth-century Greece as
shown by some cases from Book II of the pseudo-Aristotelian
Oeconomica, which proved to be less exceptional than hitherto assumed; the preponderance of foreign trade over domestic trade in
Hammurabi's Babylonia; the existence of highly organized "ports of
trade" in the second millennium B.C. in Syria, while Babylon itself
possessed no markets; the coexistence of the Mediterranean em-

porium of Tyre with its Palestinian hinterland, whose towns, as a rule, contained no marketplaces.

III. INTEGRATION OF NONMARKET ECONOMIES

The third group of propositions refers to the integration of trade, money, and market elements in the absence of a market system. This problem area was removed from all specific inquiry by the traditional assumption of the inseparable unity of trade, money, and markets. Where trade was seen, markets were assumed, and where money was in evidence, trade was assumed and, therefore, markets. Actually, over the greater part of economic history, trade, money uses, and market elements should be regarded as occurring separately. Unless trade becomes market trade and money becomes exchange-money, the question is: how does such an economy function; how, for instance, can money objects be in use for payment, other money objects be in use as a "standard," while no exchange of any appreciable amount is carried on? The role of treasure and stored staple in archaic society may provide part of the answer. Similar questions arise in regard to the large-scale functioning of trade and money in marketless economies, questions that could hardly have been formulated so long as the existence of such conditions was either denied or ignored.

The evidence in this section on trade, money, and markets aims primarily at the study of these economic institutions as they occur in nonexchange economies. This involves correlating two sets of empirical phenomena: first, the record of the historian on the nonexchange patterns of integration found in status societies—reciprocity, redistribution (and householding); second, the distinct variants of trade, money, and market institutions as they occur in status societies.

The expectation that the results obtained may also contribute towards a nonmarket economics and beyond relies, at this stage, on a formal consideration. The argument, at this juncture, falls back on a little-appreciated feature of traditional economics, not, of course, on any of its specific propositions in the theory of the market system, but rather on its broad aims. What it has successfully done for the market-ordered society still remains to be attempted, analytically and historically, for the whole range of earlier societies, where patterns of integration other than exchange have been found to prevail.

◖ 8 ◗

Traders and Trade

I. OPERATIONAL AND INSTITUTIONAL DEFINITIONS

Operationally defined, trade is a method of acquiring goods not available on the spot.[1] It is something external to the group, similar to activities we tend to associate with quite different spheres of life: namely, hunts, expeditions, and piratic raids. In every case, the point is acquiring and carrying goods from a distance. What distinguishes trade from these other activities is a two-sidedness, which also ensures its peaceful nature, absent from quests for booty and plunder.

Institutionally, under undisturbed primitive conditions, trade is like a hunt, expedition, or raid—an organized group activity. It centers in the meeting of groups belonging to different communities. One of the purposes of such meetings is the exchange of goods. These meetings, as we know, do not produce rates of exchange, but, on the contrary, presuppose them. Neither individual traders nor individual motives of gain are involved, whether the chief or king acts for the community, after collecting the "export" goods, or numerous individuals meet their counterparts on the beach. In either

---

[1] A slightly different version of this chapter, edited by George Dalton, appears in *Ancient Civilization and Trade,* ed. J. Sabloff and C. C. Hamberg-Karlovsky (Albuquerque: University of New Mexico Press, 1975), Chapter 3. An analytical essay by Dalton, "Karl Polanyi's Analysis of Long Distance Trade and His Wider Paradigm," is included in this book.

case, ceremonial and ritual elements are interwoven with the proceedings, which never lack some social or political connotation.

In primitive societies, it is readily apparent which community is actively engaged in trade and which is the passive partner. Except when trade occurs in a neutral spot, one of the two parties is a visitor, the other the host. The first carried the goods and bore the brunt of the risk and initiative; the other merely responded to the occasion. Usually the parties alternate in this role. Later on, under archaic conditions, the distinction may develop into a sharp difference between active and passive trading that involves the total organization of trade.

If it seems that we have unduly stressed "acquisition of goods from a distance" as the crucial factor in trade, it was done, inter alia, in order to work out more clearly the determinative role played by the acquisitive or import interest in the history of trade. It involves, as we saw, no less than the alternatives of peaceful versus forcible methods of satisfying that interest, alternatives that may affect the total structure of the state as well as its modes of acting in history.

The different phases in the story of nomadic civilizations, such as the Mongol and the Arabic, illustrate the point. We should distinguish here between the small-scale combination of raiding and trading, as with some Homeric Greeks and Phoenicians or Old Testament Bedouins, on the one hand, and the less obvious but much more consequential way in which the interest of great empires was served, sometimes by military, sometimes by transactional methods of acquiring goods from a distance, alternatives whose changing requirements decisively shaped their domestic and foreign policies. The permanent background factor was their acquisitive or import interest in regard to the products of their settled neighbors—their dependence on some "necessities" and, even more so, on some "luxuries" from these neighbors. Textiles and household articles belonged in the first group, gold and slaves, precious stones, silk and leather finery, cosmetics and adornments in the latter. The distinction was, of course, more slender than is sometimes realized, for what we are used to term luxuries were no more than the necessities of the rich and powerful, whose import interest determined foreign economic policy.

The acquisition of the goods on the part of the nomadic empire-builders could happen in several ways: 1. mere predatory excursions, ranging from occasional raids to permanent conquest; 2.

fostering passive trade; 3. combining predatory wars with passive trade; 4. developing active trade.

In each case, however, the character of the "empire" would tend to be different. Mere marauding expeditions, on whatever scale, do not require more than a pseudo empire such as Attila's Huns or the Avars could boast of. But a full-fledged empire of nomadic clans, such as that of Genghis Khan and his successors, which comprised farflung trade routes, would rely for its imports on passive trade organized on an enormous scale. Military power served here as a mere auxiliary of trade, policing the caravan routes, securing the debouches, and compelling the settled neighbors to grant access to their goods to all who traded in the service of the empire. A network of hostels for foreign merchants and a transcontinental postal service in the hands of the empire were designed to further the wealth of the realm through an ever-increasing volume of imports. The result was a large volume of trade, transacted by a host of traders and merchants of all nationalities along the endless trade routes of the empire, with no Mongol himself engaging actively in trade. Upon the fall of the Yuan (Mongol) dynasty in China, the Mongol clan chiefs were forced to revert to their native haunts, and the flourishing passive trade of the Genghis-khanide empire ceased forever. This situation offered a significant instance of the alternatives at issue. The fragments of Genghis Khan's steppe empire engaged in a civil war that raged for a long time between the feudal squires of the West and the Genghis-khanide princes of the East. The latter won the day, and established their ascendancy over all the khanates, for this reason: they alone could offer the prospect of a central power capable of solving the dual tasks of alternately organizing predatory incursions into the territory of their neighbors and engaging in regular commercial relations with them. Vladimirtsov emphasized that to be successful, either of these ventures—raid or trade—required not only central direction but also central "repartition," of the booty in one case and of the imported goods in the other.[2] Although the Mongols never indulged in active trade, Arabic empires, though starting from closely similar nomadic clan conditions, eventually evolved, thanks to their more democratic tendencies, a broad commercial stratum that provided for ample imports through its active trade, without recourse to predatory

---

[2] Boris Vladimirtsov, *The Life of Ghengis Khan*, trans. D. S. Mirsky (Boston and New York: Houghton, Mifflin, 1930).

methods. In this capacity for active trading, it may be surmised, lay the decisive historical superiority of the Islamic empires over the more transitory Mongol khanates, with their passive trading system.

II. INSTITUTIONAL FEATURES OF TRADE

Since, in the activities of trade, something must be carried by someone over a distance, and this movement goes in two directions, there must be 1. personnel; 2. goods; 3. carrying; and 4. two-sidedness. All these institutional features of trade permit classification according to criteria that are either sociological or technological or both. On this depends the relevance of the following analysis to the enormous variety of forms and organizations of trade in history.

A. Personnel

1. *Factor and Mercator: Status Motive and Profit Motive*

"Acquisition of goods from a distance" may be practiced by a trader either from motives peculiar to his standing in society, and as a rule comprising elements of duty or public service (status motive); or it may be done for the sake of the gain that may accrue to him from buying and selling transactions (profit motive). The typical (although by no means only) representative of the former kind of trader is the factor; the representative of the latter type is the mercator.

In spite of many combinations of the two, duty and gain stand out as sharply distinct primary motivations. If the "status motive" is reinforced by that of material benefit, the latter does not, as a rule, take the form of gain made on exchange, but rather that of gifts of treasure or landed revenue received by the trader from the master or lord by way of recompense. As it is, transactional gains usually add up to paltry sums that bear no comparison with the wealth showered upon the resourceful and successfully venturing trader by his lord. Thus, he who trades for the sake of duty and honor grows rich, while he who trades for filthy lucre remains poor—an added reason why gainful motives are under a shadow in archaic society.

The distinction between "status" motive and "profit" motive might, to the historian, seem to lose much of its relevance by virtue of the fact that most societies prior to our own were, broadly speaking, status societies where there appears to have been no room anyway for the poor trader with his profit motive. However, this would be to confuse two different functions of "status," according to whether the origin or the content of the rights and duties is meant. While in a status society the rights and duties of all groups are determined by birth, the rights and duties themselves need not, for that reason, be of an honorific character. The higher-status groups are usually expected to act from honorific motives of duty, obligation, and self-respect, but the lower-status groups may well be encouraged to indulge in gainful occupations which are looked down upon, and hardly keep their man. In ancient Greece, for instance, the status of the alien *metic* trader illustrates the point. Obversely, our modern, nonstatus societies have been, for centuries, familiar with the figure of the nonprofit trader, the agent or factor who traded for his company, not for himself, and with whom success meant not profit but preferment.

All this does not, however, affect the basic distinction between factor and mercator. The latter is engaged in trade for the sake of the profit he hopes to make on the transaction, the former trades as a part of his general duties and obligations.

2. *Upper, Lower, and "Middle" Class: Standards of Life*

The place occupied by the trader on the ladder of standards of life has been very different in different societies; indeed, even in the same society at different times. The matter is in some cases complicated by the simultaneous existence of more than one layer of trading population in the society.

In archaic society, the chief or king and his immediate entourage are alone entitled to trade, i.e., to initiate the more-or-less warlike and diplomatic ventures that lead to the "acquisition of goods from a distance." Piratic and treaty trade, whether separately or conjointly practiced, belong to the governmental sphere. The king may personally lead the venture, like Mentes, the legendary ruler of the Taphians, or only supervise its execution, as Argesilaos, authentic King of the Cyrenaika, appears to have done. But chief's or king's trade by no means implies the personal activity of the sovereign, who must in practice employ hundreds or even thousands of traders as factors or "king's merchants" to carry on trade for him. Some of them may belong to the royal family itself; others rank as princes and rulers, owning fortresses and castles, vast manorial estates; still others may count only as court personages, enjoying revenue from royal donations or, much more frequently, from the privilege of participating in the trading profits of the royal syndicate—in all cases the "king's merchants" rank with the army generals, civil governors, and other high officials among the great ones of the country.

In peasant-type societies, such as ancient Greece after the seventh century or Rome after the monarchy, king's and prince's trade ceases. Foreign trade is either discontinued, as in Rome, or reduced to passive trade. In sixth-century Greece, Solon is mentioned as a merchant, and the Peisistratids, as well as the Alkmeonids, should certainly be assumed to have at least incidentally engaged in large-scale foreign ventures in trade. But these were exceptions. Solon himself assumed that Athens was basically dependent for her food supplies on foreign corn merchants. In Israel, the inland regions developed king's trade under David that achieved a considerable level under Solomon, but after the breakup of the United Empire they became entirely dependent on passive trade. Of the three peoples, the Greeks alone produced lower-class traders in the *kapeloi*—the local retailers of food—and the *metic* class of *naukleroi*—the trading skippers. And neither of these ever developed into a middle class. This class, much idealized by Aristotle under that name, was a landed class, not a commercial class at all.

The commercial middle class of the nineteenth century is a late product of Western development. Medieval urban society typically consisted of a privileged merchant upper class of burgesses and a broad stratum of artisans and traders forming the people. Together, they were the urban community; above them ranked the landed aristocracy of the manorial countryside. Even in eighteenth-century England, the most advanced Western commercial society of the time, the successful merchant burgess rose into the landed class, leaving the "tradesman" behind him in the lower ranks of society. Not before the Reform Act of 1832 did a commercial middle class gain a standing in England.

Antiquity knows no figure of a trader other than those who belonged either to the upper or to the lower class. The first is connected with rulership and government, the other depends for his livelihood on manual labor. This fact is of the greatest importance for understanding the forms and organization of trade in ancient times.

3. Tamkarum, Metic, and Foreigner: Types of Traders in the Archaic World

The typical traders of antiquity were the *tamkarum*, the *metic*, and the foreigner. The *tamkarum* dominated the Mesopotamian region from the Sumerian beginnings to the rise of Islam, i.e., over some 3000 years. The Nile valley, too, knew only this type of trader, as did the African kingdom of Dahomey. The *metic* trader first became historically conspicuous in Athens and rose, together with Hellenism, to be the prototype of the lower-class merchant from the Indus valley to the Pillars of Hercules. In effect, it was a similar floating population of lowly merchants—not, this time, of the sea but of the land—out of which sprang the burgess merchant class of Western Europe. The third type of trader, the foreigner, is, of course, ubiquitous. He is the stranger, the bearer of "passive trade," who neither "belongs" to the community nor even enjoys the semistatus of resident alien, but is a member of an altogether different community. In the great civilizations of the East and of Africa, the leading figure of commercial life was the *tamkarum*; in Hellenic civilization it was the *metic*, but both types of civilization possessed a sprinkling of foreigners. It is against this deliberately oversimplified background, which needs many qualifications to mirror the enormous variety of configurations, that the true picture of trade in antiquity can be clearly sketched.

The *tamkarum* belonged to the factor type, he became a *tamkarum* either in a hereditary way or by appointment of the king, temple, or "great one." In his capacity of *tamkarum* he possessed a status, involving privileges and duties. His duties involved the tasks of carrying goods, from those of a porter to those of organizing caravans or fleets, and all the negotiating, information gathering, diplomacy, arrangements, haggling, and conclusion of deals related to long-distance trade. He might also serve as broker; auctioneer; keeper of safe deposits; agent of official payments, loans, and advances; and public attorney. His livelihood was not dependent on the commercial transaction in hand; it was secured by status revenue, mostly through landed property, or at least through the claim to maintenance according to his rank from the royal or temple store. If, as in Dahomey, his revenue was derived from some special commercial privilege, the transactions through which he turned that privilege to wealth were institutionally separated from the transactions he made in his capacity of *tamkarum*. Where guilds existed, to which the merchants or traders would belong by status, all this would largely be institutionalized through the guild system.

The *metic* type of trader is a resident alien. He may come from a floating population of displaced persons—fragments of dismembered peoples, political refugees, exiles, fugitive criminals, escaped slaves, or discharged mercenaries. His occupation is that of a small trader, the skipper of a small ship, and he may act as a moneychanger or moneylender with a stall in the market place.

The Athenian *metics,* primarily a population of the ports, were sometimes artisans or craftsmen, but most frequently by far they were engaged in trade and tried to earn their living from the profits to be made by buying and selling goods. Apart from being skipper and trader, the *metic* also tried his hand as a "banker," the menial occupation of testing and changing coins behind a bench in the market place. His moneychanger's commission was regulated by public authority ; as a grain dealer, he stood under strict supervision; and as a merchant skipper, he had to comply with numerous trading restrictions that would limit profits. In general he was free to follow the urge of gain, a motive thought to be appropriate to his lowly status. His life was drudgery—physical exertion aggravated by exposure to the hated hardships of the sea. Yet he was to expect no riches in recompense. He was barred from owning land or a house; he could not hold a mortgage; consequently he could possess no property that would be reckoned as wealth. An exceptional *metic* might accumulate a considerable amount of money, but that made little difference to his standard of life. As a man debarred from owning land and houses, he could not, for instance, raise horses, give feasts, or erect a mansion. Even the few rich *metics* led unglamorous lives.

4. *Trading Peoples*

Not all communities that practice trade know professional traders. One community may trade collectively; another may possess professional traders and regard them as members of a specific social class. Still other societies, even if not more than a few, make active trade the chief occupation of the bulk of the population. These last we will designate here as trading peoples.

Evidently the existence of trade does not presuppose traders, and even where professional traders are found, their relation to the community as a whole may be very different in different types of societies.

In primitive societies, as we have seen, trade is as a rule a collective undertaking, carried on either by the chief or through the general participation of the members. In the latter case, their purpose may be equally served either by crowded meetings with their trading partners on the beach or by the popular habit of carrying some local foodstuffs or manufactured articles to a neighboring island. Consequently, as a rule we do not find anyone in primitive societies specializing in the professions of trader or merchant.

It is in archaic societies that the trader makes his appearance. In this context, we have already distinguished between peasant-type societies and empires, and, in regard to the latter, between those of a nomadic and those of an irrigational kind. In peasant-type societies, the royal household may employ a staff of traders who usually disappear with the fall of the monarchy. This was probably the case in early Rome, as well as after the passing of the tyrannies in ancient Greece. In the irrigational empire, the *tamkarum* gains right of status. In the nomadic empire of the Mongols, trade was exclusively passive; no trader or merchant class made its appearance; nor did it in the early nomadic empires of the Berbers and early Arabs in Africa.

Trading peoples differ sharply from all of these; with them, trade is a source of collective livelihood. Trading peoples differ among themselves in an important respect: the trading peoples proper, as we may call them, are exclusively dependent for their subsistence on trade in which, directly or indirectly, the whole of the population is engaged. Among the others—a much more numerous group—trade is only *one* of the occupations in which a considerable part of the population engages from time to time, traveling abroad with goods over shorter or longer periods.

Examples of trading peoples proper are the Phoenicians, the Rhodians, and the western Vikings, all of whom traded by sea; the Bedouins and the Tuareg of the desert; and the eastern Vikings and the Kede of the Niger, who used river routes. Those who traded only periodically are such as the Hausa, Duala, Mandingo, and others, in West Africa; and the Malayan people. In addition, there are dislocated peoples like the Armenians and the Jews.

B. Goods

The decision to acquire goods and carry them from a distance obviously depends on the urgency of the need for the objects and on the difficulty of acquiring and transporting them. Moreover, the need must be felt by those who possess the political and technical means of organizing the trading venture effectively. The decision to acquire one kind of goods from a definite distance and region is necessarily made under concrete circumstances different from those under which another kind of goods would be acquired from another place. For this reason, archaic trade is mainly a discontinuous business, restricted to definite undertakings that do not develop into a continuous private enterprise. The Roman *societas* and the later *commenda*, for example, were trade partnerships limited to one undertaking. Before modern times, permanent trade associations are unknown. Archaic trading ventures differ, then, according to the type of goods to be acquired and transported, and they form separate branches of trade, each with its distinctive operational methods and organization.

All this may appear too obvious to deserve mentioning; yet it is useful to recall these facts if we want to interpret rightly the incisive features of nonmarket trade. Here there is no such thing as "trading in general." All trade is originally specific, according to the goods involved. It is one thing to transport slaves and cattle who, so to speak, travel under their own steam, and quite another to carry huge rocks or enormous tree trunks, perhaps over hundreds of miles of roadless country. In some cases, mules, horses, or sheep are acquired, together with their horsemen or shepherds, thus creating a social problem of some considerable complexity.

The specificity of archaic trade is enhanced, in the usual course of things, by the necessity of acquiring the imported goods in return for those that can be exported, for under nonmarket conditions, imports and exports also tend to fall under different administrative regimes. The process of collecting the goods to be exported is often quite separate from the one by which the imported goods are "repartitioned." The first is a matter of tribute, taxation, feudal gifts, or whatever the designation under which the goods flow to the center, while the "repartition" may descend in a hierarchic cascade along very different lines. Kievan Russia exported furs, flax, and honey collected by the prince and the boyars as tribute from their subjects;

their "imports" were the precious silks, cloths, jewelry, and finery of Byzantium. In the Roman empire, the food and other necessary articles that flowed from the provinces to the capital as *annona* represented an unrequited "import" of a purely political character. In this case, the imports had first to be collected in the provinces themselves before they could be shipped to Rome. Fifteen hundred years later, the African and the East- and West-Indian trade of the chartered companies of Europe ran mainly in channels determined by the ways in which tribute goods were collected from the natives, either by their princes or by the Europeans themselves, for export to Europe.

C. Transportation

In regard to transportation as in regard to goods, the market is a leveller. It obliterates all differences: what nature made distinct, the market makes homogeneous. Even the difference between goods and their transportation is done away with, since both can be bought and sold in the market—the one in the commodity market, the other in the freight market. In either case, there is supply and demand, and prices are formed in the same fashion. The various kinds of transportation services have their common denominator with the various goods in terms of costs, the *caput mortuum* of the market alchemy.

Now, such homogeneity makes for good economic theory but for bad economic history. The substantive distinctions that vanish in the the market are the very stuff of history. The different kinds of goods, as we saw, created distinctive branches of trade in archaic times. The traded goods may be needed by people of different status, whose interests are expressed through different channels, who have different means at their disposal to achieve their ends, and who, therefore, cause types of trade to develop whose organization has hardly anything in common. To ignore the difference between goods that can move, like slaves and cattle, and goods that cannot, like stones and timber, would make the early history of trade unintelligible.

In the case of transportation, i.e., *carrying* goods over a distance, the routes traveled and the means and modes of carrying are of no less incisive relevance. And here, as with goods, the geographical and technological facts interlace with the social structure. The organization of trade must be such as to cope with the perils and obstructions caused by both nature and man. In seafaring, for instance, one type of vessel was used against both the hazards of nature and those of war. The development of fighting craft separate from the merchant vessels that had served both peaceful and warlike purposes came comparatively late. In this light, the war boat's crew is only a variant of the "merchantman's" crew. Its recruitment was, therefore, not primarily a business proposition—another pointer for the history of trade.

As to the dangers from pirates and robbers, overland routes and coastal trade are almost equally exposed. Only on the high seas does attack from pirates become unlikely. (This is, of course, less true in later times, with their more frequented sea lanes.) Policing overland routes is the raison d'etre of all but the earliest empires (those which sprang directly from the political requirements of irrigation). Neither Babylonia nor Egypt nor China spread along overland routes; their transportation was predominantly riverine (the Akkadian term for a trading place is "port"). But the nomadic empires of the Turk, Mongol, Arabic, and Berber peoples were spread out as a net alongside transcontinental caravan routes. Their purpose was to "own" the routes, which meant a flow of imports—partly in the form of tolls and taxes, payment in kind for safe conduct, partly in exchange for raw materials collected as tribute from the conquered peoples by the empire builders.

Caravans thus antedate empires. Their organization was dictated by the requirements of transit through nonpoliced areas. The early caravans were doubtless set up and armed for their tasks by the public powers whether in the framework of king's trade or warrior trade. In either case, the trader would be of the *tamkarum* type. But even the later, independent caravan, often consisting of burgess merchants frequenting the traditional overland routes, remained a kind of small, wandering state, threading its way between numberless smaller or larger settlements of peoples of a more or less predatory kind. This exterritorial caravan was expected to keep strictly to the beaten track and look neither right nor left in traversing the countryside. Its participants often learned as little about the regions through which they were passing as the modern globe trotter on his conducted tour, hopping by plane from hotel to hotel. Most of the ancient slave trade was carried on by this sort of caravan. Only rarely was the "cake of custom" sufficiently tough to permit a few individual traders, without the armed accompaniment of a caravan, to lead whole slave transports across political frontiers, paying their dues to the local sovereign at each boundary. Probably in this latter type of traveling by stages lay the secret of the many hundreds of miles over which hosts of slaves were sold "down the river" on the western coast of Equatorial Africa, especially after the arrival of the Portuguese on the Congo Delta in the eighteenth century. On the Niger, the Kede colonists, as late as the nineteenth century, served the purposes of such noncaravan, riverain trade, which passed on its freighted canoes along the winding length of the river very much as the boa constrictor digests its prey.

The caravan was also, in some respects, the source of an important military development. Rostovtzeff has pointed out that the Hellenistic army was one of the most original creations of the age, the economic importance of which cannot be overrated.[3] He referred, of course, to the enormous concourse of men and beasts, numbering tens of thousands of sutlers and craftmen, which formed the wandering capital of the empire. It was a maze of markets, enmeshed in the tissues of a monstrously enlarged military headquarters. In effect, this army was nothing but a glorified caravan, the first armed formation to attempt the task of making large, wandering bodies of persons self-supporting. And yet this Seleucid *skeue,* which impressed Rostovtzeff, was relatively modest in comparison with the Grand Mogul's summer traject from his dusty Indian capital to the high mountains some two thousand years later. As described by Tavernier, this annual traject, with its near on half a millon camp followers, including the entire bazaar population of deserted Delhi, marching cross-country like some sprawling monster and camping night by night on a new site, was really an improvised city of fantastic proportions.[4]

D.   Two-Sidedness

Acquiring objects not available to the community on the spot necessarily involves the group in external relations. The pretrade forms of such acquisition are the hunt, the expedition, and the raid. Here the movement of goods is one-sided. Catching, quarrying, felling, robbing, or any other way of getting hold of the goods forms

[3] M. Rostovtzeff, *The Social and Economic History of the Hellenistic World* (Oxford: Clarendon Press, 1941). vol. I, pp. 144 ff.

[4] Jean Babtiste Tavernier, *The Six Voyages of Jean Babtiste Tavernier* (London: 1678).

one part of the action; carrying, hauling, or otherwise transporting the acquisition, the other. But trade, as we have seen, is a peaceful, two-sided activity, and it requires some specific form of organization to ensure those qualities. According to the rationale of two-sidedness, we meet with three main types of trade: gift trade, administrated or treaty trade, and market trade.

Gift trade links the partners in relationships of reciprocity, such as those of guest friends, Kula partners, or visiting traders. The organization of trading in this case is usually ceremonial, involving mutual presentations, embassies, political dealings between chiefs or kings. The goods are usually treasure, i.e., objects of elite circulation such as slaves, gold, horses, ivory, clothing, or incense; in the border case of visiting parties, the goods may, however, be of a more "democratic" character. Gift trade is widespread among tribal societies where there are no other sanctions to avoid hostile retaliatory measures; but over millennia trade between empires was carried on as gift trade—no other rationale of two-sidedness would meet the needs of the situation quite as well. Empires may secure advantages from "barbarians" through gifts, or the weaker party may excel in gifts to gain favor from the stronger, and thereby avoid paying tribute.

Administrated or treaty trade presupposes relatively stable organized political or semipolitical bodies such as chartered companies. It has its firm foundation in treaty relationships of a more-or-less formal nature. The understanding may be tacit, as in the case of traditional or customary relationships, but between sovereign bodies, trade on a larger scale assumes the existence of explicit treaties even in relatively early times (e.g., between Etruscan Rome and Carthage in the sixth century B.C.). In treaty trade, the import interest is determinative on both sides, and for that reason the trade is organized through governmental or government-controlled channels. As a rule, this organization involves the collection of the export goods as well as the distribution of goods imported—both of these falling into the redistributive sphere of the domestic economy. Accordingly, the whole of trade is carried on by administrative methods. These comprise the manner in which business is transacted: namely, arrangements concerning "rates" or proportions of units; weighing; checking quality; the physical exchange of the goods; storage; safekeeping; regulation of "payments"; credits; and "price" differentials, as well as control of the trading personnel. The traded goods are standardized in regard to quality and package, weight, or other easily ascertainable criteria. Only such "trade goods" can be traded. Equivalents are set out in simple unit relations; in principle, trade is one to one.[5]

Haggling is not part of the proceedings but, since to meet the changing circumstances it often cannot be avoided, it is practised only on items other than "price," such as measures, quality, means of payment, and profits. The rationale of the procedure is, of course, to keep the equivalents unchanged; if they must adjust to actual supply situations, as in an emergency, this is phrased as trading two to one or two and one-half to one, or as we would say, at 100% or 150% profit. This method of haggling on profits at stable "prices," which may have been fairly general in archaic society, is well authenticated from the Central Sudan as late as the nineteenth century.[6]

Once established in a region, administrative forms of trade may be practised without any previous treaty. The specific institution and the site of all administered foreign trade is the "port of trade."[7] It is a specific organ of foreign trade in nonmarket economies, usually situated on the coast, on the desert border, at a river head, or where plain and mountains meet. The diplomatic and administrative methods employed in the contacts between the government and representatives of the parties—mostly chartered companies and governments—is such as to exclude competition. The function of the "port of trade" is to offer military security to the host; civil protection to the foreign traders; facilities of anchorage, debarkation, and storage; judicial authorities; agreement on the goods to be traded; agreement concerning the "proportions" of the different trade goods in the "sortings." Market trade is the third typical form of trading. In this case, exchange is the form of integration that relates the partners to each other. This is the comparatively modern form of trade that released a torrent of material wealth over Western Europe and North America. Though at present in recession, it is still by far the most important of all. The range of tradable goods—the commodities—is

[5] Cf. Karl Polanyi, in collaboration with Abraham Rotstein, *Dahomey and the Slave Trade* (Seattle and London: University of Washington Press, 1966), pp. 146–154.

[6] Ibid., p. 148

[7] Cf. Karl Polanyi, "Ports of Trade in Early Societies," *The Journal of Economic History,* 23, (1963) pp. 30–45; reprinted in *Primitive, Archaic, and Modern Economics: Essays of Karl Polanyi,* ed. G. Dalton (Garden City, N.Y.: Doubleday, 1968), Chapter 10.

practically unlimited; the organization follows the lines traced out by the supply–demand–price mechanism. The market mechanism is adaptable to the handling not only of goods, but of every element of trade itself—storage, transportation, risk, credit, payments, etc.—by forming special markets for freight, insurance, short-term credit, capital, warehouse space, banking facilities, and so on.

Market trade presupposes, of course, both trade and markets. As to the trade, its independent origin has been shown above. Markets, on the other hand, do not necessarily spring from trade. Local markets certainly possess independent origins of their own, as we will see in Chapter 10. The catallactic notion that markets and trade are somehow the static and dynamic forms, respectively, of one and the same economic energy, is therefore erroneous.

For the economic historian, the problem lies precisely in this: when and how does trade get linked with markets? Under what circumstances do markets become a vehicle of trade movements? And at what times and places do we first meet the result—market trade?

The question will be dealt with separately in Chapter 10 in regard to external and internal markets. The external market problem is only another aspect of the port of trade and the circumstances that led to its development into regular international markets; the internal market problem, again, refers to the process by which the strictly controlled and limited *agora* of the *polis,* and the very different bazaar of the oriental world, were transformed into free meeting places of foreign traders. As we will see, trade only presents, in a striking way, a feature general to the development of economic institutions, namely, the polarity of the external and the internal lines of development. With trade the priority of the external line is clearly evident.

◀ 9 ▶

Money Objects
and Money Uses

I. MONEY AS A SEMANTIC SYSTEM

Anthropologically, money should be defined as a semantic system, broadly similar to language, writing, or weights and measures.[1] These systems differ mainly in the purposes served and the signs employed. Language and writing serve the purpose of the communication of ideas, weights and measures that of quantitative physical relationship. As to signs, language uses oral sounds; writing employs ideograms or visual characters; weights and measures, on the other hand, use physical objects as the basis of symbols.

Money resembles, but also differs from, each of these. It serves several ends, which are traditionally described as means of payment; standard of value or money of account; store of wealth; and medium of exchange. The precise meaning of these terms will be given below. We list them here only to point out that these typical "money uses" represent the "purpose" of money as a semantic system. Even though these uses are derived from the monetary theory of the market economy, it will eventually be shown that these different money uses are especially distinctive under the conditions of early society.

[1] Cf. Karl Polanyi, "The Semantics of Money-Uses," *Explorations,* October 1957; reprinted in *Primitive, Archaic, and Modern Economics,* ed. G. Dalton (Garden City, N.Y.: Doubleday, 1968) with an appendix, "Notes on Primitive Money."

Money, thus defined, resembles a metrological system in that its symbols have mostly been attached to physical objects; yet it differs from metrology as to its purpose. Though in some ways money acts as a means of measurement, that which is gauged is not how long, large, or heavy an object is, but how great its importance is to us in a definite situation. In this case, the primary use referred to is that of a standard of value or money of account.

As to systems of language and writing, money differs from them in that its symbols are, as a rule, attached not to sounds, as in speech, or visual characters, as in script, but to physical objects, such as pieces of metal, shells, or slips of printed paper. However, abstract symbols, such as "ideal units" represented by a word or cypher, may also be employed as money, a fact we should not disregard here, since it tends to occur frequently in early society.

Yet from a merely formal angle, money offers a striking parallel to language or writing. All three are elaborate semantic systems, organized through a code of rules laying down the right way to use sounds, characters, or objects as elements of the respective systems. Each employs a limited number of "all-purpose" symbols according to definite rules so as to cover a number of different uses. In the case of money, however, this is broadly true only of modern money. In contrast, the peculiarities of money in primitive and archaic societies are thrown into sharp relief.

Early society knows no "all-purpose" money. The different money uses usually fall to different symbolic objects. No one kind of object, therefore, deserves the name of money in early society; rather the term applies to a small group of them. In effect, we have here a case of "special purpose" money. It follows that, while in modern society the distinction between various money uses is more or less academic, since, as a rule, the money that serves as a means of exchange is also entrusted with performing all the other functions, in early society the position is radically different. Here one might find slaves used as a standard of value or money of account in judging substantial wealth or altogether for large amounts, while cowrie shells are employed solely in measuring small amounts in different situations. (Incidentally, the unit "slave" may stand for a conventional value, representing a unit of account, real slaves being sold at varying prices.) We might find, therefore, that while slaves are a means for the payment of tribute to a foreign overlord, cowrie shells function as a means of local payment. This need not exclude the use of precious metals for hoarding wealth, although such metals may not otherwise serve as money at all or, if they do, only in foreign trade. If the market habit is fairly widespread, money might, moreover, serve as a means of exchange in foreign trade, and to this end several trade goods might be in use that are not otherwise employed as money at all. Numerous combinations of these variants occur. No one rule is universally applicable, unless it be the general one that money uses are dispersed between a multiplicity of objects. Clearly, under such conditions the distinction between the various money uses is of great practical importance for understanding monetary institutions in early society.

The contrast to the modern organization of money could hardly be more striking. In terms of an analogy to other semantic systems; while in speech all articulate oral sounds, and in script all letters of the alphabet are eligible for use in all types of words, primitive money may in extreme cases employ one kind of object as means of payment, another as a standard of value, a third for storing wealth, and a fourth for exchange purposes. Such money would be somewhat like a language in which verbs consisted of one group of letters, nouns of another, adjectives of a third, and adverbs of yet a fourth.

There is, however, yet another significant point of contrast implied in our tentative description of a "primitive" money system. In early society, the exchange use of money is not the fundamental money use. If one use is more basic than another, it is one of the other uses, any of which may be found in communities where the exchange use of money is not practiced. Consequently, while in modern society the unification of the various uses of money regularly took place on the basis of its exchange use, in early communities we find the different money uses institutionalized separately and independent of one another. Insofar as there is interdependence between them, we find use for payment, or use for money of account, or for storing wealth, having precedence over exchange.

It might be argued that primitive money should not be described as a semantic system at all, since it was not "systematic" enough to be called a system. However, we should recall that the stuff that went into making the systems of language and writing was also originally drawn from disparate sources. Consider the role played by articulate oral sounds in uses as different as magical spells, hunters' cries imitative of wild animals, or the "counting out" rhymes practiced by children in their games. While sounds related to such uses are known to have contributed to the raw material of language, not all were eventually incorporated into it, and some have been so incorporated only by reducing their operational significance to the communication of ideas. In very much the same way, some early functions of money, such as the magical or ornamental, have been largely excluded from modern forms of currency, while all other employments of money were subordinated to the one dominant use, namely, exchange.

Thus modern money, employing the symbols of exchange for all the various uses, appears as an almost complete parallel to language and writing. But, broadly, the analogy also holds for primitive and archaic money, which differs from its modern counterpart only in the degree to which the symbolic systems are unified.

II. INSTITUTIONAL ANALYSIS OF MONEY

It behoves the student of early economic institutions, however, to exercise a more pedestrian, if careful, approach to money. Unless he holds on to the physical media themselves, such as the shells, feathers, or bits of metal, he is in danger of losing his way. For all that, he has to aim, as does the philosopher, at a functional definition; for no material object is money per se, and any object, in an appropriate situation, might function as money. To determine the uses to which the physical things are put, he will point to the situation in which the objects are used and to what effect. The functional definition of money starts from the quantifiable objects commonly designated as money and the observable operations that are performed with these objects. Below we will enlarge on the situations in which the operations are performed and on the desired effects that this has or has not on the situation. Here we wish to draw attention to what the objects look like and what is done with them or, in more technical terms, the physical aspects of the objects and the operational aspects of the performances. In either regard—objects and operations—the origins of the basic money uses take us back to that preliterate condition of society where the economy sets us problems whose resolution requires operational devices employing quantifiable objects.

Before man invented writing and learned to use mathematical symbols, he devised means by which simple manual operations produced the complex numerical results still out of the reach of his intellectual technique. Such operational devices were the gadgets of archaic life. They are manipulative short cuts in reckoning, such as the abacus, the keeping of statistical records by putting colored beads in multifarious boxes, and countless other (sometimes most ingenious) ways of handling numerical problems easily and simply with the help of such contraptions or arrangements and thus avoiding complex or time-robbing calculations. An outstanding instance is the elaborate dual system of Dahoman military and civilian administration, where symmetry served as an operational device for checking and control at almost all bureaucratic levels. Another is the ingenious Dahoman method of keeping the annual census by placing pebbles in appropriate boxes.[2]

Neither the administration nor the economy could be worked without these devices. They were not so much gadgets in the technological sense, like those used in modern times, as in the semantic sense, putting the powers of the mind in action without conceptual effort. But what semantic systems may achieve in this way with the help of symbols, the operational device attains by the use of manual operations.

However, neither the parallel nor the contrast between symbol and gadget should be overdone. Operational devices, such as slide rules, may employ symbols, just as semantic systems, such as mathematics, make use of operational devices, such as determinants.

Yet it is broadly true to say that semantic systems are on a higher level than operational devices. While vocal and gesture language, writing, weights and measures, mathematics, and the arts more or less exhaust the list of the semantic systems familiar to man, the number of operational devices is much greater, but only a few reach the level of an elaborate system. Hardly any of these have survived under civilized conditions, that is, once the art of writing, mathematics, and systems of weights and measures develop. Once that stage is reached, operational devices necessarily appear as no more than crude substitutes for writing and reckoning, great though their importance under primitive and archaic conditions undoubtedly is. They are the key to many an achievement of archaic politics and

[2] Karl Polanyi, in collaboration with Abraham Rotstein, *Dahomey and the Slave Trade* (Seattle and London: University of Washington Press, 1966), pp. 41–43, 53 ff.

economics that left the world ever after wondering how such organizational perfection was achieved without the use of writing and numerical calculation.

As for the problem of the origin and development of money uses, the connection between physical objects and the operations performed on them is crucial. The vital feature of money objects is their quantifiability, which then allows them to function as devices in each of the money uses. Each of the money uses is dependent upon definite criteria: the socially or culturally determined situation in which the need arises, the operationally defined handling of the objects, and finally, the effect thus exercised on the situation. The "situation" is a fact of general sociology, the "handling" is operationally prescribed, and the "effect" is such that the need is served.

We shall speak of money when interchangeable physical units (fungibles) are found in any one of the uses described below. *Res fungibiles* were defined in medieval law in a truly operational way as *res quae numero, pondere ac mensura consistunt.* Shells, coins, feathers, measures of barley, banknotes, or innumerable other interchangeable things shall be regarded by us as money, as long as they are employed in any of the following uses:

A. Payment

Payment is settling an obligation by handing over quantifiable objects (fungibles). "Handing over" is the operation, "settling the obligation" is the desired effect. The situation of "being under an obligation" has, however, this requirement, if money is said to be used. Unless at least one other situation is given that differs in regard to the nature of the obligation yet is capable of being met by the same means, the "settling" through handing over quantifiable objects does not constitute money payment (as when an obligation to be discharged "in kind" is so discharged).

B. Standard of Value

The standard use of money is the employment of a physical unit of a definite type as a referent in situations where arithmetical operations in regard to objects of different kinds are called for, such as "adding up apples and pears." The "handling" of the unit consists in the operation of "tagging on" a numerical value to at least one of the units with the effect that "apples and pears" can now be summed up in a meaningful way by relating them to the "standard." The effect is that barter is facilitated, since items on either side can be rated and their value added up; staple finance too, requires, as a rule, additions and subtractions of different staples, like apples and pears, and thus a "standard."

C. Store of Wealth

Storing wealth is the accumulation of quantifiable objects either (1) for future disposal or (2) simply as treasure. The "sociological situation" is one in which persons (1) either prefer not to consume or otherwise destroy such objects in the present but rather defer doing so to a future time or (2) prefer the advantages of sheer possession, especially the power, prestige, and influence accruing from it. The "operation" involved consists in keeping, storing, or conserving the objects for later use or in order that their possession and, preferably, their ostentatious display may redound to the credit of the owner and those whom he may represent.

D. Means of Exchange

The exchange use of money is the employment of quantifiable objects in situations of indirect exchange. The operation involves two consecutive exchanges, with the money objects as the middle term. However, once indirect exchange has become accepted, the sequence may start with money and end up with more of it.

Exceptionally, the term money is also applied to something other than physical units. Such "ideal units" are written signs, spoken words, or recorded deeds employed in money uses. The "operation" then usually consists of a manipulation of debt accounts formed by such units, with the effect similar to the use of physical units. In archaic society, "ideal units" sometimes occur in clearing accounts, as in early Assyrian and late Egyptian staple finance.

An apparent exception of the opposite sort may be seen when physical units that also happen to be money function in nonmonetary uses, as when coins are employed to teach children arithmetic. Those units are money because they already function in some money use, but they may also serve some other, merely operational purpose, whether statistical or simply as weights, markers, or tallies.

III. EXCHANGE MONEY

The traditional treatment regards money primarily as a means of exchange. This assumes an original situation of barter and an operation suited to facilitate it: namely, the acquisition of money objects in order to exchange them for the desired goods. This is the "indirect exchange" of the economist. In a market economy such as ours, money is mainly identified with this use, and all other uses are made dependent on this one basic use. This presumption belongs among the most powerful in the whole field of modern economic thought.

Apart from Smith and Ricardo, sociologists like Spencer, Durkheim, Mauss, and Simmel also fell victim to the catallactic fallacy that division of labour implied exchange. Hence the fateful mistake of defining money as a means of exchange, which was subsequently extended by anthropologists even to preliterate society. As Raymond Firth once expressed it, "In any economic system, however primitive, an article can be regarded only as true money when it acts as a definite and common medium of exchange, as a convenient stepping stone in obtaining one type of goods for another".[3] Professor Firth later mitigated his stand, but this narrow concept of money has created a distorted picture of the nature of money and thus raised an almost insuperable obstacle to the analysis of nonmarket economies.

According to this representative view, the exchange use of money is its essential criterion, not only in modern, but also in primitive society. Even under primitive conditions, the four money uses are said to be inseparable. Only quantifiable objects serving as means of exchange can, in this view, be regarded as money. Their function as means of payment, as standard of value, or as means of hoarding wealth is not decisive for their character as money, unless it implies their use as media of exchange. For it is this use, it is asserted, that logically unifies the system, since it allows a consistent linking up of the various functions of money. Without it there can be no true money.

We believe that such a definition is biased by a modernizing

---

[3] Raymond Firth, "Currency, Primitive," *Encyclopaedia Britannica,* 14th edition.

approach to the problem, which is partly responsible for the obscurity in which the characteristics of primitive money still abide. On a point of fact, it can be freely stated that the view which regards money primarily as a means of exchange finds but insufficient support in the early history of money uses. However, it would be a mistake to believe that the problem is merely definitional and that the obstacles to its resolution are merely conceptual. The separate and independent institutionalization of the various money uses raises questions of *fact* involving much of the mechanism and structure of early societies, as will become apparent in our examination of the other money uses in these societies.

IV.   THE PAYMENT USE OF MONEY

Payment, in the modern sense of the term, is the discharge of an obligation by handing over quantified units. Nothing seems to us more definite than the connection of payment with money and of obligation with economic transactions. Yet the origins of payment reach back to a time before quantified objects were employed in the discharge of obligations connected with such transactions. In order to cope with the variety of forms in which payment and obligation appear in the course of economic history, we shall have to trace a development that starts from preeconomic and prelegal beginnings.

Payment existed at a time when the distinction between civil law, penal law, and sacral law was not yet established. This partly accounts for the close propinquity of payment and punishment on the one hand, and obligation and crime on the other. No unilineal development should, however, be assumed. It appears rather that obligation may also have origins different from crime; that punishment may spring from other than sacral sources; and that payment includes an operational element not entailed in punishment as such. Yet historically speaking, it is broadly true that civil law followed on penal law, penal law on sacral law. Thus payment was due alike from the guilty, the impure, the weak and lowly; it was owed to the gods and their priests, the honored, and the strong. Punishment, like offense, was in sacral and social terms. It resulted in the diminution of sanctity, prestige, and status of the payer, not stopping even at his physical destruction.

Obligation may take form by spelling out the legal aspects of the offense. Many obligations, however, spring from custom and give rise to offense only in case of default on the discharge of the obligation. In neither case, it should be noted, need restoring the balance involve payment. For obligations are, as a rule, specific; and their fulfillment is not a quantitative but a purely qualitative affair which, therefore, lacks an essential of payment. Infringement of sacral and social obligations, whether toward god, tribe, kin, totem, village, age group, caste, or guild, is repaired not by payment but by doing the right thing in the right way on the right occasion. Activities like wooing, marrying, forbearing, dancing, singing, dressing, feasting, lamenting, lacerating, or even killing oneself may be the discharging of obligations, but they are not, for that reason, also payments in the monetary sense of the term.

At this point, one of the elements of the payment use of money enters, however, namely, quantification. Punishment approximates payment when the process of riddance of guilt is quantified, as when lashes of the whip, turns of the praying mill, or days of fasting dispose of the offense. But though the punishment has now become an "obligation to pay," the offense is still atoned for, not by handing over quantified objects but by a loss of qualitative life-values or of sacral and social status.

The full payment use of money is given when the units discharged by the person under obligation happen to be physical objects, such as sacrificial animals or slaves, ornamental shells, or measures of foodstuffs. Even so, the change affects only the operation of paying, but need not react on the nature of the obligation discharged. The obligations may still be predominantly non-economic, such as to pay a fine, composition, tax, tribute; to make gifts and countergifts; to honor the gods, the ancestors, or the dead. Yet there is a significant difference. For the recipient now gains what the payer loses—the operation fits precisely the legal concept of obligation to pay.

Yet the main effect of payment may be still as it was before, namely, diminution of power and status of the payer. In archaic society, an exorbitant fine did not so much bankrupt as politically undo the victim. For a long time, power and status in this way retained their precedence over economic possession as such. The political and social importance of accumulated wealth lay in the rich man's capacity to make a payment without this undermining his status. This was the condition of affairs when archaic civilization began. Treasure suddenly became of tremendous political importance. Wealth was directly transmuted into power. For a brief period of history, it was a self-sufficing institution. Because the rich man was powerful and honored, he received payments; gifts and dues showered in upon him without his having to use his power to torture and kill. Yet his wealth, used as a fund of gifts, would procure him a sufficiency of power to do so.

Once money as a means of exchange is established in society, however, the practice of money payment naturally spreads far and wide. With the introduction of the market system, a new type of obligation has come into being as the legal residue of an economic transaction. Payment now appears as the counterpart of an advantage gained in a transaction. Money is now a means of payment *because* it is a means of exchange. The very notion of the independent origin of payment is lost, and the millennia of human civilization in which payment sprang not from economic transactions, but directly from religious, social, or political obligations, have been forgotten.

V.   STORAGE USE OF MONEY

Another money use—storing wealth—has its origin partly in the need for payment. As we saw, payment is not primarily an economic term. Neither is wealth, which in early society consists largely of treasure. Like payment, it is originally more a social than a subsistence category. The subsistence connotation of wealth (like that of payment) derives rather from the frequency with which wealth is accumulated (and payment is made) in the form of cattle, slaves, and nonperishable goods of common consumption. Both that which feeds the store of wealth and that which is disbursed from that store have, then, a subsistence significance. However, this is true only within limits, since payments are still made, as a rule, for noneconomic reasons. That is the case for both the rich who own the store of wealth and the subjects who feed the store with their payments. He who owns wealth is thereby enabled to pay fines, composition, taxes, and the like for sacral, political, and social reasons. The payments he receives from his subjects, high or low, are paid to him as taxes, rents, or gifts, not for economic but for social and political reasons ranging from pure gratitude for protection and admiration of superior endowment to fear of enslavement or death.

This again is not to deny that once exchange money is present, money will readily lend itself as a store of wealth. But, as in the case of payment, the precondition is the establishment of quantified objects as media of exchange.

VI.   MONEY AS A STANDARD OF VALUE
OR AS MONEY OF ACCOUNT

Money as a standard of value seems more closely linked with the exchange use of money than is either payment or storing. Exchange is one of the two very different sources from which the need for a standard of value springs. The other is administration. The first involved barter, the latter storage. At first sight, the two have little in common. The former is an act of individual exchange, the latter of central administration. The two are therefore strongly in contrast. Yet neither barter nor storage can be effectively carried out in the absence of some standard of value or money of account. Without the help of computation assisted by money of account, how, for instance, could a piece of land be bartered against a chariot, horse harness, asses, ass harness, oxen, oil, clothes, and other minor items? In the absence of a means of exchange, the account in a well-known case of barter in ancient Babylonia shaped up like this: the land was valued at 816 shekels of silver, while the articles given in exchange were valued in shekels of silver as follows: chariot 100, six horse harnesses 300, an ass 130, ass harness 50, an ox 30; the rest were distributed over the smaller items.

The same principle applied, in the absence of exchange, to the administration of vast palace and temple stores. Their keeper handled subsistence goods under conditions which, from more than one angle, imperatively required gauging the relative importance of these goods. The famous Babylonian rule of accountancy of "one unit of silver equals one unit of barley" on the stele of Manistusu, as well as at the head of article two of the Laws of Eshnunna, illustrate the point.

Analysis of the data offered by primitive and archaic society reveals that the exchange use of money cannot claim to have given rise to the other money uses. On the contrary, the payment, storage, and accountancy uses of money had their separate origins and were institutionalized independently of one another.

VII. TREASURE AND STAPLE IN MONEY USES

It seems almost self-contradictory to expect that one could pay with money one could not use to buy. Yet that, precisely, is the implication of our assertion that money was not used as a medium of exchange but was used as a means of payment. Two institutions of early society offer a partial explanation: treasure and staple.

Treasure should be distinguished from other forms of stored wealth. The difference lies mainly in its relation to subsistence. Treasure, in the proper sense of the term, is formed of prestige goods, including "valuables" and ceremonial objects whose mere possession endow the holder with social weight, power, and influence. It is a peculiarity of treasure goods that both giving and receiving them enhances prestige. Treasure largely circulates for the sake of the turnover, which is its proper use. Even when food is "treasured" it is likely to pass back and forth between the parties, however absurd this might appear from the subsistence point of view. But food rarely functions as treasure, for interesting food (such as slaughtered pigs) does not keep, and what keeps (such as barley or oil) is not exciting. The precious metals, on the other hand, which are almost universally valued as treasure, can not readily be exchanged for subsistence since, apart from exceptionally auriferous regions such as the African Gold Coast or Lydia, display of gold by common people is opprobrious.

Nevertheless, treasure, like other sources of power, may be of great economic importance, since gods, kings, and chiefs can be made to put the services of their dependents at the disposal of the giver, thus indirectly securing for him food, raw materials, and labour services on a large scale. Ultimately, this power of indirect disposal, which comprises the important power of taxation, arises, of course, from the enhanced influence exerted by the recipient of treasure over his tribe or people.

VIII.   TREASURE AND POWER IN ANCIENT GREECE

In ancient Greece, treasure, the prestige good *kat' exochēn*, was a form of wealth that circulated only among the few. It took the form of tool money—tripods and bowls—made of gold or silver. Disposal was either in return for other treasure or for items of prestige such as access to the gods and their oracles, to kings, chiefs, and local potentates. Where prestige goods other than gold, such as horses, ivory, skilled slaves, works of art, or fine cloths, were given in return, the counterpart too would have to be a prestige good. In some regions of the world, it is not possible to acquire a slave or a horse for any amount of millet, nor can one bribe a general with silver; that requires gold. The elite circulation of prestige goods is thus met with in many archaic societies, but Greece presents a notable example.

Treasure operated in Hellenic antiquity as a portable form of power. The effects of its possession were unmediated. Whoever possessed treasure was, ipso facto, powerful, i.e., honored and feared. No doubt, the power conferred by the prestige was often an anticipation of long-range economic advantages. However, to draw a sharp distinction between political and economic power would be artificial. The difference meant little in a world where personal services of various grades formed the main economic resource, and the disposal over this particular resource was organized through relations of a noneconomic character, such as kinship, clientage, or semifeudal dependency. Not before feudalism is fully developed do the political and economic advantages that accompany the holding of land become distinctly separated through an institutional differentiation of the two kinds of dependent services. Before that time, even the economic advantages conferred by the possession of treasure were usually embodied in political power. Nevertheless, some forms of wealth, such as land or cattle, were more immediately economic than others. Yet even in the case of such clearly economic holdings, the economic and political benefits were still too closely interwoven to admit of a neat separation.

In spite of this fusion of honorific and utilitarian motives, the economic effects of the movements of treasure can be distinguished. Indeed, the key to the performance of important economic tasks, especially of such as involved massing the efforts of labor, must, in archaic society, be sought in the workings of treasure.

A perfect instance of the uses of treasure in the crowded history of sixth century Greece was the rise of the Alcmæonid house, their ousting by the Peisistratids, followed by their triumphant return under Cleisthenes—altogether a matter of two generations. Throughout, the course of events is marked by notable economic achievements.

A. The Alcmæonids

The fortune of the house of the Alcmæonids, which was legendary in the Greek world, was derived in the following way:

> Now the Alcmeonidae were, even in days of yore, a family of note in Athens, but from the time of Alcmeon, and again of Megacles, they rose to special eminence. The former of these two persons, Alcmeon, the son of Megacles when Croesus the Lydian sent men from Sardis to consult the Delphic oracle, gave aid gladly to his messengers, and assisted them to accomplish their task.[4]

The Alcmæonids bartered their political influence with the god They were not to be disappointed:

> Croesus, informed of Alcmeon's kindnesses by the Lydians who from time to time conveyed his messages to the god, sent for him to Sardis, and, when he arrived, made him a present of as much gold as he should be able to carry at one time about his person. Finding that this was the gift assigned him, Alcmeon took his measures, and prepared to receive it in the following way. He clothed himself in a loose tunic, which he made to bag greatly at the waist, and placing upon his feet the widest buskins that he could anywhere find, followed his guides into the treasure-house. Here he fell to upon a heap of gold-dust, and in the first place packed as much as he could inside his buskins, between them and his legs; after which he filled the breast of his tunic quite full of gold, and then sprinkling some among his hair, and taking some likewise in his mouth, he came forth from the treasure-house, scarcely able to drag his legs along, like anything rather than a man, with his mouth crammed full, and his bulk increased every way. On seeing him, Croesus burst into a laugh, and not only let him have all that he had taken, but gave him presents besides of fully equal worth.[5]

In this manner, Herodotus concludes, this house became one of

---

[4] Herodotus, *The Persian Wars*, VI, 125.
[5] Ibid., VI, 125.

great wealth; and Alcmæon was able to repay the Delphic god by overfulfilling his building contract, moreover bribing the Pythoness, acquiring divine influence with the Spartans, keeping horses for the chariot race, and winning the prize at Olympia, which was traditionally the door to top-rank influence at home, especially if you had a first-class foreign army to back you, such as the Spartan.

This in brief was the story of their triumphant return. The Alcmæonids had fled Athens when Peisistratus finally resumed power. They made a number of futile attempts to recapture their home country. When their fortification of Lipsydrium, in Attica, was eventually reduced by Peisistratus, they

> resolved to shrink from no contrivance that might bring them success, and accordingly they contracted with the Amphictyons to build the temple which now stands at Delphi, but which in those days did not exist. Having done this, they proceeded, being men of great wealth, and members of an ancient and distinguished family, to build the temple much more magnificently than the plan obliged them. Besides other improvements, instead of the coarse stone whereof by the contract the temple was to have been constructed, they made the facings of Parian marble.[6]

As we would say, they used their money in the contracting business, but instead of aiming at maximum monetary gain, they preferred to invest in improved public relations. Such a well-considered act of generosity would win them acclaim in the Hellenic world and thereby increase their political influence. Herodotus makes the move a crucial step in their epic struggle to regain power in Athens, and here treasure accounted even more directly for a shift in the field of power.

> These same men, if we may believe the Athenians, during their stay at Delphi persuaded the priestess by a bribe to tell the Spartans, whenever any of them come to consult the oracle, either on their own private affairs or on the business of the state, that they must free Athens. So the Lacedaemonians, when they found no answer ever returned to them but this, sent at last Anchimolius, the son of Aster—a man of note among their citizens—at the head of an army against Athens, with orders to drive out the Peisistratidae.[7]

Aristotle, otherwise reluctant to repeat anecdotic embellish-

---

[6] Ibid., V, 62.
[7] Ibid., V, 63.

ments, confirms the gist of the story of the restoration of the
Alcmæonids by the Spartan army.

> Having failed, then, in every other method, they [the Alcmeonids] took
> the contract for rebuilding the temple at Delphi, using for that purpose
> the considerable wealth which they possessed, with the view of secur-
> ing the help of the Lacedaemonians. The Pythia accordingly was con-
> tinually enjoining on the Lacedaemonians who came to consult the
> oracle, that they must free Athens; till finally she succeeded in turning
> the Spartans in that direction. . . .[8]

But this would be to overlook the part of Croesus in the circuit of
gold, honor, and safety. The god of Delphi paid the Alcmæonids
under the building contract, the enormous sum of 300 talents, much
of which came from Croesus' treasury. Alcmæon had no doubt acted
as an honest broker between Apollo and the king of Lydia. However,
Croesus misunderstood the Pythoness' unfortunate hint about the
consequences of his crossing the River Halys. Herodotus saw with
his own eyes the stupendous gifts of gold that Croesus had sent her;
they were still displayed on the temple precincts when he visited
there. But whoever was responsible for the error, the ruin of Croesus
at the hands of Cyrus the Persian did not put a stop to the transaction. The god honored his obligations. The pyre was already lit on
which Cyrus had condemned his prisoner, Croesus, to be burnt
alive, when Apollo sent rain from the skies to smother the flames—
remindful of Croesus' "genius and generosity"—as the legend had it
which inspired Pindar's ode in praise of the Pythoness.

Thus did treasure make the rounds among the few.

B.   The Peisistratids

The origin and use of treasure in the case of Peisistratus shows
similar features. The Peisistratids, being of Eupatrid extraction, enjoyed reciprocity relations with the elite, although they could not, as
did their Alcmæonid rivals, boast of the favor of Apollo. A family
conference was held shortly after Peisistratus' second expulsion, at
which it was decided to attempt to regain the sovereignty.

> The first step was to obtain advances of money from such states as were
> under obligation to them. By these means they collected large sums

[8] Aristotle, *The Constitution of Athens*, 19.

from several countries, especially from the Thebans, who gave them far more than any of the rest.[9]

State obligations owed to the Peisistratids imply reciprocal relations, maybe through prior gifts made by Peisistratus to the various states. In a much more primitive scene in the *Odyssey*, Athena, disguised as mortal Mentor, excuses herself from Nestor's proffered hospitality by proclaiming "I will go to the great-hearted Cauconians, where a debt is owing to me, in no wise new or small."[10]

Only old debts, and preferably large ones, were regarded as "good." Neither small debts nor recent ones were supposed to be due. Accordingly, ties of *xenia* between the Peisistratids and the Spartans, validated by gift giving, made the latter hesitate so long to obey the Delphic oracle's injunction to make war upon the Peisistratids.

Peisistratus' wealth consisted largely in treasure. The family estate was in Brauron in Attica, which is near the Laurion district. Whether or not he mined silver from the Laurion mines—in fact, whether or not the mines were worked in this period—is subject to dispute. But there is no doubt that he acquired properties in the rich mining district of the Pangaeus region in Thrace at some period of his long exile.

How Peisistratus acquired these properties can be conjectured from a comparable incident in the same region. Darius was anxious to recompense Histiæus, ruler of Miletus, for having saved the Persian army by preventing the destruction of the Danube bridge in their rear. Histiæus asked for—and received—the city of Myrcinus, on the Strymon river on the Thracian coast. This was the region of the Pangaeus mines. The Persian general in Thrace, Mogabazus, hearing that Histiæus was walling in the city, reproached Darius:

> What mad thing is this that you have done, sire, to let a Greek, a wise man and a shrewd, get hold of a town in Thrace, a place, too, where there is abundance of timber fit for shipbuilding, and oars in plenty, and mines of silver, and about which there are many dwellers both Greek and barbarian, ready enough to take him for their chief, and day and night to do his bidding![11]

[9] Herodotus, *The Persian Wars*, I, 61.
[10] Homer, *The Odyssey*, III, 366–368.
[11] Herodotus, *The Persian Wars*, V, 23.

This recalls Thucydides' analysis of the crucial role of wealth in archaic Greece. "Originally Pelops gained his power by the great wealth which he brought with him from Asia into a poor country."[12] A man of great wealth and ingenuity apparently could readily win followers among a poorer or more backward people, by buying over their chiefs and gods as his allies, and make them do his bidding. Of Peisistratus' Thracian stay, Aristotle remarks tersely, "Here he acquired wealth and hired mercenaries."

Storage of wealth as an institution of subsistence economy, on the other hand, starts from the collecting and storing of staples. While treasure and treasure finance does not as a rule belong to subsistence economy, storing staples represents an accumulation of subsistence goods, usually involving their use as a means of payment. For once staples are stored on a large scale by temple, palace, or manor, this must be accompanied by such use. Thus treasure finance is replaced by staple finance, i.e., the rudimentary form of money and credit finance.

Most archaic societies possess an organization of staple finance of some kind or other. It was in the framework of the planned transfer and investment of staples stored on a gigantic scale that the accounting devices were developed that characterized the redistributive economies of the ancient empires over long periods of time. Only well after the introduction of coined money in Greece, some five or six centuries before our era, did money finance begin to supersede staple finance in these empires, but especially in the Roman Republic. Ptolemaic Egypt, for example, continued in the traditions of staple finance, which it raised to unparalleled levels of efficiency.

Redistribution, as a form of integration in early society, involves the storage of goods at a center, whence they are distributed. Goods passed on as payment to the center are passed out again as payment, and fall out of circulation. They provide subsistence for army, bureaucracy, and labor force, whether paid out in wages, in solders' pay, or in other forms. The personnel of the temples use up a large part of the payments made in kind. Raw materials are required for the equipment of the army, for public works, and for government exports: barley, oil, wine, wool, dates, garlic, and so on are distrib-

---

[12] Thucydides, *The Peloponnesian War*, I, 9.

uted and consumed. The means of payment are thereby destroyed. Maybe some of them are eventually bartered privately by their recipients. To that extent, "subsidiary circulation" is started that may become a mainspring of local markets.

The relevance of treasure and staple to the question of money uses is therefore this: they explain the functioning of the various money uses in the absence of a market system. Treasure goods may be used for payment. They serve simply to swell the hoard of treasure, and do not necessarily enter into the chain of economic exchange. The much larger sector of payments in a nonmarket economy concerns, of course, subsistence goods. Such quantifiable objects, when used for the discharge of obligations, are taken care of by the payments from the center implied in redistribution. Thus treasure and staples, between them, offer broadly the answer to the problem posed by the conditions of early society, where means of payment may be independent of the exchange use of money.

The absence of money as a means of exchange in the irrigational empires also stimulated the use of money of account, and it helped to develop a kind of banking enterprise—actually, large estate managements practicing staple finance—in order to facilitate transfer and clearing in kind. It might be added that similar methods were employed by the administration of the larger temples. Thus clearing, book transfer, and nontransferable checks were first developed, not as expedients in an exchange economy but, on the contrary, as administrative devices designed to make redistribution more effective and, therefore, the development of market methods unnecessary.

IX.   MONEY AND STATUS

The mutually reinforcing effects of status situations and patterns of integration were a source of the vigor of early social structures. Status was underscored by the institutions that supported the patterns. Money, price, and trade, for instance, contributed to class stratification. Archaic money created and maintained the span of prestige, separating wealth and poverty through elite circulation and poor man's money. Not only did stratification derive energy, but rates of exchange even gained stability from the general structural tenacity.

We should distinguish two broad groups of money institutions. First, as we have seen, are the money uses "which turn fungibles into money" and moneys that differ precisely in regard to these uses, namely, all-purpose money that is employed, as modern money is, in all three uses, and special purpose moneys that are employed only in one or another of these uses. Second, are money institutions deliberately designed to regulate status.

In Old Babylonia, money was common, but it was special purpose money: grain was the fungible most widely used for payment, as, for instance, wages, rent, or taxes; silver was universally employed as a standard, both in barter and in staple finance; most staples, at fixed equivalents, were used in cases of exchange, with no preference accorded to silver.

The differentiation of money institutions in their relation to status is met at an early stage in society. A ranking of moneys was described by Paul Bohannan among the Tiv of the Benue valley.[13] The different kinds of fungibles employed as currency there can be said to have an effect on status insofar as they are appraised according to rank. Food and craft goods rank lowest; cattle, slaves, and brass rods next; women to be possessed as wives, with a man's right to their offspring, rank highest. Two distinct moral categories of transactions emerge: transactions in which goods are exchanged for goods of the same rank ("conveyance") and goods exchanged for goods of a higher rank ("conversion"). The first kind of "money use" is morally neutral; the latter proves a man's strength of character and enhances his status. Exchanges in the opposite direction, which are of course inevitable, are rationalized as the fulfillment of obligation towards one's kin, who are to be given subsistence. This is morally right, but it does not enhance personal prestige. In view of the circles of exchanges, Tiv society can be regarded as multicentric.

On a more advanced level of societal development, the idea of ranked money may also find application. Fully six centuries before our time, Ibn Batutah recorded thin and thick copper wires of a definite weight functioning as currency side by side on the Middle Niger in Gogo, a city in the Negro empire of Mali (1352). Thin wires were poor man's money, exchangeable for firewood and common

---

[13] Paul Bohannan, "Some Principles of Exchange and Investment Among the Tiv," *American Anthropologist*, 57 (1955), pp. 50–70. See also Paul and Laura Bohannan, *Tiv Economy* (Evanston: Northwestern University Press, 1968).

millet. Thick wires bought anything, including horses, slaves, or gold, indeed all the elite goods that convey standing. In Homeric Greece, a conventional exchange of elite gifts existed unrelated to money. In its emphatically status-creating form, elite circulation was a feature of archaic trade: fast horses, precious metals, jewelry, objects of treasure, skilled slaves, or heirlooms could be acquired only for goods of a similar brand. Diamonds were available in seventeenth century India only for gold, not for silver. In West Africa, horses could be acquired only for slaves. Closer to the money range was the Mesopotamian practice of temple loans, given to peasants in barley while the free citizen received silver. Incidentally, this may solve the mystery of the twofold rate of interest that, paid in silver, amounted to 20%, while, paid in barley, it was 33⅓%. The answer to this economic conundrum may be that the debtors were of different status and that silver could not be purchased with barley. In the city state of Alalakh, the peasant and craftsman seem to have received small loans of a conventional amount, while persons of "family" aspired to loans of an amount in a distinctively higher bracket. Royal status in Dahomey entitled one to the use of round figures plus one, a privilege also traceable with the Big Ones in Babylonia. Also, the Yoruba King of Oyo burdened the defeated King of Dahomey with a yearly tribute of 41 boxes containing 41 muskets each. Upon ascending the throne, the King of Dahomey symbolically "bought" the land from the people for the traditional sum of 201 cowries. Again, loans made to peasants of Alalakh by the palace amounted to 10 or 20 shekels, while a gentleman could count on 41, 51, or 61, shekels. This custom of "plus one" weathered a span of several millennia and travelled far, from Alalakh to Abomey. It may have been one of the many cultural curiosities of early social structures that explain the marvellous stability of monetary exchange rates. An ounce of gold cost 32,000 stringed cowries in Dahomey for as far as our records reach, i.e., the lifetime of the dynasty, which was about three centuries. Today, the introduction of money into the economy is associated with a tendency to fluidity and instability; in archaic society it was, on the contrary, a source of stability that needed no bureaucratic controls to rely on.

Still other unsuspected money institutions emerge in any discussion of price and trade, revealing ever new aspects of the formation of money rates, built-in profits, "ideal" units to link basic standards with a variety of limited currencies, to breach the gap between fundamental, unchanging regional units and local trading moneys. Most of this remained necessarily invisible under the formula of "money, a means of exchange."

X. SUMMARY

The independent meanings of payment, standard, store of wealth, and exchange are thus borne out by their institutionally separate origins and purposes served. Of these we now have fairly solid knowledge.

Payment occurs in connection with some institutions of early societies, mainly bridewealth, wergeld, and fines. A person may thus be under an obligation to hand over quantifiable objects mostly, though not always, of a utilitarian character (usually employed also in the settlement of some other obligation). In the archaic law books, composition, damages, and fines are regularly set out in one and the same physical terms, like oxen, sheep, or silver. These three main sources of obligation survive in archaic society and are, moreover, enormously expanded through the introduction of taxes, rent, and tribute, which offer many more occasions for payments in discharging obligations, and, therefore, money uses—social and political— for stores of wealth.

The standard use of money is vital to the staple finance that accompanies large-scale storage economies. No assessment and collection of taxes, no budgeting and balancing of manorial households, no rational accountancy comprising a variety of goods is possible without a standard. Since it is not the number of things but their values that are here subjected to arithmetic, this operation requires the setting of rates relating the various staples to one another. Such figures, representing rates, are in effect available in most archaic societies. Whether by virtue of custom, statute, or proclamation, fixed equivalents designate the rate at which the necessities of life can be mutually substituted, one for another. It is only when prices develop in markets (i.e., relatively late) that money as a standard can be taken for granted, as it is today.

Exchange develops, as a rule, within the framework of organized trade and markets, apart from which indirect exchange is only occasionally met. Hence the exchange use of money is of but little importance under fully primitive conditions. Even in highly stratified archaic societies, such as Sumeria, Babylonia, Assyria, the Hittites, or Egypt, storage economies prevailed; and, in spite of a large-scale use of money as a standard, its use for indirect exchange was negligible. This may, incidentally, explain the complete absence of coins in the great civilizations of Babylonia or Egypt at a time when the poor and semibarbarous Greek world indulged in a variety of artistic coins.

A comparative study of early money institutions must start from the fact that, while modern money is "all-purpose" money, i.e., the medium of exchange is also employed for the other money uses, primitive and early moneys tend to be "limited purpose" moneys, i.e., different objects are employed in the different money uses. Hence the widely disparate role of money institutions in modern Western societies, on the one hand, and early non-Western societies, on the other. All-purpose money makes for more homogeneous forms of social organization; in contrast, limited purpose moneys, in spite of a much lower degree of monetarization, tend to enrich the articulation of society, particularly the differentiation of its kin and class structure. Early money may show, therefore, more specialized institutional forms than does money in our own society. A developmental study bears out this fact.

Neither reciprocity nor redistribution is workable without some kind of "rates" that are valid as between different goods. On this level, "rates" are an operational necessity. Even the game yielded by a single hunt cannot be distributed without some kind of rates relating the different parts of the body of the animals to be cut up. This holds good irrespective of whether the distribution is intended to be strictly egalitarian (1:1) or not (e.g., 3:1). At the same time, rates between elite goods automatically maintain higher status if circulation is limited to interchange between such goods (elite circulation); lower class status, too, is maintained by restricting living standards to the coarse food and bare necessities that native money is allowed to purchase (poor man's money). The same device may serve to distribute food rations to the poor at official rates during famine. Equivalencies here are an absolute necessity, since the standard use of money is impossible without them. The variety and often minute articulation of money institutions thus help to achieve integration and stabilize status privilege without the use of open force; make provision against famine; and extend the scope of operational devices that substitute for writing. This again makes staple finance possible, together with large-scale taxation. In literate societies, where money becomes a means of exchange, most of those devices become obsolete and lapse into oblivion together with the manifold moneys and monetary practices of primitive and archaic communities.

☙ 10 ☙

Market Elements and Market Origins

I. INTRODUCTION

The origin of market institutions is an intricate and obscure subject, even though markets are not so old as mankind and had specific origins in human history. On this point, markets may be said to differ from the trickle of trade and the modicum of money uses found in human communities even of the simplest and earliest kind. Some two-way acquisition of goods from a distance, i.e., trade, is inseparable from wooing gifts and dowry goods, those accompaniments of a universal exogamy. Blood money and fines, again, involve the employment of quantifiable objects, i.e., money units used either in payment or as equivalencies. Trade and money, we may say, were always with us. Not so the market, which is a much later development. Nevertheless, as we will see, it is hard to trace its beginnings.

This observation holds good of the market in both its current meanings, very different though they are. The first is that of a *place*, typically an open site, where the necessaries of life, mainly foodstuffs or prepared food, can be bought in small quantities, as a rule, at set rates; the second is that of a *supply–demand–price mechanism*, through the instrumentality of which trade is carried on, though that

123

mechanism is not necessarily tied to a definite location or restricted to the retailing of food.[1]

For the historian of economic organization, the two sets of facts are far apart. In the one case, the empirical phenomenon to which he can hold on is a physical spot where crowds once met for the purpose of exchange; in the other, he is looking for a variant of trade that works through a specific *mechanism*. The latter is also an empirical fact, but it is too intangible, too much in the nature of a mere statistical event, to lend itself easily to historical research. A marketplace is in the reach of the archaeologist, but a market mechanism is beyond the most nimble spade. While it may be comparatively easy to locate an open space where, sometime in the past, crowds were wont to meet and exchange goods, it is much less easy to ascertain whether, as a result of their behavior, exchange rates were fluctuating and, if so, whether the supply of goods offered was changing in response to the relative or absolute up or down movement of those rates.

Obviously, the market as a *place* preceded any competitive *mechanism* of the supply–demand type. It was some 2000 years after the first noticeable appearance of the market as a mechanism facilitating the distribution of grain in the Eastern Mediterranean that the self-regulating system of price-making markets evolved in Western Europe and spread over a great part of the globe. It must be strongly emphasized that such a system—the term we are using here for liberal capitalism—is far more than a mere variant of trading. The principle of exchange implied in trade is, under capitalism, put to a wholly different use from the acquisition of goods from a distance. A full market system encompasses its society. Here land and labor are allocated through the supply–demand–price mechanism; risk bearing is organized as a market function; the supply of money and credit, as well as all the complex services summed up under banking, are provided through markets. And eventually the market becomes, at least for a time, the fundamental institution of Western society.

Naturally, in our time, interest turns toward this self-regulating system of markets that dominated the nineteenth century. Yet our

[1] Cf. Walter Neale, "The Market in Theory and History," in *Trade and Market in the Early Empires*, ed. K. Polanyi, C. M. Arensberg, and H. W. Pearson (Glencoe, Ill.: Free Press and Falcon's Wing Press, 1957), Chapter 17.

inquiry here stops far short of the emergence of a market economy. At best, we reach a point of vantage from which a new vista opens up on that system. Historically, that economy lies as far ahead of mere market trade as market trade itself was ahead of its primitive origins.

A warning as to method is imperative at this point. The temptation, in our own age, to regard the market economy as the natural goal of some three thousand years of Western development is overwhelming. In regard to such institutions as local food markets or market trade, Western thought is almost incapable of conceiving of them in any manner, except as the small beginnings that eventually grew into the world-encompassing economy of the modern age. Nothing could be more mistaken. Market trade itself, and eventually the modern market economy, were the results, not of a process of growth from small beginnings, but rather of the convergences of originally separate and independent developments that cannot be understood apart from an analysis of the institutional elements that went into their making. To avoid this teleological pitfall, as in the cases of trade and money discussed above, an institutional and operational approach seems most appropriate.

In the institutional sense, the term *market* does not necessarily assume a supply–demand–price mechanism. It is a conjunction of definite institutional traits, which we will call market elements. They are a site, physically present or available goods, a supply crowd, a demand crowd, custom or law, and equivalencies. Thus a market, in institutional terms, merely postulates an exchange situation; exchange is taken here not in the catallactic but in the purely operational sense of the term. This implies no more than a bare vice-versa movement of goods between "hands" at rates that may be determined by custom, administration, law, or by the market institution itself. Whenever the market elements combine to form a supply–demand–price mechanism, we speak of price-making markets. Otherwise the meeting of supply and demand crowds, carrying on exchange at fixed equivalencies, forms a non-price-making market. Short of this we should not speak of markets, but merely of the various combinations of the market elements the exchange situation happens to represent. In the case of auctions, for instance, we have a demand crowd with no supply crowd; with sutlers provisioning an army in the field, a different situation, with many market elements, appears; similarly, with the operation of ports of trade, the "provisioning at the gates" in some redistributive oriental economies, and the institution of the bazaar. All of these have market elements; none are markets proper.

The market institution has its origin in two different sets of developments: the one external to the community, the other internal. The external is intimately linked with the acquisition of goods from outside, the internal with the local distribution of food. This latter took two very different forms: the first was general in the irrigational empires and centered on storing and distributing staples; the second is to be found from the earliest times in peasant and bush communities, and focused on the local sale of fresh victuals and prepared food. These varied sources of origin contributed different constituent elements to the institution of the market.

II. LOCAL MARKETS

One type of local market is the means by which the retailing of food—whether foodstuffs or precooked food—was practiced in the societies of ancient Greece and Rome. We will briefly call this commercial site *agora,* and contrast it with the kindred institutions of the *gates* and the *bazaar* in the irrigational empires.

The *agora* type of local market was primarily a feeding place for the population. Fresh milk and eggs, fresh vegetables, fish, and meat were offered for sale; frequently the food was prepared. In principle, this excluded goods from a great distance, which would have to be conveyed by carrier to reach the market. In general, the articles held for sale were products of the neighborhood and often, in peasant societies, they were provided by women who carried them to market on their heads. The customer who looked for his food to the market was the poor laborer or transient who had no household of his own to turn to. Neither the trader coming from afar nor the well-to-do resident frequented the early local market; it served the needs of the common people.

The battle for and against food distribution through a market was waged in Athens, for example, largely on party political grounds. The democratic machine was handicapped, since owners of manorial households made a practice of inviting their neighbors and hangers-on to free meals. Cimon, the aristocratic leader, was famous for this type of political hospitality. Pericles, his democratic opponent, to right the balance, fostered the market habit and had all citizens provided with a small daily allowance for public service that would keep them going through the day as long as it bought them a meal in the marketplace. We have no knowledge from other *poleis* of similar caucus maneuvering that involved the food market. For Athens, it is well authenticated, as we shall see.

A. Markets for Mercenaries

Outside of Attica, especially in the Greek-speaking regions of Asia Minor, the chief promoters of markets were the Greek armies, notably the mercenary troops, now more and more frequently employed as a business venture. By the turn of the fifth century, towards the end of and just following upon, the Peloponnesian War the self-equipped hoplite army, traditionally engaged only in brief campaigns on a sack of barley meal brought along from home, was changing into an expeditionary force, only the cadres of which consisted of Spartans or Athenians proper, while the bulk was recruited from mercenaries. The employment of such a force, especially if it was supposed to cross friendly territory, raised novel logistic problems.

This question—the relationship between armies and markets— has been surprisingly neglected by historians of antiquity. A tentative examination of Thucydides and Xenophon suggests that a tremendous impetus to the development of markets and market elements came from the armies. Apart from the somewhat hypothetical question of development, this study has revealed a great deal of significance with respect to the operation and general character of ancient markets.

The economic impact of the Greek army may be analyzed from two separate angles: the disposal of booty captured by the army; and the provisioning of the army. The first contributed greatly to the development of a demand crowd; the other to that of a supply crowd.

We have commented elsewhere on the quantitative importance of war booty. It is sufficient to point out here that booty remained perhaps the greatest single means of enrichment throughout the classical period. Early in the period, Cimon rose from genteel poverty to tremendous wealth through his military exploits; almost a century later, mercenary service became commonplace as a means of acquiring wealth.

Booty, in the Homeric and archaic periods, consisted of treasure, cattle, and slaves; these were used directly or circulated among the elite. There was little or no change in the articles taken as booty in the classical period except that slaves perhaps increase in importance; there is a substantial change in the method of disposal, however. The administrative problems presented by the safekeeping, moving, and distributing of slaves, cattle, and treasure must have been great; the risks of loss through escape or illness equally large; even more pressing were the tactical and, in fact, often also strategic problems raised by the safekeeping and transportation of the booty. The growth of foreign trade and of market elements provided an alternative to direct handling: the booty could be sold and the money distributed instead. The number of incidents in Thucydides' history in which a captured population is sold into slavery suggest that this was the standard method of disposing of captured populations.[2] The practice apparently became somewhat distasteful towards the end of the Peloponnesian War, and in 411 B.C. we find an instance in which only the former slaves (and the goods) are seized, the free population being left alone.[3] Thereafter, until the battle of Mantinea in 223 B.C., this rule seems to have been generally observed.[4] In all probability, enslavement of a Greek population remained legally possible in wartime, the prohibition being essentially a moral one: enslavement of Greeks was a serious violation of good taste. When it happened, therefore, the fact that the people in question were of "a mixed Hellene and barbarian stock" was offered by way of explanation.[5] In the late fifth century, the decision whether or not to sell the inhabitants, seems to have rested with the general.[6]

Xenophon's accounts provide rather more details on the actual techniques of booty sale than those of Thucydides. Thucydides does relate that when the Athenians took Hyccara, a town on the north coast of Sicily, they transported the enslaved population to the city of Catana, where the main Athenian fleet was based, and sold the slaves there for 120 talents.[7] Transporting the slaves or other booty

[2] Thucydides, The Peloponnesian War, I, 55; I, 98; IV, 48; V, 116; V, 31; VI, 62; VII, 85.
[3] Ibid., VIII, 62.
[4] Polybius, II, 56–58.
[5] Xenophon, Hellenica, II, 1. (The incident is dated 405 B.C.)
[6] Ibid., I, 6.
[7] Thucydides, The Peloponnesian War, VI, 62.

to an emporium seems to have been the preferred method. Thus, Xenophon tells us that when his army reached the emporium of Chrysopolis near the mouth of the Bosporus, they "halted seven days while they disposed of their booty by sale."[8] Somewhat earlier, they had halted for ten days at the Sinopian colony of Cerasus on the Black Sea, where, besides reviewing and counting the troops to determine the number of casualties, "they divided the money accruing from the captives sold."[9] From the context of the preceding passages, it seems very likely that the slaves were sold there. The Spartan king and mercenary, Agesilaus, in fact, created a scandal when he followed an alternative procedure in order to enrich his friends. Having captured tremendous wealth in a campaign in Phygia in 396 B.C., he ordered the booty sold on the spot, informing his friends that immediately after the sale he would march to the seacoast where the booty could be resold at a substantial price. The army auctioneers were told to turn over the goods on consignment, simply keeping a record of the purchaser; Agesilaus' friends thus didn't have to pay until after they had resold the goods on the coast. Through this technique, Xenophon remarks, "his friends reaped an enormous harvest."[10] There are indications, however, that auction on the spot was a regular procedure in the Spartan army. Spartan constitutional practice provided that anyone taking booty in the field turn it in to the official booty-vendors (laphyropolai),[11] who apparently registered the name. That such registration entailed considerable honor is indicated by the fact that some of Agesilaus' principal allies in Asia Minor deserted because of the insult received when Spartan officers seized their booty from them, in order to have to themselves the honor of turning a large quantity over to the auctioneers.[12] The auctioneer must have frequently sold the booty on the spot, either to the soldiers themselves or to accompanying merchants. This is the procedure used, for example, when Xenophon's army is paid in kind for its past services with 600 head of cattle, 4000 sheep, and 120 slaves.[13]

The growth of the scale of warfare, together with the growth of the marketing habit, caused a thorough revision of the traditional

---

[8] Xenophon, *Anabasis*, VI, 6.
[9] Ibid., V, 3.
[10] Xenophon, *Agesilaus*, I, 18 ff.
[11] Xenophon, *Constitution of the Lacedaemonians*, XIII, 11.
[12] Xenophon, *Hellenica*, IV, 1.
[13] Xenophon, *Anabasis*, VII, 7.

methods of army supply. Early in the Peloponnesian War, the Spartans bring their provisions with them when they invade Attica and retire when these have been used up; the procedure is repeated the following year.[14] Such a method clearly must have been unsatisfactory, and in the ill-fated Sicilian expedition we find the Athenians relying on two methods: buying food in markets provided by the inhabitants of the region through which they were traveling; or buying from sutlers who accompanied the army. The former is clearly the preferred method, but it is not completely reliable: the availability of a market in neutral or hostile territory cannot be taken for granted, but is instead the subject of elaborate diplomatic negotiations. Negotiating for markets is a major responsibility of an army commander; our clearest picture of the proceedings is contained in Xenophon's *Anabasis*. After the death of Cyrus, the Greek mercenaries who had been serving him desired to return; the Persian king was himself apparently anxious to rid the country of a group that could only do mischief, hence he granted them safe conduct through his territory.

> You may now, if you like take pledges from us, that we will make the countries through which you pass friendly to you, and will lead you back without treachery into Hellas, and will furnish you with a market; and wherever you cannot purchase, we will permit you to take provisions from the district. You, on your side, must swear that you will march as through a friendly country, without damage—merely taking food and drink wherever we fail to provide a market—or, if we afford a market, you shall only obtain provisions by paying for them.[15]

We cannot imagine that such a treaty failed to fix equivalencies—and probably measures as well. A while later, Xenophon argued for breaking the treaty, asking

> is it better to be buying provisions in a market of their providing, *in scant measure and at high prices*, without even the money to pay for them any longer; or, by right of conquest, to help ourselves, applying such measure as suits our fancy best?[16]

When they were coming to the country of the Macrones, a truce was negotiated in which the Greek mercenaries gave a lance in pledge to

---

[14] Thucydides, *The Peloponnesian War*, III, 1.
[15] Xenophon, *Anabasis*, II, 3.
[16] Ibid., III, 2.

show that their intention was merely to pass through on their way to the sea. The Macrones in turn pledged a lance as witness of their peacefulness. "After the pledges were exchanged," Xenophon relates,

> the Macrones fell to vigorously hewing down trees and constructing a road to help them across, mingling freely with the Hellenes and fraternising in their midst, and they afforded them as good a market as they could, and for three days conducted them on their march. . . .[17]

The city of Trapezus also afforded a market. Xenophon defends his army against the charges of plundering leveled at them by Sinope.

> At Trapezus, they gave us a market, and we paid for our provisions at a fair market price. In return for the honor they did us, we requited them with much honor. . . . But wherever we come, be it foreign or Hellenic soil, and find no market for provisions, we are wont to help ourselves, not out of insolence but from necessity. They have been tribes like the Carducjians, the Taochians, and Chaldaeans, which, although they were not subject to the great king, yet were no less formidable than independent. These we had to bring over by our arms. The necessity of getting provisions forces us; since they refused to offer us a market. Whereas some other folk, like the Macrones, in spite of their being barbarians, we regarded as our friends, simply because they did afford us the best market in their power, and we took no single thing of theirs by force. But, to come to these Cotyorites, whom you claim to be your people, if we have taken anything from them, they have themselves to blame, for they did not deal with us as friends, but shut their gates in our faces. They would neither welcome us within nor furnish us with a market without.[18]

Clearly, the location of the market is also a matter of importance. As a rule, a neutral or hostile city will provide the market outside the city, in order to avoid admitting the soldiers inside the gates. On one occasion, when the city of Heraclea became angered by the mercenary demands, the city "dismantled the market outside and transferred it within, after which the gates were closed."[19] Moving the market outside the gates was the general rule during the Sicilian campaign; Rhegium and Messina, for example, forbade the Athenians to enter

[17] Ibid., IV, 8.
[18] Ibid., V, 5.
[19] Ibid., VI, 2.

the city, but provided a market outside the gates.[20] On occasion, the market might have been moved closer to the fighting area. Thus, the Syracusan fleet won an important naval battle by attacking the Athenian fleet before the latter had the chance to eat: the Syracusans gained time by persuading the nearby city "to move the sale market as quickly as they could, down to the sea, and oblige every one to bring whatever eatables he had and sell them there, thus enabling the commanders to land the crews and dine at once close to the ships, and shortly afterwards, the selfsame day, to attack the Athenians again when they were not expecting it."[21]

The type of market provided by the local residents varied very widely: at one extreme, what must have been the crude food market provided by the Macrones, which Xenophon pointedly calls the best the barbarians could do, and at the other extreme, the market town provided by Ephesus for Agesilaus' army.

> Thereupon it was a sight to see the gymnasiums thronged with warriors going through their exercises, the racehouses thronged with troopers on prancing steeds, the archers and javelin men shooting at the butts. Nay, the whole city in which he lay was transformed into a spectacle itself, so filled to overflowing was the marketplace with arms and armour of every sort, and horses, all for sale. Here were coppersmiths and carpenters, ironfounders and cobblers, painters and decorators—one and all busily engaged in fabricating the implements of war; so that an onlooker might have thought the city of Ephesus itself a giant arsenal.[22]

It is clear from Xenophon's experiences that total reliance on markets provided on the spot by the local inhabitants posed considerable risks for the army. Wherever possible, therefore, other methods had to be used. Thus, we find at the outset of Cyrus' expedition that his Asian army is accompanied by a moving food market manned by the par-excellence retailers of Asia Minor, the Lydians, a market that also provisions the Greek mercenaries.[23] But Cyrus also took along 400 wagons of grain and wine to distribute to the mercenaries "in case of extreme need overtaking the expedition."[24] Direct distribution of food was kept in reserve as an

---

[20] Thucydides, *The Peloponnesian War*, VI, 44.

[21] Ibid., VII, 39, 40.

[22] Xenophon, *Agesibaus*, I, 25 ff.

[23] Xenophon, *Anabasis*, I, 5.

[24] Ibid., I, 10.

emergency measure. Traveling markets manned by sutlers must have been, in fact, quite common. It is clear that in the incident described above, in which Timotheus issued a bronze coinage to his army, the same sutlers who bought the booty were also retailers of food.[25]

The Athenian expedition against Syracuse, in 415 B.C., the biggest naval expedition of antiquity to that date, relied primarily on markets provided on the spot, and this was a major tactical problem.[26] But the expedition included thirty "ships of burden laden with grain," manned in part by bakers and millers drafted into service for pay "in order that in case of our being weatherbound the armament may not want provisions, as it is not every city that will be able to entertain numbers like ourselves."[27] From the description, it seems probable that this grain and other food were sold to the members of the expedition by state commissary agents at fixed prices, and the grain ground and baked into bread by the drafted bakers, again at fixed prices.

The techniques of army supply offer striking evidence of the proliferation of markets throughout Greece, Sicily, and Asia Minor in the late fifth and the fourth centuries. An army could hardly depend on buying its food in markets on the spot, without assurance that the markets would actually be there. At the same time, the growth in the scale of warfare must have provided an impetus to the further development of markets, both from the provisioning and especially from the booty-sale side.

Cause-and-effect analysis of this material can be only speculative. But some of our assumptions regarding the character of markets in this period are strengthened. It seems quite clear from the Thucydidean and Xenophontian writings that the term market (*agora*) everywhere and always means a *food market*. Its specificity as to site, place, authority, and goods is demonstrated with particular clarity: the market is moved inside or outside the gates, down to the shore; a particular army is admitted to or excluded from the market; the market is provided for a set period of time. What is of particular interest are the diplomatic negotiations necessary before trade can begin: a treaty must be established setting the time and place,

[25] Pseudo-Aristotle, *Oeconomica*, II, 1350a.
[26] Thucydides, *The Peloponnesian Wars*, VII, 14.
[27] Ibid., VI, 44, 23.

specifying where the purchasers can go and where they cannot, and—we strongly suspect—setting the terms of trade as well. Certainly this latter must have figured importantly in the Asia Minor expeditions, where different systems of weights and measures, as well as of coinages, must have existed. The food markets provided for traveling armies thus take on some of the characteristics of the West African ports of trade, designed to provide a market for the foreigner, but to exclude them from the territory of the city so far as possible.

B. Gates

Another more distant ancestry, yet still a local one, connects the market with the methods of food distribution practiced in the redistributive empires. The market was here the offshoot of an essentially different institutional arrangement, which then underwent an almost complete transformation. We refer to the storage-cum-redistribution methods practiced in early Sumeria and its Mesopotamian successors. In these irrigational empires of antiquity, central government and grain growing on a large scale made for an elaborate system of storage at the *gates,* whether of temple, palace, or city. The need for storage is caused by fear of famine as well as the pressure of the food requirements, for soldiers or for work parties organized by palace or temple to deal with flood water, irrigation, or drainage. Gates consist of tall towers for protection of entrance and exit; massive cellars for dry storage, sometimes insulated by a coat of asphalt; an open space in front of the outer gates for ceremonial meetings and court sessions; sometimes a regular gateway situated behind the outer gates, that is, a narrow passage with gates at both ends connecting two walls. At the gates a few main staples—necessaries that keep—are both received and handed out, often against some fixed equivalent (such as silver) in terms of which accounts may be kept; or the equivalents may be in kind, such as one *gur* of grain being equal to ten *ka* of oil in Babylonia. Simple quantitative equivalencies for grain, oil, wine, and wool allow the staples to be substituted for each other. Tax and rent payments, in the one direction; rations to laborers or soldiers, in the other, are thus taken care of. Although food is distributed, this is no food market, since there is no "meeting of supply and demand crowds."

C. Bazaars

In the *bazaar*, there was such a meeting. However, it was not a food market but emphatically one for manufactured articles, the products of craftsmen. It was also different from any modern market, inasmuch as there was no one price for any type of object, and competition was excluded by its very organization. Sale took place not "in the open" but in the shop, the head of the craftsman's family acting as broker. The craftsmen were, as a rule, strangers—either transplanted as part of a conquered people, or settled under treaty. Physically, the bazaar was a covered place. In the absence of other accommodation, the alleys of the walled city were roofed over from one side to the other. From the beginning, however, the essential point is that the bazaar lacked a distinctive element of the market— one price—whether that price, or equivalence, is provided by law, custom and authority, or by suppliers and customers interacting collectively, as in the price-making market of modern times.

Gates and bazaars together represented the institutional apparatus by virtue of which the necessities of everyday life were distributed over enormous periods of time in the Eastern cradles of our civilization. But at some rather late period of history, a change is noticeable in the function of the bazaar. The intrusion of the *polis* into the long coastal areas; the establishment of manorial seigniories in the Turkicised regions of continental Asia; lastly, the enfranchisement of the "commercial classes" by Islam tended to dissolve the centralized storage system and fuse it in more than one way with the bazaar. Almost imperceptibly, the craftsmen's bazaar took on the additional function of a local food market—sometimes the one, sometimes the other feature predominating in the new set-up—as can still be vividly seen in the Central Asian and Central Sudanese markets up to this day. Finally, the bazaar absorbed the sale of foreign goods when ports of trade were outmoded as a result of world market development.

III.   MARKET TRADE—EXTERNAL MARKETS

A supply–demand–price system implies fluctuating prices that control supply, if not production itself. Where did such a system originate? And when and how did trade—a millennial institution of great scope and power, which had developed entirely on expedition-ary, gift–countergift, and administrative foundations—link up with it? When and how did trade come to base itself on methods so foreign to its whole history?

As to the origins of the supply–demand–price mechanism, for the historian of antiquity the only practicable way to go about locat-ing such a mechanism is to follow the tracks of trade. Traces of the market mechanisms of the past elude us. Library documents are few and lack the necessary precision. Even in our own days, the presence or absence of a market for a definite good is sometimes difficult to ascertain, as business men know all too well; for the distant past it would be almost a hopeless endeavor. Trade is an altogether different matter: personnel, goods, routes, and vehicles are manifest. Wherever trade was seen to take its course, we might expect to find pools of goods—the source and sink, as it were, of the flow. If we can then find trade determined by the price differential obtaining be-tween goods, we can speak of market trade.

So much for the method to look for the beginnings of price-making markets. But, even assuming these to have been much more widely spread than the evidence seems to warrant, there is still the question of how trade, organized in an entirely different way before, was massively reorganized in this new form.

Once again we must shun the teleological temptation, which may, in retrospect, easily be overwhelming, and would do away with most of the question. For, was not the course of trade bound to be caught up in the meshes of the market mechanism? And, once that decisive link was forged, was it not merely a question of time before an unbreakable tissue of market trade should pervade the economy?

Teleology, as always, would invite a manner of euphoria that makes the researcher rely on the working of time and circumstance to evolve the inevitable result. Yet to assume such a natural affinity between market mechanism and trade is a purely arbitrary simplifi-cation, which ignores the complexity of both. As to the market, we have been made aware, by the social scientist, of the intricate psychological implications of that apparently obvious mechanism. And as to trade, in whatever form it be carried on, it necessarily represents a definite convergence of personnel, goods, equivalen-cies, and transactions—each of which is embedded in technologically and socially defined conditions with a history and logic of their own. A conjuncture of market mechanism and trade is, therefore, a highly specific development, in no way to be speculatively inferred but, on the contrary, to be deduced from historical and institutional conditions ascertainable only by factual research.

The emergence of market trade, although historically a more recent event than the emergence of local food markets, is almost equally obscure in its beginnings. It must have happened first in one region rather than another; in respect to some types of goods rather than others; moreover, which is decisive, it must have come by degrees, affecting one or another component of trade. We are thus faced with the picture of a highly variegated development. As we will see, with institutional analysis it can, however, be put in relatively simple terms.

Trade, then, will again be regarded as the composite of personnel, goods, equivalencies, and transactions. In respect to each of these constituents, one can speak of a transition from administered to market forms of trade. We will take these constituents in their transition separately, always keeping in mind the unavoidable distortions inherent in the use of historical data, and regarding institutional problems in their comparative and developmental aspects. This may serve as a rough approximation of the institutional problems encountered in the emergence of market trade.

IV.   PERSONNEL, EQUIVALENCIES, AND TRANSACTIONS

Tamkarum was, in Mesopotamian and Near Eastern antiquity from Sumerian times, the name of a status figure sui generis, around whom revolved the organization of trade and finance. The term is common to all three main groups of documentary sources, namely, the Sumerian Temple of Bau at Lagash in the time of Urukagina; later, the Assyrian, so-called Cappadocian tablets, and the roughly contemporary Code of Hammurabi of Babylonia. The *tamkarum's* activities, according to the context, are those we would describe as factor, agent, broker, auctioneer, safekeeper, banker, trustee, referee, travelling merchant, official slave dealer, tax collector, bailiff of the royal household—the term being employed indiscriminately to describe all these activities. As is apparent, some of them would fit in equally well with a commercial system of the conventional sort. The *tamkarum* could thus easily be mistaken by modern scholars for a private merchant, as long as the presence of markets was taken for granted. But the realization of the absence of market institutions in the Mesopotamian civilization is leading us to a reappraisal of the figure of the *tamkarum*, with important consequences for interpreting the data in the whole field of the economy.

In this regard, it is vital what interpretation be made of the Code of Hammurabi and the richly documented activities of the "Cappadocian" trade settlement in Central Anatolia.[28] According to the traditional reading, the Code of Hammurabi's *tamkarum* is a merchant, and the Cappadocian settlement consisted of Assyrian merchants, or traders, making profits in the usual way as intermediaries between the proto-Hittite natives and the far-off city of Ashshur. For the rest, in view of the differences in time, place, conditions, and dialect, no identifying of the *tamkarum* of the Code with that of the Cappadocian tablets could be postulated.

Turning to the Cappadocian tablets, the alternative here suggested is based on the assumption of a marketless trade, consisting in buying and selling for cash at equivalency rates, the trader's revenue being derived from commissions he charged the Assyrian exporter—maybe the city of Ashshur itself—on the consigned goods.

To the uninitiated, there is a particularly confusing fact that should briefly be brought to attention: the traders of the Cappadocian settlement are called by their personal names and are *never* designated as *tamkarum*. On the other hand, there is also a *"tamkarum"* who gives those traders important assistance in their business, who, however, remains nameless! He is invariably mentioned only as "the *tamkarum*." No completely satisfactory answer to this puzzle has yet been offered. The Codex Hammurabi contains, as we said, many references to the *tamkarum*, whose function is in trade, but never satisfactorily clarifies his activities. The question arises whether the *tamkarum* of the Code and the anonymous *tamkarum* of the Cappadocian tablets should not be regarded as identical figures, in spite of the admittedly special conditions of the Cappadocian colony and the fact that the active traders are never designated there by that name. If so, the assumption that the Mesopotamian economy was marketless might help to unravel the skeins of the *tamkarum* mysteries in the Code and Cappadocian tablets alike. Herein may lie the key to the status and activities of the *tamkarum* under the Code,

---

[28] Cf. Karl Polanyi, "Marketless Trading in Hammurabi's Time," in *Trade and Market in the Early Empires*, Chapter 2.

and perhaps to the organization of Babylonian business life, which is still obscure to us.

Be this as it may, and whatever the concrete activities of the *tamkarum* in various circumstances may have been, his chief characteristic is generally recognized as that of a status figure whose function was connected with public duties in trade and business life. This is a far cry from the modern merchant who makes a living from the differences between buying and selling prices; shoulders the risk on prices on the one hand, bad debts on the other, and is neither briefed to do so by public authority nor endowed with landed income or treasure to carry the burden of the task.

This brings us to the question of the transition from the one situation to the other. For nothing is more certain than that, at some time before our era, the figure of the *tamkarum* was replaced by a figure resembling that of the merchant. Many avenues of change suggest themselves. The *tamkarum*, while retaining his chief function, may have been permitted to carry on private trade, either in some definite kind of goods, or above some definite amount of goods traded; or change may have come in some other way that would still institutionally safeguard the public interests involved.

Some instances may be adduced from anthropology and history. In West Africa, up till recently, custom required an Ashanti to carry on his head 40 kola nuts for the government; anything above that was for his private gain.[29] China caravan men of the Eastern Turkestan route may be participants in a caravan that consists of numerous camel-owning merchants. A camel–puller, who is expected to tend up to eighteen camels, may own up to six of these and receive hire for them. Moreover, he is permitted to *soo-che*, i.e., to take along goods of his own, up to half a camel load going one way, a whole camel load coming back. If he owns more than six camels, he ceases to be paid for his work. If he owns more than the full complement of 18 camels, which is a lien, he becomes an independent partner who contributes his share to the overhead.[30] Nearly 4000 years ago, Cappadocian merchants allowed their junior employees, the *be'ulatum*, to trade on consignment, for their own advantage, with a limited sum of goods entrusted to them interest free, a benefit that served as a reward for

[29] Robert S. Rattray, *Ashanti Law and Constitution* (Oxford: Clarendon Press, 1929).

[30] Owen Lattimore, *The Desert Road to Turkestan* (Boston: Little Brown, 1929).

their traveling services, thus raising them to a status of some independence. Other evidence seems to point to a distinction between trading in goods monopolized by the government—goods given on consignment to the trader—and trading in free goods, which he could do in his own name. A similar practice was a feature of Persian export trade to Europe in the seventeenth century A.D. Silk was a government monopoly and was sold abroad on the government account by Armenian traders; other goods they could trade abroad freely.[31]

Another avenue of emergence might have been brokerage and auctioneering. Both activities are widespread in archaic societies. The Code of King Bilalama of Eshnunna, prior to the Code of Hammurabi, required that some religious dignitaries, who were barred from business, sell ale through brokers (Article 45). This may have been to save the religious man from defilement, which trading would bring about. The broker is an intermediary by profession. In some of the biggest Central Sudanese markets, when a scant supply of the necessaries of life threatens to give out at the valid equivalency, it falls to the broker to ration the goods in question without further ado. This assures the poor a minimum supply of food, firewood, and the like that might otherwise be scooped by the well-to-do.[32] A similar function falls to the broker in regard to the interloper who might either scoop or swamp the market and disorganize long-run supply. But the broker may also be expected to cooperate in the adjustment of equivalencies in an ordered fashion. Here the principle of auctioning enters, i.e., sale to the highest bidder. In premarket trade, it consists in the public display of the goods and their sale to the highest bidder without further formalities. The broker may supplement the usual sale at equivalency in the fixed price market by enquiring after likely buyers in the market neighborhood to ensure a good bid. Thus auctioning often merged with brokerage. It should be noted that, under conditions of equivalency exchange, goods are supposed to be sold neither below nor above "price." Even to sell cheap is forbidden, in view of the producers' interests, whether those of guild brethren or, more generally,

---

[31] Jean Babtiste Tavernier, *The Six Voyages of Jean Babtiste Tavernier* (London: 1678).
[32] Heinrich Barth, *Travels and Discoveries in North and Central Africa* (New York: Harper and Brothers, 1859).

suppliers of the raw materials. It suffices to recall these requirements of the medieval "just price" economy to recognize the stringency of these rules. Nevertheless, with the gradual lapse of such principles in favor of bargained prices, brokerage combined with auctioning would lead to more ordered forms of market trading.

A different avenue of adjustment might have opened up by way of so-called bankers. Originally, banking is a premarket activity. When barter is general, where money is used only for paying and as a standard, a specialized service is required, first for making payments, and second for dealing with debts. For the difficulty of barter, as an everyday transaction, is that there may be discrepancy between the two sides over the goods to be bartered, because there is either a lack of equivalency or a time lag to be bridged. In the first case, a balancing payment is in order, in the other, a debt is incurred. Whether payment is in kind, in silver by weight, or, later on, in miscellaneous coins, making up both the "difference" and honoring the debt involves, in "oral" civilizations, some professional witnessing of the act. The banker, in fifth century Athens, paid over to the creditor, in the presence of the debtor, the sum previously deposited with him by the debtor for this purpose. In an even simpler fashion, the money tester or money changer at his "bench" (usually a slave) is entrusted by public authority with the function in question.

In primitive societies, credit, through which debt is formalized, is provided originally by the reciprocity practiced within clan and neighborhood. In the archaic state, temple and palace are the chief providers of harvest credit. In the Cappadocian trading colony, long-term credit appears to be a matter for the *ummeanum,* whose seat was probably in the city of Ashshur itself, while advances were made according to circumstance by the *tamkarum.* The Codex Hammurabi appears to make it the duty of the *tamkarum* to provide mortgage credit up to the value of the harvest to the citizen–farmer. While, operationally, money-testing, money changing, payment, and crediting in premarket times are no different from these activities at much later times, in regard to the question in hand, their function is altogether different. With the emergence of price-making markets, money is primarily employed as a means of exchange, while both payment and credit take on functions of a new character. Credit is now a by-product of the process of the exchange of goods and their production; the time lag to be bridged is no longer due to the discrepancy in the value of the goods to be bartered, even less is credit a matter of reciprocity between kin and villager or of palace and temple distribution. Modern banking, far from making markets unnecessary, as archaic banking did, is a means of expanding the market system beyond any simple exchange of goods in hand. In the end, there is not much to show that in Mesopotamia banking did actually prove itself an avenue to the changeover from administered trade to market trade. Neobabylonian merchant bankers dealt directly with farming. Roman banking hardly reached the Athenian level. Only in the late Middle Ages did wholesale trading over long distances provide a source of capital that sought employment in more speculative channels, thus helping to demolish the preserves of the protected urban economies.

II

TRADE, MARKETS, AND MONEY IN ANCIENT GREECE

Introduction

In surveying well-known facts of Greek history from an angle somewhat different from the traditional, a singular circumstance will come sharply into light: namely, the Hellenic origin of both economic systems, the rivalry and the possible combinations of which are the problem of our time—the one system based on markets, the other on scientific, overall planning.

This remarkable fact was due, only to a minor extent, to the anything but commercially minded citizens of Athens and Sparta. Rather it came with the spread of the Greek language and elements of Greek culture to the ethnically non-Greek populations of the eastern Mediterranean, within the comparatively brief period of the flowering of Hellenism.

The outstanding facts are, on the one hand, that trade and money, mainly through the use of small coin, were linked with market elements in the Athenian agora; on the other, that not much later in Egypt, and again under Greek leadership, the methods of storage and redistribution inherited from the ancient Pharaohs were raised to the level of sophisticated economic planning.

The significance of this development, important in itself, is greatly enhanced by its formative influence on Rome, and, eventually, on the whole of Europe and North America. Even the earlier Babylonian and the ancient Egyptian institutions reached the western Mediterranean almost exclusively through Hellenic channels. In effect, apart from some traits of Etruscan and Carthaginian origin, the economic history of Rome over ten centuries might be said to feature methods either of Hellenic marketing or of Hellenic central planning. The conclusion can hardly be resisted that the Greeks of antiquity, whose genius was already credited with giving birth to our politics, philosophy, science, and art, were also the initiators of all advanced human economy.

Only an initiating role can, of course, be claimed for the Greeks, since the market never became more than a secondary feature before the modern age. Nevertheless, the part played by market elements, even at that early time, was of importance to the economy as a whole.

The conjunction of circumstances that made the warrior and peasant state of Athens, with its modest food market and moneychangers, into a significant factor in this development was anything but obvious or simple.

Indeed, as late as the opening of the seventh century, no sign of a market development was forthcoming in Greece. For at least a thousand years before that time, the continental empires of Mesopotamia, Asia Minor, Syria, and Egypt, and the seafarers of Ugarit and Crete carried on large-scale trade without the use of money as a means of exchange or of the market as the regulator of supply and demand. And it was not in backward Attica, but in Asia Minor, that we first meet, as late as the seventh century B.C., the use of coined money and the retailing of food in the local market of Salamis. Yet by the end of the fourth century, the Attica practice of distributing food through markets was already giving rise to an altogether new venture in the economic scheme of things. The use of coins of small denomination for retailing food and other everyday necessities in the market, which is in evidence soon after the end of the Persian Wars, now resulted in the marketing of grain in the eastern Mediterranean—the first known system of exchange of goods in history that deserves to be called an organized world market. Paradoxically enough, this great commercial venture was initiated in Greek Egypt under the sway of the most extreme system of bureaucratic central planning known to history, which characteristically employed the methods practiced by Athenian private bankers to increase the efficiency of a purely state-run economy.

Although market trade and an elaborate planned economy— twin themes of this book—were thus hardly more than a by-product of the history of ancient Greece, their joint beginnings may well throw new light on that nuclear institution of Western civilization— the Attic *polis* economy.

ᴄᴉ 11 ᴄᴉ

The Hesiodic Age: Tribal Decay and Peasant Livelihood

For the gods have hidden the livelihood of men.

Hesiod, *Works and Days*

I. THE WORLD OF *WORKS AND DAYS*

A world ignored by the Homeric epics comes into view in the works of Hesiod, the seventh century Boeotian poet. It has endured unchanged to the present, at least in wide regions of the planet. This is the world of the independent peasant householder, fiercely individualistic, moralistic, superstitious, ever complaining, and thrifty.

In perspective, *Works and Days* is a documentary manifestation of the birth of the isolated individual—a painfully anomalous figure in tribal society. A bitter ingredient accrues to the existence of the vast majority of men: individual concern for livelihood. It reflects the novel threat of lonely starvation, a contradiction in terms under tribal conditions. Its specter haunts the glorious rhythms of *Works and Days* and invests them with an eerie note of prophecy.

With the decay of the tribe, a new kind of uncertainty is born, which gnaws at the core of existence while forcing into being, even if in an uncouth form, an element latent in the human frame: personality. Under tribal conditions, economic fate had been collective, not individual: when it shifted, with the turn of the pastures, the run of the seasons, the favor of sun, wind, and rain, it shifted for all. Henceforth it was to become a fearful companion of the individual, who could no longer rely on the traditional tissue of redistribution and reciprocity to keep stark hunger away.

Hesiod discovered hunger as a part of the human condition. In the *Odyssey*, the pressing need for food makes its appearance only on the fringes of the community. It is a shameful event that befalls the outcast, the out-of-town beggar, the unaccepted guest. The urgency of its animal impulsions stamps the owner of the belly as a man *sans* kin, law, and hearth. "To belong" is to get one's food in the natural course of things; "not to belong" is to be concerned for one's food. Apart from the whine of the warrior doomed to die at the hands of the victorious foe, or the laments of the wandering hero whose return to his home is cut off by a god's spite, no outcry is so bitter as the hungry man's curse of his own belly that betrays his shame by its craving for food. The arrival of a stranger, guest, or wanderer is conventionally staged in the *Odyssey* as a step-by-step change from the wretched individual denouncing his belly to his eventually being welcomed and encouraged to partake freely of the food, offered to him ungrudgingly however much he decided to eat.

Though Hesiod registers realistically the symptoms of tribal decay, he was too close to the underlying process of dissolution to understand it in natural terms. Hence the mystery of the doom, the finality, and the unspeakable horror of the Iron Age. How was man thrown back upon himself for his nourishment? Had (in Hesiod's words) Zeus in his anger hid the bread of life, for that Prometheus of crooked counsel had deceived him? "For the gods have hidden the livelihood of men!" Man is alone, and care must never leave him. "Pass by the smithy and its crowded lounge in winter time, when the cold keeps men from field work—for then an industrious man can greatly prosper his house—lest bitter winter catch you helpless and poor, and you chafe a swollen foot with a shrunk hand" (493–497). To ward off starvation is the meaning of human life.

Hesiod's poetry records the appearance of isolated households on the scene of human affairs; there is no mention of common pasture; soon grain would be bought and sold. Almost contemporaneously with him, Amos, first of the great prophets, was calling down Jehovah's wrath on those who bought and sold the produce of the land. But by the middle of the fifth century, the temple state of

Judah had returned to redistributive methods, except for subordinate local food markets in Jerusalem. Israel stopped traffic in food and returned to the earlier ways. Some Greeks alone went on experimenting with market elements. So far as the historian is able to date changes in the awareness of the human race, it was in Hesiod's Greece that the "economic" as a concern of personal existence rose from the deep. For better or worse, a stark force of nature, the fear of hunger, had been unfettered.

II. THE COMING OF THE IRON AGE

Historically, the somber horror of the Hesiodic age probably lay in the conjuncture of two extraneous and otherwise disparate events, the one a political catastrophe, the other a technological revolution. The effects of the Dorian invasion and of the coming of iron combined to make his verse pregnant of ultimate despair. The Dorians had destroyed civilization, its arts and crafts as well as its order, justice, and administration; about the turn of the millennium, central Greece must have been a heap of ruins; the Dark Ages were on. A century or two later, the spread of iron tools and weapons began in many subtle ways to degrade men's lives in war and work. The incidence of this slow technological change, that centered on the western Caucasus and maybe the eastern Alps, made itself felt in Greece in the opening centuries of the first millennium B.C., gripping one geographical area and sphere of human activity after another. The effects were extremely varied and comparable, in their violent impact, only to that of the Industrial Revolution some 25 centuries later. For reasons that we cannot yet trace with precision, the growing use of hardened iron appeared in many cases to intensify some processes of everyday life nefariously, outweighing the liberating effects for which, in spite of all, the modern machine remains conspicuous. Thus war and agriculture were the two realms revolutionized by the spread of iron instruments and tools. An entirely new kind of discipline seems to have been forced upon tillers of the soil, with the growing of grain outside of irrigated areas where no iron-edged plow was needed and several harvests made for abundance. Stripped of its poetic glamor, *Works and Days* is an almanac of heartbreaking drudgery, spelled out in strident notes of warning to such as are fated unremittingly to toil on the land. It is the record of some cruel change that has interfered with the natural flow of life as it was lived by pastoralists, hoe gardeners, or seminomadic, crop-snatching folk. To tend animals and to grow plants is one thing; to depend for subsistence on harvesting grain from poor soil is another. The free man, laboring on his own land, had fallen into an almost unbearable form of servitude to the soil. It communicated to him its dictates through the rigor of the procession of the seasons and of plant life. This fierce regime of constraint was exacerbated by the whims of the weather, which trapped him into the eternal vigil of a humiliating uncertainty. Man as the servant of the machine is well understood as a modern problem; what we have forgotten is his subjection to nature in the early forms of agriculture.

III.   THE PASSING OF TRIBAL ORDER

Such may have been the forces responsible for that long ebb tide of Greek life of which Hesiod has bequeathed to us the dirge. The loosening of the clan tie, precipitated by the political and military upheavals, in no way released the more ample flow of life that sometimes accompanies the successful transition from a purely tribal organization to all-round feudalism. The dim recollections of a glorious past and the continued advance of culture overseas may have created, on the contrary, an almost insufferable sense of desolation.

Himself an independent peasant farmer, Hesiod was concerned with the political and social problems of the peasantry, above all with the growing insecurity of the prospects of the individual's livelihood, the dangers of indebtedness, and consequent loss of land, to his luckier neighbor. There are also ominous hints at a differentiation in the higher orders of society, through the amassing of wealth by masterful individuals outside of tribal relationships. The emergence of a crude individualism, however traditionalist, was the consequence of the passing of the tribal order. The rich peasant enserfs the poorer, the princely robber holds sway over tribal chiefs. The philosophic sections of the poem deal with the problems of conduct raised by this disturbing new feature of life.

We repeat: Greek social history from the Homeric age down to the beginning of the fifth century B.C. is mainly the story of the village neighbor and citizen gradually replacing kin. Somewhere on this continuum the peasant had to ask himself, who now was friend, who foe?

> Call your friend to a feast; but leave your enemy alone; and especially call him who lives near you: For if any mischief happen in the place, neighbors come ungirt, but kinsmen stay to gird themselves. (342–345)

Personal safety now depends on the neighbor, not on the mutual protection offered by the clan.

The good neighbor is an economic asset:

> A bad neighbor is as great a plague as a good one is a great blessing; he who enjoys a good neighbor has a precious possession. Not even an ox would die but for a bad neighbor. (346–348)

Few institutions are as deeply rooted in tribal life as marriage; in fact, marriage order is tribal order. Yet Hesiod, explaining precisely at what age to marry, and what sort of woman, advises his brother: "and especially marry one who lives near you" (700).

Only very gradually does the neighbor take the place of the kinsman. Already in the *Odyssey* Telemachus is asked

> the name by which they were wont to call thee in thy home, even thy mother and thy father and other folk beside, the *townsmen and the dwellers round about.* . . . And tell me thy country, thy people, and thy city. . . .
>
> (VIII. 550–555, K.P.'s italics)

Yet, by and large, for the aristocracy the blood tie still prevails.

With Hesiod the hold of the tribe weakens, but its lingering comes in for many subtle ambiguities. Blood feud is enjoined, but the revenge is made more personal: he who is hurt should retaliate, not any more the members of the clan, by virtue of their relations to the injured party. But even the injured man should fit his action to the circumstances:

> . . . do not wrong him first, and do not lie to please the tongue. But if he wrong you first, offending either in word or in deed, remember to repay him double; but if he ask you to be his friend again and be ready to give you satisfaction, welcome him. (708–712)

Not even the tie of brotherhood is excepted:

Let the wage promised to a friend be fixed, even with your brother—and get a witness; for trust and mistrust alike ruin men. (370–372)

The new individualism disrupts the closest bonds of kinship: no one should ever be trusted.

The structure of the family itself undergoes a change; Malthusianism is expressly advocated. One son constitutes the desirable family, "for so wealth will increase in the home" (375). Life is still possible if there are two sons; but only if the father manages to grow old. In that case, the advantages of division of labor may outweigh the burden of the fragmentation of the land through inheritance.

IV.   THE DECLINE OF RECIPROCITY

One of the great themes of the poem is the injustice of the times. Tribal bonds were wearing thin while feudal bonds had not yet had time to develop. The greed and cruelty of the princes, the helplessness of the individual against their rapacity were equally great. Hesiod describes the callous rich and the helpless state of the poor in magnificent imagery.

And now I will tell a fable for princes who themselves understand. Thus said the hawk to the nightingale with speckled neck, while he carried her high up among the clouds, gripped fast in his talons, and she, pierced by his crooked talons, cried pitifully. To her he spoke disdainfully: "Miserable thing, why do you cry out? One far stronger than you now holds you fast, and you must go wherever I take you, songstress as you are. And if I please, I will make my meal of you, or let you go. He is a fool who tries to withstand the stronger, for he does not get the mastery and suffers pain besides his shame." So said the swiftly flying hawk, the long-winged bird. (202–212)

The traditional political structure of tribal settlements had been viciously distorted by the "gift-devouring princes," who now failed to return the law and justice that was their responsibility. The empty forms of chieftainship remained; but meaning and content were gone. The tribal obligations expressed by those forms had faded. Justice became an abstract ideal to be pursued, and was no longer the institutional setting for the life of the tribe.

There is a noise when Justice is being dragged in the way where those who devour bribes and give sentence with crooked judgments take her. (220–221)

Politics now is for the wealthy: "Little concern has he with quarrels and courts (*agorai*) who has not a year's victuals laid up betimes" (30–31)—gone and forgotten is the popular assembly of tribal Ithaca.

The common meal apparently survived as an occasional, if somewhat poor affair; Hesiod must plead: "Do not be boorish at a common feast where there are many guests; the pleasure is greatest and the expense is least" (722–723).

But vanishing tribal reciprocity could not be simply transferred from kin to neighbor, from clan to village. In vain does *Works and Days* attempt to base reciprocity on neighborhood.

> Take fair measures from your neighbor and pay him back fairly with the same measure, or better, if thou can; so that if you are in need afterwards, you may find him sure. (349–351)

Interchange of gifts has here been transformed into a somewhat erratic transaction in which interest shyly makes its appearance. This kind of mutuality is necessarily selective and unpredictable: one must be very careful to whom one gives.

> Be friends with the friendly, and visit him who visits you. Give to one who gives, but do not give to one who does not give. A man gives to the free-handed, but no one gives to the close-fisted. (353–355)

Note the emphasis on the stringent necessity of fully returning a gift: this is in contrast to tribal reciprocity, with its absence of all precise equivalency. There one who consistently gave inadequate countergifts would be regarded as stingy, and perhaps completely lose face—but the gifts must continue, since they are decreed by the situation in which the giver finds himself. Hesiod's version, in fact, more closely resembles the modern idea of personal mutuality than the impersonal, but rigidly effective, reciprocity of the tribe.

And so Hesiod ends on a note of bitter warning: There may come a day when

> In bitter anguish of spirit you, with your wife and children seek your livelihood amongst your neighbors, and they do not heed you. (399–400)

> For it is easy to say: "Give me a yoke of oxen and a wagon," and it is easy to refuse: "I have work for my oxen." (453–454)

No one but the individual himself, through unceasing hard work, can avert "debt and joyless hunger": "And whatever be your lot, work is best for you." (314) . . . "Work that hunger may hate you . . . for hunger is altogether a meet companion for the sluggard." (299–302)

Such a concept of work is strikingly new—a far cry from the Homeric ethos which knows not, for the truly free, compulsion to work. Hesiod spells it out in so many words that "work is no disgrace: it is idleness which is a disgrace" (311). Work must be steady and carefully scheduled:

> Do not put your work off till tomorrow and the day after; for a sluggish worker does not fill his barn, nor one who puts off his work: industry makes work go well, but a man who puts off work is always at hand-grips with ruin. (410–413)

Independence is understood almost as much in negative as in positive terms. Positively, independence means a full barn; negatively, the avoidance of the loss of one's land, the avoidance of debt and of hunger. Work, as suggested above, can prevent hunger; proper organization of work can provide a larger measure of independence, in which "you . . . will not look wistfully to others, but another shall be in need of your help" (477–478). But the help and good will of the gods themselves is needed to avert the greatest evil, loss of land. Evil deeds must be avoided, and Hesiod warns

> As far as you are able, sacrifice to the deathless gods purely and cleanly, and burn rich meats, and at other times propitiate them with libations and incense, both when you go to bed and when the holy light has come back, that they may be gracious to you in heart and spirit, and so you may buy another's holding and not another yours. (336–341)

The meaning of these neatly phrased alternatives is identical with the Biblical hope that "thou shalt lend to another, and not another to thee."

V. THE HOUSEHOLD

The economic unit is the small household, whose members should be carefully selected. The danger of having more than one, or at most two, sons was mentioned above. A wife should be chosen

with great circumspection, not only to avoid the neighbor's censure
(and one should preferably marry a neighbor), but also because

> . . . a man wins nothing better than a good wife, and again,
> nothing worse than a bad one, a greedy soul who roasts her man
> without fire, strong though he may be, and brings him to a raw old age.
> (702–705)

A man should not marry until the age of thirty; first it is necessary to acquire the proper servants and the proper tools.

> First of all, get a house, and a woman, and an ox for the
> ploughing—a slave woman and not a wife, to follow the oxen as well—
> and make everything ready at home, so that you may not have to ask of
> another, and he refuse you, and so . . . you are in lack . . . (405–408)

This woman should have no children (602). Besides her, Hesiod
suggests a male servant of forty, since he will be interested in his
work rather than in his friends.

In such a small household, not a moment can be wasted
throughout the year if the struggle against debt and hunger is to be
won: the idle man "garnereth many sorrows for his soul." Prepara-
tions for the winter begin in summer. "While it is yet midsummer,
command your slaves: 'It will not always be summer, build barns' "
(502–503). But winter is no time for relaxation, either: Hesiod warns
his brother to shun the smithy, where men gather. And the public
assembly (agora) must be avoided at all times; for "little concern has
he with quarrels and courts who has not a year's victuals laid up
betimes" (30–31).

Besides work, thrift is enjoined: this was an entirely novel idea.
Wealth had been acquired by fraud, violence, or gifts. Yet Hesiod not
only risks the paradox that fraud and violence are the wrong way of
acquiring wealth, but also says that "if you add only a little to a little
and this often, soon that little will become great" (361–362). Rarely in
economic history has a departure of great consequence been put in
simpler terms.

Still another new chord is struck by Hesiod; competition serves
as a stimulus to work, clearly playing an economic role in Greek
society for the first time. Hesiod has trouble describing this new
phenomenon. He observes in the very beginning of the poem that
there are two kinds of strife on earth, one of which is to be praised,
the other "blameworthy," increasing evil war and contention. The
new kind is "the elder daughter of dark Night," who

stirs up even the shiftless to toil; for a man grows eager to work when he considers his neighbor, a rich man who hastens to plow and plant and put his house in good order: and neighbor vies with his neighbor as he hurries after wealth. Strife is wholesome for man. And potter is angry with potter, and craftsman with craftsman, and beggar is jealous of beggar, and minstrel of minstrel. (12–25)

None was offering to underbid his competitor. Each wished to excel in prowess, to retain the privilege of being regarded as the best, or at least the best liked. Hesiod's own minstrelsy was the famed prototype of this kind of strife.

VI. TRADE AND THE SEA

Trade is, of course, in evidence, but certainly not as a force in peasant life. Hesiod distinguishes two forms of trade, neither of which is very desirable in his eyes. The one he refers to simply as "seafaring"; this is limited to an occasional bartering of surplus by coasting along the shore in a small ship, in the proper season.

But if desire for uncomfortable seafaring seize you when the Pleiades plunge into the misty sea to escape Orion's rude strength, then truly gales of all kinds rage. Then keep ships no longer on the sparkling sea, but bethink you to till the land as I bid you. Haul your ship up on the land and pack it closely with stones all round to keep off the power of the winds. . . . You yourself wait until the season for sailing is come, and then haul your swift ship down to the sea, and bestow a convenient cargo in it so that you may bring home profit. . . . Admire a small ship, but put your freight in a large one; for the greater the landing the greater will be your piled gain, if only the winds will keep back their harmful gales. (618–645)

The other form, which he specifically calls trading (*emporia*),[1] appears to be more of an occupational affair. Even this is not a regular occupation, but only a last resort for the unfortunate.

If ever you turn your misguided heart to trading and wish to escape from debt and joyless hunger, I will show you the measures of the loud-roaring seas, though I have no skill in seafaring nor in ships. (646–649)

[1] This is the first instance in which *emporia* is employed in the sense of trade. H. Knorringa, *Emporos* (Amsterdam: H. J. Paris, 1926), p. 13.

In any case, the season for seafaring is very limited. The only time Hesiod approves of at all is July and August; unless Poseidon is determined, it is possible to escape death during that period, but one must be sure to return before the autumn winds. Those who are really desperate sail during the spring also, but Hesiod warns against it.

> Such a sailing is snatched, and you will hardly avoid mischief. Yet in their ignorance men do even this, for wealth means life to poor mortals; but it is fearful to die among the waves. (684–687)

Only a small part of one's goods should be carried on any voyage, because of the risks.

⊂ 12 ⊃

Local Markets: The Political Economy of *Polis* and *Agora*

I have never yet been afraid of any men, who have a set place in the middle of their city, where they come together to cheat each other and forswear themselves.

Cyrus, great King of the Persians, gave this answer to a Spartan embassy that came to warn him not to attack the Greek cities of the Asia Minor coast. The scene was Sardis, the captured capital of Lydia, the time 546 B.C. Lest anyone mistake the import of this symbolic meeting of east and west, Herodotus added a note:

> Cyrus intended these words as a reproach against all the Greeks, because of their having market-places where they buy and sell, which is a custom unknown to the Persians, who never make purchases in open marts, and indeed have not in their whole country a single market-place.[1]

There is a deep significance in this scene for the understanding of the *polis*. Herodotus proved to be, in the end, not only a more reliable historian than he was credited to be, but also a more resourceful writer. Cyrus fatefully underrated the moral fiber of his opponents, because of a doubtful point in their social equipment, the market habit. And indeed, but for the surpassing inner discipline of the *polis*, which curbed and regulated the market, it might have very

[1] Herodotus, *The Persian Wars*, I, 153.

well been, as Herodotus indicates, both the sign and the source of moral debility. As matters stood, those who confidently expected such debility in the Hellenes and built on it their hopes of victory over them were bound to be disappointed.

I. HERODOTUS AND THE HELLENIC MIND

Herodotus' use of the Sardis episode is a masterly performance in manner and content. His great work comprises no less than the picture of the known world and the course of its events. His philosophy of history is an interplay of the envy of the gods and the hubris of mortals, winged with the words of double-edged oracles. The vast panorama of events is arranged around the story of the Persian Wars, made to fit the same pattern. As Croesus the Lydian was made to pay for his success, which had outraged the gods, so in their turn, were his conquerors, the Persians, to be punished for their overweening self-confidence. It was not by chance that in the Sardis episode Herodotus bracketed *agora* and *polis,* as he did, striking up his leitmotif in a minor key. He succeeded to marvel: by a simple literary device he gave Cyrus' rebuff that touch of hubris and ambiguity that should not be quite absent from the first clash between Hellenes and barbarians. The conflict between East and West was made to echo the theme of universal history, powerfully, and not without subtlety.

Herodotus was a Greek patriot, and in spite of all their failings he deemed his people worthy of the splendid heritage that had fallen to them in the Aegean. But his masterpiece was meant as a monument, not to the Hellenes alone, but rather to human civilization, which, according to him, originated in Egypt and whose marvelous works adorned the great cities of Persia. His was not anti-Persian work. He was publishing the result of his research, he wrote, in the hope "of preventing the great and wonderful actions of the Greeks and barbarians from losing their due need of glory." Such an impartial appraisal was appropriate to an *oikoumene* in which similarities and contrasts were curiously intermingled. While the Persians had a passion for justice and veracity, the Greeks' lifeblood was discussion and freedom. Athens was a democracy, Persia a despotism. The Persian empire, still at its heights and unsurpassed in power and efficiency, had been defeated once only—but then by the Greeks—and it was now out of Europe. Yet in wide areas, Greek and barbarian culture, religion, and morals interpenetrated. Lydia itself, the Asiatic neighbor of Ionia, was more Greek than Asian, though in contrast to Greece, Lydia knew premarital prostitution. "The Lydians have very nearly the same customs as the Greeks" wrote Herodotus, "with the exception that these last do not bring up their girls in the same way."[2] As to the Persians, he held, "there is no nation which so readily adopts foreign customs" as they do.[3] A century after Herodotus' death, Alexander the Great made his name immortal by his attempt to marry Greeks and Persians and make them one nation.

Certainly to Herodotus the Persian wars were not a struggle between light and darkness. The Greeks were filled with wonderment at the moral ideas of the Persians. In Persian education, abstract ethical requirements were added to sporting and military prowess. "Their sons are carefully instructed, from their fifth to their twentieth year, in three things alone—to ride, to draw the bow, and to speak the truth."[4] Shades of Odysseus! Was this not to overwork the virtue of veracity? Herodotus' text is rich with overtones: "They hold it unlawful to talk of anything which it is unlawful to do. The most disgraceful thing in the world, they think, is to tell a lie; the next worst, to owe a debt; because among other reasons the debtor is obliged to tell lies."[5] Plato, somewhat later, may have responded to ideas such as these, but on the whole, to the Athenian, a life without liberty to explore the avenues of mind and fancy, as well as the freedom to go into debt at his leisure, would have meant death of boredom, and mere truthfulness cold comfort.

Herodotus avoids striking an ethical balance. The text bears a slight inflection of irony, at the expense of both sides. The Laconian warriors, notoriously slow of wit, must have been at a disadvantage when they found themselves mistakenly branded as marketeers. Herodotus makes Sparta—of all Greek cities the least addicted to the market habit, and no little proud of that—the butt of Cyrus' sally; although it would have been more appropriate to their Athenian rivals. Be that as it may, it was quite true that the market habit sometimes went with an informality of the oath, which Persians would take in no place other than the temple, and which the Greeks,

[2] Ibid., I, 94.
[3] Ibid., I, 135.
[4] Ibid., I, 136.
[5] Ibid., I, 139.

too, traditionally surrounded with a greater solemnity. In addition, the freedom of the marketplace left the quality of wares—and often also their ratios or, as we would say, their price, as well—to the uninformed judgment of the parties.

But Cyrus, the prim barbarian, shot beyond the mark. He contemptuously defied the Hellenes as a people, for the habit of forswearing themselves and publicly defrauding one another. This was one of those aspersions with which puritan barbarian propaganda, in its pristine vigor, was trying to discredit the Greeks. Actually, the Athenian reader was well aware that numerous officials were checking on market dealings and that proceedings in the market stood under strict supervision and moral self-control. But, while this was so, no one could deny that the market was also open to abuse; that it carried its temptations; that the spurious practice of concluding deals under oath smacked of profaneness. All the evidence goes to show that to many people the market was suspect, or at least a controversial institution. Plato, in the next century, still insisted on banning oaths from the market, and the exclusion of citizens from selling in the market, this being below their status. Aristotle, though he often disagreed with Plato on matters of the *polis,* urged the separation of the political *agora* from the marketplace and wished to have all artisan and commercial classes excluded from citizenship. Both were decrying the weaknesses of the very institution that Cyrus had chosen as his target.

Yet Herodotus' point was well taken. In the person of Cyrus, that wise and generous ruler, founder of the Persian Empire and, perhaps, greatest of living men, the Persian people were trapped into eventual defeat as were the powerful and cultured Lydians before them. Croesus, their king, had attacked the Persians and was now their prisoner in his own capital. Misled by the double talk of the Delphic oracle into that ill-fated crossing of the river Halys, he had indeed destroyed a great empire, his own. But was not Cyrus preparing a similar discomfiture for his own nation? The Persian misjudged his opponents; and so, assuredly, did his luckless successors, Darius and Xerxes. And their fateful error hinged not the least on that dubious Greek novelty, the market. By discounting the capacity of the Hellenes to master that unruly and ambivalent institution, the Persians, to their undoing, blinded themselves to the civic discipline and staying power of the Greek *polis.*

II. THE AGORA AND THE GREEK WAY

To understand the *polis* is to understand the place the market occupies in it. The historian must confess to an embarrassing ignorance of its actual development. While there are numerous mentions of the *agora* in the Homeric epics, the word in every case refers to a place of assembly;[6] the same is true of Hesiod's *Works and Days,* where the industrious man is warned to avoid the *agora,* that site of futile politics. We do not know when and where the word was employed to denote a marketplace. While the *tyrannis* episode in Greek history was a prerequisite to the later establishment of the peculiar Greek type of market system, it was, in origin, rather in the nature of an antimarket development. Peisistratus' rural resettlement program could hardly have stimulated the development of the market, which was situated in the city of Athens proper; on the contrary, the rehabilitation of the countryside may have been conceived as an alternative to the market growth of the Solonic and post-Solonic periods.

Whereas the invention of coined money swept the Greek speaking world, the market appears to have been regarded as a doubtful asset. At least in the aristocratic view, markets tended to sap a people's virility. When Cyrus thought of destroying the conquered Lydians because of their proclivity to revolt, Croesus, their captured emperor, who had become a friend and adviser to his conqueror, Cyrus, proposed to him as an alternative:

> Grant, then, forgiveness to the Lydians, and to make sure of their never rebelling against you, or alarming you any more, send and forbid them to keep any weapons of war, command them to wear tunics under their cloaks, and to put buskins upon their legs, and make them *bring up their sons to lyre-playing, harping, and shop-keeping [kapéleuein]. So you will soon see them become women instead of men,* and there will be no more fear of their revolting from you. (K.P.'s italics)

Cyrus, we are told, acted upon this advice; he

> summoned to his presence a certain Mede, Mazares by name, and charged him to issue orders to the Lydians in accordance with the terms of Croesus' discourse.

[6] Knorringa, *Emporos* (Amsterdam: H.J. Paris, 1926), p. 11.

Mazares entered Sardis, Herodotus continues,

> and first of all he forced the Lydians to obey the orders of his master,
> and change (as they did from that time) their entire manner of living.[7]

The Lydians, one infers, must have been notorious in the middle
of the fifth century as musical entertainers and retailers of cooked
food; occupations were looked down upon as unworthy of their virile
past. Herodotus himself stressed that up to the time of Croesus they
ranked as the best cavalrymen of Asia Minor. Not for nothing had the
downfall of Croesus been the international morality play of the sixth
century. Just as the ancient empire of the Assyrians on the Tigris had
dissolved into thin air, after the fall of Nineveh in 606 B.C., so the
glittering realm of the Lydians in Asia Minor now disappeared overnight, and its displaced population drifted into keeping market stalls
and playing stringed instruments in cookshops.

To the Hellenic reader, Herodotus abounded in topical allusions
and unavoidable exaggerations. The Lacedaemonians, affecting their
Dorian mannerisms, he twitted by fathering the promiscuous market
habits upon them, while it was common knowledge that their rivals,
the Athenians, fostered these habits, much to the satisfaction of
Spartan malice. In effect, loafing in the marketplace was becoming
almost a fashion in Athens, at any rate in democratic circles. But even
in Athens the market had yet to make the grade. It took another
century before a textbook on public finance laid down that "For
guarding, it will be well to adopt the Persian and Laconian systems.
Athenian housecraft has, however, some advantages. For, selling,
they buy . . ."[8]

By that time, Athens had become foremost among the democratic *poleis,* and it seems certain, on our evidence, that among these it
was Athens that pioneered the commercial *agora* as a way of life.

A curious connection between practical democracy and the rise
of the market as we find it in classical Athens should be noted.
Pericles was not only the Pericles of the Funeral Oration, that
Thucididean monument to the idea of a free and cultured community; he was also a party politician who recognized the tactical
advantage of a local food market in undermining the "Tory" election
machine.

---

[7] Herodotus, *The Persian Wars,* 155–157.
[8] Pseudo-Aristotle, *Oeconomica,* I, 6.

His opponent, the aristocractic leader Cimon, to come to the aid of the genteel poor who had been forced to fall back on buying their food in the market,

> . . . took away the fences from the fields, that strangers and needy citizens might have it in their power to take fearlessly of the fruits of the land; and every day he gave a dinner at his house—simple, it is true, but sufficient for many—to which any poor man who wished came in, and so received a maintenance which cost him no effort and left him free to devote himself to public affairs. But Aristotle says that it was not for all Athenians, but only his own demesmen, the Laciadae, that he provided a free dinner.[9]

Be that as it may, it was a spirited show:

> He was constantly attended by young comrades in fine attire, each one of whom, whenever an elderly citizen in needy array came up, was ready to exchange raiment with him. The practice made a deep impression.

But Cimon did more than offer his hospitality as an alternative to the cookshops and their popular atmosphere. He penetrated into the very camp of the enemy, the marketplace:

> These same followers also carried with them a generous sum of money, and going up to poor men of finer quality in the market-place, they would quietly thrust small change into their hands.[10]

The lordly patronage practiced by Cimon, based on his manorial *oikos*, called forth an original response from Pericles, the democratic leader. Himself a member of the great house of Alcmaeon, Pericles espoused the humble institution of the market. Plutarch says that despite his occupation with politics, he was able to preserve his inherited estate unimpaired, through the novel organization of his household:

> This was to sell his annual products together in the lump, and then to buy in the market each article as it was needed, and so provide the ways and means of daily life. For this reason he was not liked by his sons when they grew up, nor did their wives find in him a liberal purveyor, but they murmured at this expenditure for the day merely and under the most exact restrictions, there being no surplus of supplies at all, as

---

[9] Since Plutarch expressly contradicts Aristotle (*Constitution of Athens*, XXVII, 3) on this point, we may assume that other sources supported Plutarch's interpretation.

[10] Plutarch, *Cimon*, X, 1–3.

in a great house and under generous circumstances, but every outlay and every intake proceeding by count and measure. His agent in securing all this great exactitude was a single servant, Evangelus, who was either gifted by nature or trained by Pericles so as to surpass everybody else in domestic economy.[11]

Pericles' methods remained exceptional for "great houses" throughout Athenian history. Pseudo-Aristotle, after observing that the Attic system is to sell the produce and then buy what is needed, adds: "the smaller households keep no deposits in store."[12] The *agora*, then, made it possible for the small households to be self-sufficient: food and other necessities could be purchased from day to day, as needed. Side by side with this provisioning through the market, the self-sufficient *oikos* of the manorial type survived, of which Cimon's was an instance.

While the market was beginning to play a key role in provisioning the poulace, we should not exaggerate its part in the economy as a whole. Market trade and the *agora* were purely internal to the *polis*, bounded by its physical and political limits. The *agora* was hardly more than a device, facilitating the operation of the redistributive system, which remained dominant. Responsibility of the city for the livelihood of its citizens was an abiding principle of the Greek city economy. This responsibility was exercised in every direction: not only was the supply of necessary imports as a whole kept under public supervision, but the livelihood of the citizens themselves was to a considerable extent ensured by the state.

Polis economy, then, in the case of Athens, was made up of three strands, which today we would regard as disparate: redistribution in households of a manorial type; redistribution on the state level; and market elements. The three were coexistent in an organic whole that should be regarded as a distinctive type of political economy.

Not that the relationship of these three strands had been fixed and settled. The class struggle between the democrats and the oligarchs, which plays so prominent a role in Athenian history, may perhaps be best understood in relation to those three institutional patterns. The primacy of the principles underlying redistribution was beyond argument, as it had been with the tribe; the market—a later development—was never more than an accessory. But how and

[11] Plutarch, *Pericles*, XVI, 4–5.
[12] Pseudo-Aristotle, *Oeconomica*, I, 6, 2.

through what institutions the redistribution was to be organized, was another matter.

In Homeric Greece, there is already evidence of the distinction between redistribution of a tribal and of a manorial kind. The *polis* inherited the tribal traditions, both aristocratic and democratic; while the manorial household organized around family property existed outside of the tribal nexus and remained a disruptive force throughout most of Greek history. Cimon's case, as recounted by Plutarch, represented the one method: redistribution through the overgrown households of the rich. Such a system would make the households into manorial establishments and reduce the peasantry to the status of dependent clients, if not of serfs. On the other hand, redistribution by and through the state would be on a countrywide scale, and thus transcend the feudal parochialism of the petty lords. However, it still might mean one of two things: the superdemesne of a monarch, even though he be favorable to the popular interest, as most tyrants were; or a democracy in the classical sense of the term, namely, the administration of everyday life as executed by the people themselves.

Between these two variants, the crucial difference lay in regard to the method by which the distribution of food was organized. The monarch—whether king, despot, or tyrant—needed for this purpose a central bureaucracy, as in Egypt, or he had to leave untouched the local tribal organizations, as in Persia. In a democracy, where the citizenry was expected to do the administering itself, the distribution of food required the market; for how else could the citizens—some of whom were, at least periodically, engaged all day in public affairs and in need of support by the state—procure their provisions and maintain themselves? In modern terms, the distinction might be phrased as one between large-scale bureaucratic planning, as in Egypt, and small-scale democratic planning, with the market playing an important role in the distribution of food, as in classical Athens. This made the place which the market occupied in it crucial to the political constitution of *polis* democracy.

III. THE POLIS IN HELLENIC LIFE

Before the functioning of the *polis* economy can be fully understood, some remarks on what is meant by the civic discipline of the *polis* are required. The Greeks believed with deep conviction that it was the *polis* that made civilization possible; in fact, that the two were identical. Nowhere is this view more concisely expressed than in the first book of Aristotle's *Politics*. Remember that whenever he speaks of *the state*, he means the *polis*; when he uses the term *political*, he simply means pertaining to the *polis*:

> It is evident that the polis is a creation of nature, and that man is by nature a political animal. . . . A social instinct is planted in all men by nature, and yet he who first founded the state was the greatest of all benefactors. For man, when perfected, is the best of animals, but when separated from law and justice, he is the worst of all. . . . But justice is the bond of men in states, for the administration of justice, which is the determination of what is just, is the principle of order in political society.[13]

Civilization, in other words, requires law and justice; the determination of what is just and its execution through law constitute the principal function of the *polis*.

One hardly ever left the world of the *polis* in the fifth century unless expelled; in practice this meant that one took service either with another *polis*, or with the Persian empire, as witness Alcibiades and Themistocles.[14] Only exceptionally could an alien win citizenship rights in a Greek city; even the great democrat, Pericles himself, closed the citizenship rolls of Athens to anyone who could not prove Athenian descent on both sides. At no time could an alien—i.e., a Greek of another city—own land outside his own city—with rare exceptions. Law existed only in the *polis*; outside his own *polis*, or its sphere of influence, the citizen was subject to no laws, hence he was also defenseless, unless protected by special treaty. Aristotle's remarks thus were no mere patriotic aphorisms.

The *demos* was heir to the tribal tradition of equality. The dichotomy between the *demos* and the oligarchs was fundamentally a continuance of the archaic distinction between the tribe and the manorial households that grew up outside the tribal confines. Speaking of the classical period, Westermann observed that *polis* law "ex-

---

[13] Aristotle, *Politics*, I, 2.
[14] Kurt Riezler, *Über Finanzen und Monopole im alten Griechenland* (Puttkammer und Mühlbrech, 1907), Part I—a pioneering monograph.

pressed the sense of 'justice' as the will of the tribal citizen body, namely, the *polis*."[15]

Law in the *polis* had almost a self-enforcing character. Rostovtzeff put the question in this way:

> In Greece, laws are made by men. If a law offends the conscience of the majority, it can and must be changed; but while it is in force, all are obliged to obey it, because there is something divine in it and in the very idea of law. To break its injunctions entails punishment not only from men, the guardians of law, but also from gods. This rule of law in the city—or law created by the whole body of citizens—is one of the most characteristic features in the public life of Greece.[16]

The discipline of the *polis*, then, was boundless, the subordination of the individual to the *polis* complete. No concept of rights inherent in the individual ever developed in Greece; freedom came to the individual through his participation in the state. This must not be interpreted as a denial of individual liberty. Rather, the individual was inconceivable as existing apart from the *polis*. The modern concept of individual rights, of a basic antagonism between the individual and the state, would have appeared to the Greek as a contradiction in terms.

This unique discipline comprised not only the political and military sphere, but also the economy. Far from relying on a nonexistent supply–demand–price mechanism, it insisted on ensuring adequate supply at a set price. This made it possible for the *polis* to look to the market as a helpful device for provisioning the citizens.

Herodotus' underlying faith in *polis* discipline put Cyrus in the wrong. For in an emergency, the market could be—and was—transformed at a moment's notice into a redistributive device. The speed and ease with which a new coinage could be substituted for an old one draws a laugh in Aristophanes' *Ecclesiazusae:*

> And a bad job for me that coinage proved.
> I sold my grapes and stuffed
> My cheek with coppers and then I steered away
> And went to purchase barley in the market.

---

[15] W. L. Westermann, "Greek Culture and Thought," *Encyclopaedia of the Social Sciences* (New York, Macmillan), 1931, Volume I, p. 18.

[16] M. Rostovtzeff, *A History of the Ancient World* (Oxford: Clarendon Press, 1928), Volume I, pp. 205–206.

> When just as I was holding out my sack
> The herald cried: "No coppers allowed.
> Nothing but silver must be paid or taken."[17]

The second book of the Pseudo-Aristotelian *Oeconomica* still tells of numerous instances in which prices were fixed, coinage doubled, halved or otherwise altered, goods collected or rationed—and invariably with instant effect—peremptorily and without exemptions.[18]

If it was impossible to separate the individual from the community—neither tribe nor manor knew such a separation—the responsibility of the *polis* for the livelihood of its members was evident. The primacy of redistribution was such a tribal legacy. Rostovtzeff was aiming at this point in somewhat different terms:

> One of the main features of the economic development of the ancient world consists in the leading part taken by the State . . . [which] both as an organizing and stimulating and as a restrictive and destructive economic force was paramount . . .

The city state, he adds, practiced

> interference by the State in the economic activity of individuals which has no parallels in modern economic development. And this interference is not secondary, not an insignificant handicap to the development of private economy; it is the paramount and directing activity. "Redistribution of land and abolition of debts" was not only a revolutionary slogan, it was a pre-eminent, though bitter, event in the economic life of most of the Greek cities. . . . And such facts as the liturgies, the distribution of grain by the State, the close watch kept by it on grain commerce and on commerce in other foodstuffs which it organized so carefully, were all apt to change thoroughly the methods and evolution of private husbandry.[19]

Hardly anything was excluded from the scope of municipal redistribution. Goods, services, and money were collected at the center or, alternatively, the right to allocate them. Money and treasure were stored in the state treasuries; precious metals were cast into statues and other works of art that could be melted down when needed; grain, the staple food, was often kept in state storehouses and, in an emergency, could be brought there for storage by the householders.

---

[17] Aristophanes, *Ecclesiazusae*, pp. 816–822.

[18] See Chapter 15.

[19] M. Rostovtzeff, "The Decay of the Ancient World and Its Economic Explanations," *Journal of Economic and Business History*, II (1930), pp. 204–206.

Distribution of food—both directly and indirectly through the state organization of supply—played a decisive part; and increasingly, the citizens' subsistence derived from cash payments made by the state for military, administrative, and judicial services.

We shall now turn to the center from which, and the channels through which, this all-embracing redistribution operated in the *polis*.

IV. PUBLIC ADMINISTRATION

We have dwelt on the need for a centralized administration if redistribution was to be effective. The tribal form of redistribution had not been able to withstand the disruptive effects of self-sufficient manorial households; these grew up outside of the tribe and were capable of organizing a redistribution of their own on a small scale. Democracy, to the Athenian of the classical period, meant the supplanting of these households by the power of the *demos* organized in the *polis*. The Cleisthenic constitution completed the establishment of the democratic power of the *polis;* but the antidemocratic challenge of the manorial households persisted.

We have seen Cimon as a public benefactor acting in his role as a private host. But his services to the community went further than that. He filled in the swamplands south of the Acropolis at his own expense, and "beautified the city" by planting trees in the *agora* and "by converting the Academy from a waterless and arid spot into a well watered grove, which he provided with clear running-tracks and shady walks.[20] The first undertaking, meant to facilitate the construction of the southern wall of the Acropolis, made necessary the dumping of "vast quantities of rubble and heavy stones" into the swamps. This required the efforts of a large number of men, as did the embellishments in the *agora* and the Academy. Whether the laborers were permanently aattached to Cimon's household, like the host of artisans who followed Demaratus from Corinth, we cannot know. But the picture is unmistakably that of a manorial type of household—we need only keep in mind Cimon's youthful entourage who so generously exchanged cloaks in the market place. Cimon's princely wealth, it should be noted, was entirely derived from his

[20] Plutarch, *Cimon,* XIII, 7–8.

share of the booty that fell to him as commanding general of military expeditions. Although of noble birth, he had been so poor in his youth that, as some said, he lived with his sister as man and wife because their poverty prevented her getting a husband suitable to her rank.[21]

Oligarchy, Aristotle says, is the rule of the wealthy on account of their wealth, while democracy is the rule of the poor.

> . . . wherever the rulers owe their power to wealth, whether they be a minority or a majority, this is an oligarchy, and when the poor rule, it is a democracy.

The distinction is not, he insists, between rule of the few and rule of the many, but between rule of the rich and rule of the poor. In actual fact, the rich are almost invariably few and the poor many, but this need not be so, and is anyway beside the point—it is wealth that holds the key.[22]

But how does wealth provide the means to power in a *polis* that possesses a democratic constitution? How was democracy to counter such a development without losing its character of a *polis* democracy, that is, without a bureaucratic establishment? Once a large number of citizens were maintained in order that they could participate in public life, their support had to come either from the public hand or from the private means of the manorial lords. If these citizens were to remain free and equal citizens, and not to sink into manorial dependence, their support had to come from the public hand. Owing their support to the manorial lord, they would owe him allegiance in a feudal relationship. Such dependence can reach a pitch at which the legal rights of the citizenry are reduced to ineffectiveness. An instance is offered by Republican Rome with its patron–client relationship, a factor first in patrician and later in caesaristic rule.

In brief, democracy, in the Greek sense, required material safeguards to prevent the bribing of the public by the rich. As the only effective guarantee, the wealthy were to be prevented from feeding the politically active populace that was engaged in sitting on the jury, voting in the assembly, administering in the *Prytany*. To the Athenian mind, two seemingly contradictory requirements followed—the distribution of food had to be done by the *polis* itself,

---

[21] Ibid., IV, 7; X, 1.
[22] Aristotle, *Politics*, III, 8.

yet bureaucracy was not to be permitted to enter. For democracy meant rule of the people by the people, not by their representatives nor by a bureaucracy. Both representation and bureaucracy were looked upon as its antithesis. Rousseau, the fount of all modern thought resting on the idea of popular sovereignty, still rigidly adhered to this principle. But how could this distribution by the state be accomplished without a bureaucracy? In Athens the food market served as an answer.

A similar dilemma was at the root of the alternatives Rostovtzeff so rigidly drew between tax farming and financial bureaucracy as two sharply opposed administrative alternatives in the ancient world. For how, except through farming out their collection to privates, can taxes be collected if a bureaucratic development is to be avoided? Similarly, how could the necessary public works be constructed, except through letting out contracts to private persons?

In precisely the same way, we may add, money payments to the citizenry may represent an alternative to the distribution in kind of food and other necessaries. The payment may be for military, political, or other services, or may simply be a daily fee. Money is thus used for payment—an alternative to payment in kind—the market supplying the goods. The one or two or three obols a day received by the citizen from the state could thus be transformed into food. No bureaucracy was needed, yet the state provided for its citizens' livelihood. The democratic form of redistribution would then depend on the use of the market.

So complete was the avoidance of any bureaucratic element in ancient Athens that state offices were taken in turn by the citizens and filled by lot.[23] Offices could not be held a second time until the other citizens had held them.[24] Only few exceptions from these rules were made. Election by lot was considered the embodiment of true democracy, since every man thereby had an equal chance of holding office, regardless of ancestry, rank, or special ability. Rotation of office meant that every Athenian had familiarity with the intricate workings of public administration—at the same time, the growth of a permanent civil service was avoided. The Athenian could have no

[23] The treasurer of the military funds; the treasurers of the theatre fund; the superintendent of the water supply; military officials were also elected by vote. Aristotle, *Constitution of Athens*, XLIII, 1.

[24] Military offices could be held without limit; Council membership could be held twice. Aristotle, *Constitution of Athens*, LXII, 3.

doubt as to what the state was, or what the administration of justice was; justice was not embodied in distant institutions, but rather in such as every citizen had inside knowledge of. Henry Pericles could say:

> We alone regard a man who takes no interest in public affairs not as a harmless, but as a useless character; and if few of us are originators, we are all sound judges of a policy. . . . I say that Athens is the school of Hellas, and that the individual Athenian in his own person seems to have the power of adapting himself to the most varied forms of action with the utmost versatility and grace.[25]

The survival of tribal traditions of redistribution is illustrated in the famous story of Themistocles' diversion, to defense purposes, of the revenues from the silver mines of Laurium. As Plutarch tells it,

> . . . the Athenians were wont to divide up among themselves the revenue coming from the silver mines at Laurium, he, and he alone, dared to come before the people with a motion that this division be given up and that with these moneys triremes be constructed . . .[26]

So deeply rooted was tradition that Themistocles was not even able to use the Persian danger—genuine though it was—as the reason for the ship building, but rather had to use the more intimate challenge of neighbouring Aegina. No wonder that, as Plutarch comments, "there was no public treasure at that time in Athens."

According to Aristotle, the event occurred in 483/2 B.C., when "the mines of Maroneia were discovered and the state made a profit of a hundred talents from the working of them."[27] One hundred triremes were built with this money, according to both Aristotle and Plutarch; in Herodotus' version, the surplus was large enough to provide ten drachmas for each citizen and was used to build two hundred triremes.[28] All the gifts of persuasion of the wily Themistocles were needed in order to induce the Athenians to forego redistribution of a surplus fund. Yet without this action, Persia would have conquered Greece, since, as Aristotle tersely remarks, "with these ships . . . they fought the battle of Salamis against the barbarians." The mines themselves were state property, being leased to

---

[25] Funeral Oration, in Thucydides, *The Peloponnesian War*, II, 40–41.
[26] Plutarch, *Themistocles*, VI, 1.
[27] Aristotle, *Constitution of Athens*, XXII.
[28] Herodotus, *The Persian Wars*, 144.

individuals for either three or ten years; both letting the leases and paying the rentals were under rigid supervision. We should not be surprised to find that, in an emergency, the market was looked upon merely as another means of distributing food to the commonalty without bureaucratic intervention.

V. PRESENTS FROM THEIR OWN PROPERTY

To many students of antiquity the expansionism of Athenian democracy appeared almost as a contradiction in terms. Classical democracy developed a great maritime empire and kept her allies in subjection. The modern mind tended to regard this as a total defection from democratic principles. In regard to the internal constitution of the confederacy, this certainly holds good. But, in general, such a view, while understandable in the light of early nineteenth-century liberalism, ignored the historical aspect. After the warning of the Persian Wars and the narrow escape, Athenian democracy, if it was to survive, had to create an empire. This was, above all, a defense measure designed to prevent an annihilating revanche on the part of the Great King. And the corresponding economic policy of Athens, which aimed at securing grain supplies and maintaining financial support of the defenders themselves, was altogether a military and strategic necessity.

Defense, as Athenian experience had shown, demanded that food from overseas be ensured, as well as a livelihood for a large part of the population, which was bound to devote itself to the enormously expanded public services. Empire therefore meant, first, control of the import of grain; second, additional revenues to support the citizenry. The first will be discussed when the organization of the grain trade is examined. For the latter—that is, the general background of imperial policy and its financial aspects, to which we now turn—our chief authority is Aristotle. His works offer an elaboration of the entire problem.

The period before and after the battle of Salamis was one of political struggles between two rival "leaders of the people," Aristides and Themistocles. The latter, Aristotle remarks in the *Constitution of Athens*, "devoted himself to the conduct of war, while the former had the reputation of being a clever statesman and the most upright man of his time."[29] Themistocles, the hero of Salamis, was responsible for the development of Athenian sea power. Having established the fleet and led it to victory at Salamis, he proceeded to develop an adequate anchorage and harbor, which Athens lacked, since the insignificant vessels of the past had simply run up on the beach at Phalerum.

According to Plutarch,

> he equipped the Piraeus, because he had noticed the favorable shape of its harbors and wished to attach the whole city to the sea; thus in a certain manner counteracting the policies of the ancient Athenian kings. For they, as it is said, in their efforts to draw the citizens away from the sea, and accustom them to live not by navigation but by agriculture, disseminated the story about Athena, how, when Poseidon was contending with her for possession of the country, she displayed the sacred olive tree of the Acropolis to the judges, and so won the day. But Themistocles did not, as Aristophanes the comic poet says, "knead the Piraeus onto the city," nay, he fastened the city to the Piraeus, and the land to the sea. And so it was that he increased the privileges of the common people as against the nobles and filled them with boldness, since the controlling power now came into the hands of skippers and boatswains and pilots.[30]

To describe the city as "fastened" to the port was an exaggeration; but Plutarch's remark, that the development of sea power fostered democracy, reflects a fundamental truth. Aristotle, in tracing the growth of an extreme democracy at Athens in his *Politics*, observes that this was "largely due to circumstance," not to the reforms of Solon, "for the people having been the cause of the naval supremacy in the Persian War became proud and adopted bad men as popular leaders . . ."[31] And in his *Constitution of Athens*, he said of the Periclean expansion of Themistocles' naval program that, through it, he "caused the masses to acquire confidence in themselves and consequently to take the conduct of affairs more and more into their own hands."[32] The antidemocratic pasquil which goes under the authorship of the "Old Oligarch" explains the power of the populace as being due to the importance for Athens of the fleet.[33]

[29] Aristotle, *Constitution of Athens*, XXIII, 3.
[30] Plutarch, *Themistocles*, XIX, 2–4.
[31] Aristotle, *Politics*, II, 12.
[32] Aristotle, *Constitution of Athens*, XXVII, 1.
[33] Pseudo-Xenophon, *Constitution of Athens*, I, 2.

But navy and empire went together, lest both be destroyed by a bottling up of the fleet and a blockading of the capital. Most ancient and modern scholars have given the greater share of their attention to Themistocles' achievement in developing the Piraeus and the Athenian navy. But Aristotle demurs; Aristides, he insists, should be given the credit for the growth of the classical form of democracy. He used the establishment of the empire—undoubtedly his greatest achievement—to transform the character of Athenian democracy. The empire, as he conceived it, provided the funds that could maintain the entire population. He proposed, in fact, a sort of *synoecism*, in which some of the rural inhabitants would move to Athens, the tribute paid by the allies largely providing for the cost.

> After this, seeing the state growing in confidence and much wealth accumulated, he advised the people to lay hold of the leadership of the league, and to quit the country districts and settle in the city. He pointed out to them that *all would be able to gain a living there*, some by service in the army, others in the garrisons, others by taking a part in public affairs; and in this way they would secure the leadership. This advice was taken; and when the people had assumed the supreme control they proceeded to treat their allies in a more imperious fashion, with the exception of the Chians, Lesbians, and Samians. . . . *They also secured an ample maintenance for the mass of the population in the way which Aristides had pointed out to them. Out to the proceeds of the tributes and the taxes and the contributing of the allies more than twenty thousand persons were maintained.* There were 6000 jurymen, 1600 bowmen, 1200 knights, 500 members of the Council, 500 guards of the dockyards, besides fifty guards in the city. There were some 700 magistrates at home, and some 700 abroad. Further, when they subsequently went to war, there were in addition 2500 heavy armed troops, twenty guard-ships, [each carrying 200 marines], and other ships which collected the tributes, with crews amounting to 2000 men, selected by lot; and besides these there were the persons maintained at the Prytaneum, and orphans, and gaolers, since all these were supported by the state. In this way the people earned their livelihood.[34] (K.P.'s italics)

The juncture of seapower and democracy recognized by Aristides was also manifested in Periclean policies. It was under this greatest of all *demagogues* that the Athenian thalassocracy reached its

---

[34] Aristotle, *Constitution of Athens*, XXIV. Aristotle is here describing the ultimate results of the adoption of Aristides' policy, since payment for some of the services he mentions was not adopted until later in the fifth century.

peak. Aristotle's analysis of the manner in which Pericles rose to power is of particular interest to us; it takes us a long way towards an understanding of *polis* democracy.

> After this Pericles assumed the position of popular leader, having first distinguished himself while still a young man by prosecuting Cimon on the audit of his official accounts as general. Under his auspices the constitution became still more democratic. He took away some of the privileges of the Areopagus, and, above all, he turned the policy of the state in the direction of naval domination, which caused the masses to acquire confidence in themselves and consequently to take the conduct of affairs more and more into their own hands . . . *Pericles was also the first to institute pay for service in the law courts, as a bid for popular favor to counter-balance the wealth of Cimon.* The latter, having private possessions of royal splendor, not only performed the liturgies magnificently, but also maintained a large number of his fellow demesmen. Any member of the deme of Laciadae could go every day to Cimon's house and there receive a reasonable provision; and his estate was guarded by no fences, so that anyone who liked might help himself to the fruit from it. Pericles' private property was quite unequal to this magnificence, and accordingly he took the advice of Damonides of Oia . . . which *was that, as he was beaten in the matter of private possessions, he should make presents to the people from their own property;* and accordingly he instituted pay for the members of the juries.[35] (K.P.'s italics)

The conflict between Cimon and Pericles is pointedly expressed in terms of the contrast between the two centers of redistribution: manorial *oikos* and democratic *polis*. Pericles—the democratic leader—was kept from power by Cimon's wealth, redistributed through the conservative leader's household and by his generous performance of *leiturgies*. The two are of one piece: leiturgies, too, were performed only by the rich, and tended to reduce the common people to something akin to dependence. Pericles' policy is presented as a clear alternative to Cimon's: to "make presents to the people from their own property," and so to give them more power; for "under his auspices the constitution became still more democratic." Moreover, redistribution by and through the *polis* was on the lines of *polis* tradition; by contrasting pay for serving on a jury with Cimon's lavish *leiturgies*, Aristotle really implies that the performance of public services by the populace was no more than an

---

[35] Aristotle, *Constitution of Athens*, XLIII, 1.

extension of the *leiturgy* principle to the masses. Voluntary performance of duties was the poor man's *leiturgy*.[36]

Hence, to some extent, Pericles carried the Aristidean ideas into
effect. Some twenty years had gone by though, because of the oligar-
chic reaction following the Persian War. Although naval expansion
did favor democratic power, the Areopagus[37] had regained a large
measure of its former influence because of the prestige that it won
during the wars. For when the Athenian fleet was about to disband
for lack of pay, the Council of the Areopagus stepped in and donated
eight drachmas to each member of the crew.[38] Its power, though
gradually diminishing, lasted some 17 years after the Persian Wars.[39]

Plutarch, who echoes Aristotle's account of Periclean ascen-
dency, gives many more details of his redistributive policy:

> In the beginning . . . pitted as he was against the reputation of Cimon,
> he tried to ingratiate himself with the people. And since he was the
> inferior in wealth and property, by means of which Cimon could win
> over the poor,—furnishing a dinner every day to any Athenian who
> wanted it, bestowing raiment on the elderly men, and removing the
> fences from his estates that whosoever wished might pluck the fruit,—
> Pericles, outdone in popular arts of this sort, had recourse to the
> distribution of the people's own wealth. . . . And soon, what with
> festival grants and jurors' wages and other fees and largesses, he bribed
> the multitude by the wholesale, and used them in opposition to the
> Council of the Areopagus.[40]

To what degree Aristides' *synoecism* was carried out, and country people moved into the city, cannot be ascertained. Thucydides
writes that at the opening of the Peloponnesian War, most of the
population maintained households in the country.[41] Undoubtedly
many moved to Athens, since much of Pericles' attention was taken
up by the presence of idle throngs of commoners. He sent out 60

---

[36] In the early classical period the liturgy was a coveted honorific duty voluntar-
ily assumed by the rich; it was only later that it became semicompulsory and that the
wealthy sometimes tried to evade it.

[37] The high council of nobles, distinguished from the Ecclesia, the assembly of
freemen—ED.

[38] Aristotle, *Constitution of Athens*, XXIII.

[39] Ibid., XXV.

[40] Plutarch, *Pericles*, IX, 2–3.

[41] Thucydides, *The Peloponnesian War*, II, 16.

triremes each year, "on which large numbers of the citizens sailed about for eight months under pay, practising at the same time and acquiring the art of seamanship," and dispatched colonies to the Chersonesus, Naxos, Andros, Thrace, and Italy, altogether several thousand men.

> All this he did by way of lightening the city of its mob of lazy and idle busybodies, rectifying the embarrassments of the poorer people, and giving the allies for neighbors an imposing garrison which should prevent rebellion.[42]

Gomme infers a steady increase in the urban proportion of the population in the fifth and fourth centuries.[43]

But "that which brought most delightful adornment to Athens and the greatest amazement to the rest of mankind" was Pericles' great program of construction. From it were born the Parthenon and the Propyleion on which the fame of Athens forever rested. Pericles himself had conceived it as a long-term program of public works designed to maintain a large portion of the population.

> And it was true that his military expedition supplied those who were in the full vigor of manhood and abundant resources from the common funds, and in his desire that the unwarlike throng of common laborers should neother have no share in the public receipts, nor yet get fees for laziness and idleness, he boldly suggested to the people projects for great constructions, and designs for works which would call many arts into play and involve long periods of time, in order that the stay-at-homes, no whit less than the sailors and sentinels and soldiers, might have a pretext for getting a beneficial share of the public wealth. The materials to be used were stone, bronze, ivory, gold, ebony, and cypress-wood; the arts which should elaborate and work up these materials were those of carpenter, molder, bronze-smith, stone-cutter, dyer, worker in gold and ivory, painter, embroiderer, embosser, to say nothing of the forwarders and furnishers of the material, such as factors, sailors and pilots by sea, and, by land, wagon-makers, trainers of yoked beasts, and drivers. There were also rope-makers, weavers, leather-workers, road-builders, and miners. And since each particular art . . . kept its own throng of unskilled and untrained laborers in compact array . . . it came to pass that for every age, almost, and every capacity there the

---

[42] Plutarch, *Pericles*, XI, 4–5.
[43] A. W. Gomme, *The Population of Athens in the Fifth and Fourth Centuries* B.C. (Oxford: B. Blackwell, 1933), Chapter 2, esp. pp. 46–47.

city's great abundance was distributed and scattered abroad by such demands.[44]

The funds for this gigantic endeavor were extorted from the tribute and dues of Athens' allies or dependents. The amount of wealth Athens derived from her empire is shown by the size of her state treasure at the time of the Peloponnesian War; she had 6000 talents of coined silver in the Acropolis, treasure objects valued at 500 talents, the removable gold ornaments of Athena, containing forty talents of pure gold, as well as other temple treasures.

Pericles was "ever devising some sort of pageant in the town for the masses, or a feast, or a procession," Plutarch reports.[45] If we accept Wilamowitz's view, the *theorikon*, a two-obol gift to enable the poorer citizens to pay the admission to the Theater of Dionysus, was instituted by Pericles. The Funeral Oration could exalt Athenian ways:

> And we have not forgotten to provide for our weary spirits many relaxations from toil; we have regular games and sacrifices throughout the year; our houses are beautiful and elegant; and the delight which we daily feel in all these helps us to banish melancholy.[46]

And an emergency distribution of land in Aegina, and of money, was made at the start of the Archidamian War in 431 B.C.[47]

Lest there be any doubt as to the rationale of these activities, here is Pericles' own defense of the uses to which he put the allies' contributions:

> And it is but meet that the city, when once she is sufficiently equipped with all that is necessary for prosecuting the war, should apply her abundance to such works as, by their completion, will bring her everlasting glory, and while in process of completion will *bring that abundance into actual service,* in that all sorts of activity and diversified demands arise, which rouse every art and stir every hand, *and bring as it were, the whole city under pay, so that she not only adorns, but supports herself as well from her own* resources.[48] (K.P.'s italics)

To our era, which not so long ago was concerned with the

---

[44] Plutarch, *Pericles*, XII, 5–7.
[45] Ibid., XI, 4.
[46] Thucydides, *The Peloponnesian War*, II, 38.
[47] Plutarch, *Pericles*, XXXIV, 1.
[48] Ibid., XII, 4.

problem of "boondoggling," Plutarch's remark on the achievements of this great state program is worth quoting.

> So then the works arose, no less towering in their grandeur than inimitable in the grace of their outlines, since the workmen eagerly strove to surpass themselves in the beauty of their handicraft. And yet the most wonderful thing about them was the speed with which they rose. Each one of them, men thought, would require many successive generations to complete it, but all of them were fully completed in the heyday of a single administration . . . they were created in a short time for all timer.[49]

Not only was this state planning, but state planning on a very high level of efficiency. Lord Keynes in his *General Theory* might well have offered the Parthenon instead of the pyramids as a historical parallel to our modern public works.

Other regular payments were added by Pericles' successors. Cleophon, who followed Cleon as demagogue, began the payment of the much vilified *diobelia* about 410/9 B.C.[50] The *diobelia*, a universal payment of two obols per day, seems to have been an emergency measure designed to take care of the throng of displaced persons crowding into Athens from the overrun countryside; it remained in force for several years. The *diobelia* had its precedent in the Persian War; when the Athenian women and children were removed for safety to Troezen, before the battle of Salamis, the citizens of that city "voted to support them at the public cost, allowing two obols daily to each family."[51] And at the very beginning of the Peloponnesian War, when Pericles induced the country inhabitants to move into Athens, a large part of the Piraeus, as well as land between the long walls from Athens to the Piraeus, was distributed among them.[52]

Sometime about 400 B.C., a one-obol payment for attendance at Assembly meetings was begun, and rapidly increased to two and then to three obols by 390.[53] By Aristotle's day, the payment amounted to one drachma for ordinary meetings and one and a half for the monthly "sovereign" meeting, at which grain supply and foreign policy were on the agenda. Jurors, who had received one or

[49] Ibid., XIII, 1, 3.
[50] Aristotle, *Constitution of Athens*, XXVIII, 3.
[51] Plutarch, *Themistocles*, X, 3.
[52] Thucydides, *The Peloponnesian War*, II, 17.
[53] Aristotle, *Constitution of Athens*, XLI, 3.

two obols per day during the Periclean age, had their pay raised to three obols by Cleon, and it remained at this figure throughout the fourth century. By Aristotle's time, also, Council members received five obols per day, while those whose turn it was to serve on the Prytany, the chief executive council, received an additional allowance of one obol per day, as well as meals taken in common at public expense. The archons received four obols each, along with the services of a flute player and a herald; the deputies to Delos received a drachma a day, while magistrates on foreign service received an unspecified maintenance.[54] "Invalids," the *adynatoi*, received a daily payment of two obols; they were subject to examination by the Council in order to determine their eligibility.[55]

VI.   THE KAPĒLOS

All this bears out the view that the Athenian *agora* was largely a retail market for the sale of foodstuffs ready for consumption; and the *kapēlos*, whose never clarified figure was domiciled in the *agora*, was in the first place a retailer of cooked food.

The Aristidian semisynoecism, as Wilamowitz-Moellendorff referred to it, followed upon the forced evacuation of Athens, whose population took to the ships and was rescued from starvation by the miracle of Salamis. Short of a public consciousness to which the bare question of food supply had a dramatic poignancy, the political contest between Cimon and Pericles could hardly have centered on anything so trivial as the retailing of provisions in the market. Yet it did center precisely on that, though there is remarkably little direct evidence on this point, so basic for the understanding of the *polis* and its economy. Nor do we possess certainty on that central figure of the *agora*, tje *kapēlos*.

For some insight we must turn to Aristophanes, who in his *Acharnians* brought on the stage a monumentally exaggerated *kapēlos*, unmistakable and oversize, but—to heighten the comic effect—avoided naming him. *Acharnians* was written and performed in the first half of the Peloponnesian War, in Athens, the capital of the warring *polis*. Periclean strategy involved yearly evacuation of the

---

[54] Ibid., LXII, 2.
[55] Ibid., XLIX, 4.

countryside, the inhabitants taking refuge in Athens. The martial inhabitants of the township of Acharnae, chief sufferer from the yearly Spartan raids, belonged to the war party, while the hero of the comedy is a citizen farmer, Dicaeopolis, who has had enough of the war. Eventually he concludes a private truce with the Spartans and devotes himself altogether to his own private life. He is the citizen philosopher who solves the problem of war and peace in his own common sense fashion. He is, in effect, the *zoon apolitikon*. He shuns the very word *polis*, as if to use it would run him into trouble. Normally, he would live on his plot of land and till the soil in blissful self-sufficiency, never bothering about town and market. But for these six years he has found himself embroiled in high politics, cut off from his despoiled homestead by the annual enemy incursions, and reduced to turn, even for his oil and vinegar, to the market of the town, to which he is now time and again compelled to repair. To say nothing of the foolish embargo that the Athenian government clamped on imports from Megara, thereby forcing our hero to forego all "enemy" dainties and relishes of the table. Piglets from Megara and eels from the Boeotian marshes are no more than a memory.

In this politicophilosophical burlesque, where anything goes, Dicaeopolis happens to contribute information on the fifth century *agora*, and even rarer knowledge on the exact nature of the catering business carried on there by the *kapēlos*. By natural inclination, Dicaeopolis decries the market habit, recalling the happy times in his rural home when he lived unharassed by the cares of the kitchen and the jostling crowd. Yet the logic of this exuberant farce, with its loosely knit scenes of realism and absurdity, lands him in the very center of the marketplace. The time is the present, 426, B.C., the place is the Pnyx, just before the assembly is due to open. The political theme of the play is, of course, peace; the tiresome, inconclusive truce talks; and the insensate policies of the leaders, Pericles, Cleon, and the rest of them. Dicaeopolis is in vain making a single-handed stand to deflate the insincere peace promises of the "war-mongers"; the fraud of the alleged negotiations to acquire allies; the junketeering of those roaming embassies, stretched out over a decade, evading the dire rigors of the war at home, wasting their time and the country's money in futile diplomatic missions abroad. Our man is surfeited with these pretences. He concludes his private truce with the Spartan enemy at the cost of only eight drachmas; he openly boasts a campaign of treasonous negotiations; he smuggles in peace offers from abroad, both short-term and long-term ones; eventually, he sets up a regular "pool of peace" from which he dispenses ounces and drams of that precious elixir to those he deems worthy. His extravagant joke of exporting spies and informers as the Athenian staple, wrapped in straw like pottery to prevent breakage; his refusal to sell delicatessen from his private mart to members of the war party; his riotous domestic feasts; his disporting himself in the beggar's rags fashionable in the high tragedy of his pet target, Euripides, and mocking, in this attire, his genteel neighbors' pompous uniforms; the bountiful cakes and viands he lavishes on peaceful picnics, follow in a fantastic sequence. The main performance, however, is his playing the part of a *kapēlos* whose private market supplies him with all the blessings of peace and, at the same time, gives him a monopoly of catering cooked food for the crowd, as dream-like as a pleasure and as profitable as business.

First of all we see him setting up his private mart.

> *Dicaeopolis.* These are the confines of my marketplace. All Peloponnesians, Magarians, Boeotians, have the right to come here and trade, provided they sell their wares to me and not to Lamachus. As market-inspectors I appoint these three whips of Leprean leather, chosen by lot. Warned away are all informers and all men of Phasis. They are bringing me the pillar on which the treaty is inscribed and I shall erect it in the center of the market, well in sight of all.[56]

A Boeotian, who enters with a slave "carrying a wide assortment of articles of food," asks Dicaeopolis whether he will buy "some chickens or some locusts." Dicaeopolis asks what he brings.

> *Boeotian.* All that is good in Boeotia, marjorem, penny-royal, rushmats, lampwicks, ducks, jays, woodcocks, water-fowl, wrens, divers.
> *Dicaeopolis.* A regular hail of birds is beating down on my market.
> *Boeotian.* I also bring geese, hares, foxes, moles, hedgehogs, cats, lyres, martins, otters, and eels from the Copaic lakes.
> *Dicaeopolis.* Ah, my friend who brings me the more delicious of fish, let me salute your eels.[57]

Soon we see Dicaeopolis revealed as a veritable master cook. He calls on the children and women of the household to busy themselves.

[56] Aristophanes, *The Acharnians,* 719–728.
[57] Ibid., 860–882.

Dicaeopolis. . . . Quick! let the hares boil and roast merrily; keep them turning; withdraw them from the flame; prepare the chaplets; reach me the skewers that I may spit the thrushes.

First Semi-Chorus. I envy you your wisdom and even more your good cheer.

Dicaeopolis. What then will you say when you see the thrushes roasting?

First Semi-Chorus. Ah! true indeed!

Dicaeopolis. [*to a slave*]. Slaave! stir up the fire!

First Semi-Chorus. [*to the other Semi-Chorus*].
See how he knows his business, what a perfect cook!
How well he understands to prepare a perfect dinner!
. . . .
Dicaeopolis. [*to a slave*]. Pour honey over this tripe, set it before the fire to dry.

Second Semi-Chorus. You hear how he gives his orders?

Dicaeopolis. [*to the slaves within the house*]. Get the eels on the gridiron. . . . Have this fired and let it be nicely browned.[58]

The pros and cons of the market as an institution are not at issue here. The poet does not preconize the merits of the market as such. Witness his complaints about the hardships of townlife catering. Nor does he, in this play, deprecate the ways and habits of market people, keepers of stalls, runners of taverns and cookshops, indistinguishable though they often are from the rabble of the ports. On the balance, this happens to be rather a promarket play, featuring the deprivations caused to the citizenry by Olympian Pericles' banning of the Megarians "from earth and sea, the mainland, and the mart." At the same time, the poet's overflowing wit introduces a strain of anticompetition into his hero's private market, with all the contradictions of such a twist. But all the more we are on solid ground when it comes to the trivial detail. The chorus extols, in rapturous terms, the perfection of our hero's *eudaimonia*. He has indeed contrived for himself a situation of matchless felicity. His are the profits of the market without its toil; the ample supplies, acquired with no effort; freedom from spies and informers, from the milling crowd and public nuisances; no sales pressure for him to exert, no dearth of supplies to satisfy the customer.

By virtue of his treaty-making he is supplied with all foreign merchan-

---

[58] Ibid., 1005–1040.

dise to retail it off [*diempolan*] whether to be made up in the household, or consumed tepid [*chliara*].[59]

Thus he retails in lots the goods that flow to him from everywhere. But this is not the whole story. The necessaries he is engaged in selling are food stuffs, and they are dealt with in two different ways. Some of them are carried off by the customer to be cooked at home. The others, and this is essential, are fit to be eaten—meal and viands, ready cooked, not piping hot yet still comfortably warm, whether fish or fowl, roasted or broiled.

This, then, is the only literary closeup of the *kapēlos* we possess. The term *kapēlos* itself was anything but honorific, and its associations were all too obvious. To increase the effect, it was here deliberately avoided by Aristophanes. To picture the war-weary peasant in the part of a sly *kapēlos*, whose private market device gives him the profile of a benign philosopher and the dignity of a wholesale merchant, must have caused an uproar of mirth. However, this requirement of true comedy may account for the fact that, in later times, the part played by Dicaeopolis in these scenes remained unidentified.

The *agora* was first of all a cooked-food market, not very different from markets of the African Guidea Coast. Rigid boundaries; specifications of who may and who may not trade, and with whom; official market inspectors as well as municipal spies; commodities—mostly foodstuffs—sold directly by the peasant either for money or in barter, such were the features of the classical *agora*. The heights reached by the civilization of Athens should not blind us to the primitive character of the market institution that a Pericles deemed worthy of his personal support.

---

[59] Ibid., 972–973.

◖ 13 ◖

Local Markets and
Overseas Trade

The marketplace in Athens was not meant to be the cradle of a market system. The local market was one thing, foreign trade another. They had their separate and independent origins. Whether in the open space reserved for public meetings—or rather, in its immediate neighborhood—grain was distributed or at times sold at a fixed price; whether victuals were or were not offered for sale in the commercial *agora*, may have depended upon many factors, each of them of domestic political concern. Among these factors were the frequency with which shortages of supplies arose from the over-crowding caused by religious festivities, the influx of refugees, or a dislocation of the rural population; the manner in which public works on city walls or temples happened to be organized; the charac-ter of the labor employed there, and the kind of authority responsible for the undertaking; or the availability of small coin for purchases. These, and perhaps other reasons, were responsible for the devel-opment of a local food market.

I. KAPĒLOS AND EMPOROS

Trade was an altogether different affair. It probably antedated the market; it reached the coasts of Attica from outside; it was a foreigner's show; the authorities would see to it that traders did not

189

turn raiders or kidnappers, that they were discouraged from roaming the country, that after getting a chance of displaying their wares at princes' courts and in manorial halls they were sure to depart again in peace. Active trade also may have been carried on occasionally by kings or chiefs in search of metals or other military stock. But such events would be even less related to the *agora* than those much more regular actions of the foreign trader. Market and trade had nothing in common. There was no reason to suspect that the time would come when the two would not only appear to be, but actually would be, comprised in one and the same institution, the market system.

The distinction between local and overseas trade was most clear-cut with respect to the person of the trader. Their designations were different, as were the identity, and probably the status, of their persons. The local trader was the *kapēlos*, the overseas trader was the *emporos*. Plato defined the *kapēloi* as "those who planted in the *agora*, serve us in buying and selling," the *emporoi* as "those who roam from city to city."[1] *Emporos* originally meant *traveler*,[2] an etymological root that is by no means rare, since the purpose of traveling was invariably supply. For example, of the four words used to connote trade or trader in the elaborate description of Tyre, the great emporium, in Ezekiel 27, two words have as their root "to roam about" and two others "to intertwine, tie together." The two groups of words are used distinctively. In the one case, the reference is to distance and carrying, in the other, to dealing and negotiating—two functions that later merged in the term *trade*. The researches of Knorringa,[3] Hasebroek,[4] and Finkelstein[5] have confirmed the fact that the distinction between *kapēlos* and *emporos* referred primarily to locality—not to retail versus wholesale trade, as was assumed. Plato refers the local trader to the *agora*. Xenophon, too, distinguishes in the *Memorabilia* between the *emporoi* and the "traffickers in the marketplace."[6] Since throughout antiquity the volume of

---

[1] Plato, *Republic*, 371 D.

[2] H. Knorringa, *Emporos*, p. 114.

[3] Ibid., passim.

[4] Hasebroek, *Trade and Politics in Ancient Greece*, trans. L. M. Fraser and D. C. Macgregor (London: G. Bell and Sons, 1933), pp. 1–8.

[5] M. I. Finkelstein, "Emperos, Naukleros, and Kapēlos," *Classical Philology*, 30 (1935) 320–36. Finkelstein qualifies this judgment somewhat by adding, "How carefully the distinction was retained is another matter" (p. 336).

[6] Xenophon, *Memorabilia*, III, 7, 6.

overland trade was negligible,[7] the phrase *to roam* referred to those engaged in trading by river or sea. Of the small volume of overland trade—excepting expeditionary and caravan trade—the bulk must have consisted of peasants trudging to the local market to dispose of their surplus crops and purchase some other articles they needed.

However, the distinction was not merely functional. According to an Athenian law, ascribed to Solon and reenacted by Aristophon, no alien was permitted to offer goods for sale in the market.[8] This was qualified in the period from which our evidence stems, the middle of the fourth century, so as to forbid aliens from selling in the market unless they paid a tax.[9] This amounted, in practice, to a licensing arrangement; thus in one case the defendant refutes the charge that his mother, a ribbon-vendor, was an alien by saying that "If she was an alien, they ought to have examined the market-tolls, and have shown whether she paid the alien's tax, and from what country she came. . . "[10] That having a stall in the *agora* was, at some periods, the citizens' prerogative seems evident; granting the right to an alien on payment of a tax was a qualification of that right. That resident aliens did actually vend in the market in the early fourth century is borne out by Lysias' speech against the grain dealers, where the grain retailers admit they are metics; however, they are all the more strictly to be kept in hand. Also, the grain trade may have stood under special rules.

Differences of sex may well have entered into the matter of *agora* regulations. Traveling traders are, with rare exceptions, men. Retailers in the marketplace, on the other hand, need not be of the male sex; indeed, in some regions of the Sudan they are exclusively women. The distinction between the institutions of trade and market there runs rigidly along the lines of sex: traders are males, market vendors are females. In Hammurabi's Babylonia the innkeeper was a female. In Sardis, and maybe in Halicarnassus whence the institution of retailing food in the market probably spread to Greece, the *kapēlos*, up to the middle of the sixth century, almost certainly was

---

[7] Finkelstein, "*Emporos*," p. 328, n. 37 for Greece. For the ancient world in general, cf. Max Weber, *General Economic History,* trans. Frank H. Knight (Glencoe, Ill.: The Free Press, 1950), Chapters 15, 16.

[8] Demosthenes, *Private Orations*, trans. A. T. Murray (Cambridge: Harvard University Press, 1964), LVII, 29-31.

[9] Ibid., 33–34.

[10] Ibid., 34.

a woman. Herodotus made great play, as we have seen, of an anecdote, dated about that time, which turned on the emasculating effect of practicing *kapēlikē*. The inference appears to be that *kapēlikē* originally had been a female occupation. For Herodotus held that retailing in the market was a custom of ancient Lydian origin; the gold dust, he said, was carried from Mount Tmolus right into the *agora* of Sardis. Yet allegedly it was only much later, after their defeat at the hands of the Persians, that the Lydian men were forced by Cyprus to become shopkeepers in order to make them effeminate. As to Athens, at times both sexes were permitted to keep stalls in the market, and the practice may well have varied, possibly even according to the wares offered for sale. Lydian premarital prostitution appears to have been an adjunct of the market habit. Aristophanes certainly never missed an opportunity to twit Euripides about the fact that his mother sold vegetables in the market. Demosthenes' speech against Eubulides would be beside the point unless a female person could keep a stall in the commercial *agora*. In classical Attica, then, it may be said that the *emporos* was a man, while the *kapēlos* was either a man or a woman, depending upon the goods sold or other circumstances of the case.

Though the *kapēlos* was at most periods a citizen-trader, in Attica he was not, for that reason a trader by status. Rather than acting from duty or for honor, he sought merely to make a living from gains made "off the other man" (*ap' allēlōn*). Accordingly, the regard in which he was held could not have been lower. The long-distance trader, on the other hand, was in classical times rarely a citizen—and hardly ever a citizen of high standing, as he had certainly been in the archaic days of chieftains' trade. He was now, as a rule, a foreigner, i.e., a citizen of another state, or a resident alien. By and large, the *emporos* was a Greek of the islands, Magna Graecia, Asia Minor, or some mainland city such as Corinth—at the same time, he only exceptionally would be of lesser standing than a trader by status in the country of which he was a citizen.[11]

The fact that in classical times the vast majority of *emporoi* were Greeks has led to considerable confusion, and to much misunderstanding of the structure of Greek trade. We are concerned here largely with Athens, which was the great trade center of the Greek

[11] This assertion may need qualification for the case of the Rhodians, who appear to have been a "trading people."

world in the fifth and fourth centuries. Yet, although this was so—although the Piraeus was the great emporium for the Greek world—only infrequently do we find a citizen actively engaged in trade, except to grant sea-loans. And an examination of Demosthenes' private orations reveals that even the majority of sea-loans were made by metics or foreigners. That in Attica traders were foreigners, and, on the other hand, that citizens were as a rule *not* traders, emerges with power and clarity from an examination of a few important sources. Outstanding among them is *Ways and Means,* a mid-fourth-century pamphlet which justly, it seems, has been ascribed to the aged Xenophon, and to which we will return presently.

II. METICS AND FOREIGNERS

The two main types of traders, we submit, were the foreigner and the metic. The metic—the resident alien—was one of the results of the almost ceaseless warfare between and within the Greek cities. Nowhere in known history were these two forms of strife so intimately linked over long periods of time as they were among the Greek city states. Party struggles inside many Greek states, as well as regular wars between the petty states, produced a multitude of stateless men, a floating population of the ports, who had no alternative but to turn to trade for a living. We have seen how the dissensions of the Solonian period produced hosts of exiles, men who "no longer spoke the Attic tongue—so wide had been their wanderings."[12] The fierce nativism of the Periclean democracy—and Pericles' rigid exclusion from citizenship of all men who were not second-generation native born, could hardly have been exceptional—meant that normally no higher status than that of metic was open to the exile. That intrastate and interstate warfare remained an abundant source of metic populations seems evident from Xenophon's confident conclusion that, if his proposals to improve the status of metics in order to attract them were adopted, "all without a city would covet the right of settling in Athens."[13] We may assume that the foreigners trading at Athens were largely metics hailing from some Greek city, the balance

[12] Aristotle, *Constitution of Athens,* XII, 4.
[13] Xenophon, *Ways and Means,* II.

being made up of full-fledged citizens of such a city, or even of a Greek trading community such as Rhodes.

Athens herself had a considerable metic population, mostly settled in the Piraeus. Many of them were *emporoi*, mainly grain importers; more than a few made sea-loans, essential to the functioning of foreign trade.

Much of our knowledge of foreign trade, sea-loans, banking, and traders comes from the forensic orations of Demosthenes.[14] Almost all traders appearing in these speeches are metics or foreigners, a motley crew mostly of hardworking folk who travel with their goods and handle the goods themselves. The goal of most trading skippers seems to be to accumulate a small fortune, enough to permit them to retire from seafaring and apply themselves to making sea-loans.[15] The small scale of operations of the trader is indicated by his utter dependence on the sea-loan; one lender boasts

> The resources required by those who engage in trade come not from those who borrow, but from those who lend; and neither ship nor shipowner nor passenger can put to sea, if you take away the part contributed by those who lend.[16]

While this is undoubtedly exaggerated, it must have a measure of truth.

One of the most important of private orations is the speech against Dionysodorus.[17] The case involves default on a sea-loan. The plaintiff—the lender—is a metic. In his peroration he warns the jury of the unfortunate consequences that would ensue from their failure to give him the verdict.

> . . . while you are today deciding one case alone, you are fixing a law for the whole port, and . . . many of those engaged in overseas trade are standing here and watching you to see how you decide this question.[18]

If he, the plaintiff, loses, overseas traders will be convinced that nothing can prevent the voiding of contracts, hence none will be

---

[14] No attorney was permitted in Athenian courts; plaintiff and defendant had to plead for themselves. Accordingly, the habit developed of hiring a skilled speaker to prepare the speech for the individual, who then memorized it.

[15] Demosthenes, *Private Orations*, XXXIII, 4.

[16] Ibid., XXXIV, 51.

[17] Cf. Chapter 14.

[18] Demosthenes, *Private Orations*, LVI, 48.

willing to risk their money in sea-loans, and so trade will cease to be carried on. Do not permit this, he warns. The passage is conclusive:

> . . . for it is not to the interests of the mass of your people any more than of those engaged in trade, who are a body of men most useful to your public at large and to the individuals who have dealings with them. For this reason you should be careful of their interests.[19]

The plaintiff appears to be contrasting the group of traders with the citizen body, but he insists that the interests of the citizens are in this instance identical with those of that group. He seems to be hired by the big merchants, who also make sea-loans to the mass of the smaller merchants.

It was the metics who manned the tiny cargo boats—and therefore helped man the navy in time of war—and performed many of the myriad jobs that go with the operation of a great port. The shrewd "Old Oligarch" refuses to express surprise at the freedom accorded to slaves and the crowd of metics in his newfangled democracy. The Athenians, he says,

> have established an equality of speech between our slaves and free men; and again between our metics and citizens, because the city stands in need of her metics to meet the requirements of such a multiplicity of arts and for the purposes of her navy.[20]

This shows how little the citizens of substance thought of themselves as traders. Their complaint against democracy was not that it promoted the metic to the status of a trader, but that democracy, by doing so, was strengthening the navy, and thereby its hold on the nation.

III. WAYS AND MEANS

Nothing could be more decisive on the whole issue, however, than the pamphlet ascribed to Xenophon. It leaves no doubt about the status of trade in Athens. For a long time, scholars denied the authenticity of *Ways and Means* because they deemed its proposals unworthy of the famed author. Yet if its attribution to Xenophon by the ancients was mistaken, it was rather, we submit, for the opposite reason, namely, that nothing else we possess from his pen can

---

[19] Ibid., 50.
[20] Pseudo-Xenophon ("The Old Oligarch"), *Constitution of the Athenians*, I.

compare with this pamphlet in sheer power of conception and execution.

Its originality lies in the thought that wealth, power, and security can be the product of peace rather than of war. That force was not the best means of acquiring wealth was an idea that Hesiod had first conceived in regard to the individual in his maxim of "little by little"; but in regard to the state, this idea had hardly even occurred to the Greeks.

The structure of the pamphlet shows great vigor. It was probably a political pamphlet issued by the extreme pacifist party of Eubulus; it would therefore offer the strongest possible arguments for a peaceful increase in state revenues. It takes its stand on moral grounds: the acts of injustice committed by the Athenians themselves towards their supposed allies but actual dependents had been a subject of acrimonious debate. Xenophon concedes some weight to the argument that Athens was compelled to act as she did in order to sustain her population. First preference should be given to the question

> whether by any means the citizens might obtain food entirely from their own soil, which would certainly be the fairest way. I felt that were this so, they would be relieved of their poverty, and also of the suspicion with which they are regarded by the Greek world.[21]

He then, after a brief eulogy of Attica's allegedly great natural resources, suggests three major methods of increasing Athens' revenues: attracting more metics to the Piraeus,[22] attracting foreign traders,[23] and taking measures to make the silver mines more profitable to Athens.[24] There is nothing to show that the plan suffered from any inherent defect that would have condemned it as utterly impracticable. After arguing the almost certain success of these measures, he shows that one and all they would depend on, and be furthered by, the maintenance of peace. War, on the other hand, only serves to deplete resources.[25] Thus, if his suggestions are followed, "we shall be regarded with more affection by the Greeks, shall live in greater security, and be more glorious."[26]

But only some of his proposals bearing directly on trade interest

---

[21] Xenophon, *Ways and Means*, I.
[22] Ibid., II.
[23] Ibid., III.
[24] Ibid., IV.
[25] Ibid., V.
[26] Ibid., VI.

us here. Let us consider the first two. The one would be to take positive steps to encourage the settlement of aliens.

> But instead of limiting ourselves to the blessings that may be called indigenous, suppose that in the first place, we studied the interests of the resident aliens. For in them we have one of the very best sources of revenue, in my opinion, inasmuch as they are self-supporting and, so far from receiving payment for the many services they render to states, they contribute by paying a special tax.[27]

To attract aliens, all disabilities placed on metics should be lifted, unless this would cause a financial loss to the state. Exempt them from infantry duty, but permit them to enter the cavalry—an honorific organization. Give them the right to own property that is not being used, provided they build houses on it. Lastly, appoint an order of guardians of foreigners, comparable to the guardians of orphans, with honors going to those who attract the greatest number of foreigners. Such a plan "would increase our revenues."[28]

The other proposal, closely linked with the first, is to attract foreign merchants in large numbers in addition to the metic merchants. "The rise in the number of residents and visitors would of course lead to a corresponding expansion of our imports and exports, of sales, rents and customs."[29]

To effect this, only a few carefully thought out measures would be needed. Prizes awarded to the judges in the Athenian commercial court who decide controversies with the greatest expedition would induce foreigners to trade in the Piraeus, since they would not be unnecessarily detained.[30] Merchants and shipowners who bring particularly important cargoes to Athens should be honored with seats of distinction at public events.[31] And a fund should be established, in order to build lodging houses for sailors around the harbor in the Piraeus, as well as others for merchants convenient to the emporium; "public houses for entertainment for all that come to the city" should also be built.[32] If, along with these measures, peace is maintained, prosperity would be assured. For,

---

[27] Ibid., II, 1. (The metic-tax was 12 drachmas a year for men, and, under some conditions, 6 for women.)

[28] Ibid., II, 7.

[29] Ibid., III, 5.

[30] Ibid., III, 3.

[31] Ibid., III, 4.

[32] Ibid., III, 12.

if the state is tranquil, what class of men will not heed her? Shipowners and merchants will head the list. Then there will be those rich in corn and wine and oil and cattle; men possessed of brains and money to invest. . . . Besides, where will those who want to buy or sell many things quickly meet with better success in their efforts than at Athens?[33]

Nowhere in this discussion is there as much as a hint that the Athenians themselves were engaged in trade. Even less is there a suggestion that the revenues might be increased through the increased commercial activities of the citizens. On the contrary, foreigners should be induced to visit, or to settle in Athens. The visit or residence of traders would increase revenue by way of the 2% tax on imports and exports and the harbor taxes, while additional revenues could be obtained from renting the state-owned inns and public houses. Export interests are, as it were, nonexistent. Sole emphasis is on the income to be derived from foreigners buying and selling in the Piraeus; insofar as the interest is in the trade itself rather than the revenues to be derived from it, it is the import of essential commodities that is discussed. Attracting metics has the further advantage of the considerable revenue derived from the metic residence tax.

Apart from the absence of any suggestion that citizens take up or extend their volume of trading—and this is even more impressive—there is no sign of any fear of the damaging effects foreign competition might have on native traders. Considering the degree to which the state acted as the guarantor of the citizens' livelihood—the proposals themselves were aimed at securing alternative means for a state guarantee of livelihood—it is inconceivable that Xenophon's plan could have harmed Athenian trade. Trade, to Xenophon, meant trade carried on by foreigners, from which Athens would benefit partly directly, through the importation of a variety of goods, partly indirectly, through the revenues derived from trade.

To sum up: Different types of traders, then, were engaged in local and in foreign trade. The two forms of trade were sharply distinct. Local trade—and no other trade—was market trade. Overseas trade was partly administered trade, partly gift trade; and the stray market elements that made appearances here were relatively unimportant.

[33] Ibid., V, 3–4.

⊂₤ 14 ⊂₤

Securing Grain Imports

Why did Athens, the site of what was perhaps the first city market in history, her famous *agora*, herself never become a pioneer of market trade? Why did her extreme dependence on imported grain, combined with her pioneering experience in the use of food markets, not make her take the lead in establishing an international grain market which, one would think, should have solved her problem? Indeed, why did she strike out, rather, in the opposite direction, obstructing the Egyptian initiative in setting up such a market? One need not share an unhistorical prejudice in favor of commercial methods to see the problem of Athenian grain trade in these common sense terms.

Accordingly, our points of inquiry are to what extent did the conditions of the grain trade in classical Greece permit the development of market trade? Or, conversely, how far did those circumstances discourage such a development and require the use of administrative methods of trading to ensure the supply of grain?

The answer, we submit, lay in the geographical and political configuration of the regions in which grain supplies and routes of communication were situated. These conditions, under which military and diplomatic means had to be employed to ensure that supplies were forthcoming, as well as the safety of the trade routes themselves, determined the methods and organization of the grain trade.

Nine-tenths of the matter is comprised in the geographical circumstances that kept Attica at all times keenly anxious about the provenance of her daily bread from overseas and made her eventually seek out, as sources of supply, the Black Sea, Egypt, and Sicily, in succession. The rest may be summed up in the recognition that, while Athenian foreign policy was first and foremost grain policy, it was hardly ever affected by commercial considerations or inspired by so-called trade interests. The reason for this apparent paradox will be manifest from a bare outline of the history of the grain trade.

I.   GRAIN PRODUCTION AND CONSUMPTION

Greece, as a whole, lacks agricultural land, and Attica's soil, especially, is best suited to the production of oil and wine. At no time after the Solonic crisis did Athens raise more than a fraction of her grain. Yet grain, supplemented by fresh and dried fish, constituted the staple of her diet. If we were to postulate any one determining factor in the foreign policies of most of continental Greece, it would unquestionably be that area's dependence on grain imports for its food supply.

Greek social and political thought may well have reflected this unalterable circumstance. The Greeks, one is tempted to conclude, never developed a concept of economics because at no time could the country rely for its food supply on the market, which is the true subject of that discipline. Instead, they turned to political theory, which almost to this day has retained the cast of the Attican *polis*. Her ever unassuaged need for an adequate food supply made the principle of self-sufficiency the basic postulate of her existence and, therefore, of her theory of the state. Autarchy became, for the Greek mind, the *rationale* of the *polis*. On this point Aristotle agreed with Plato— they shared the conviction that the citizen population of the *polis* ought to consist of farmers. Indeed, from the history of Athens no other lesson could be drawn.

There is agreement among scholars of Greek antiquity over this extreme dependence on grain imports. Rostovtzeff has shown that, as late as the third century, this inadequacy was still so pronounced that not a trace of commercial rivalry could be found between the two greatest grain producers, Egypt and the Crimea.[1] Grundy insists that every Greek mainland state, with the possible exception of Thessaly,

---

[1] Rostovtzeff, "Great Sightseers in Egypt," *Journal of Egyptian Archeology*, 14, (1928), p. 14.

was, to a greater or lesser extent, dependent on imports.[2] Of Attica, Jardé has asserted that she could always absorb any amount of the available imports without their causing a failure of domestic prices.[3]

It is possible to make a crude estimate of the Athenian deficit in grainstuffs. Since statistical accuracy cannot be attained for antiquity, the figures can do no more than indicate orders of magnitude.

On the population of Attica, the calculations of A.W. Gomme remain authoritative. There is a striking fluctuation of the total, as well as of the parts. He estimates the total population in 431 B.C. as 315,500, of which 172,000 were citizens, 28,500 metics, and 115,000 slaves. Six years later, after the plague, the total had fallen to 218,000, with 116,000 citizens. In 323, the total is back to 258,000, 112,000 citizens, 42,000 metics, and 104,000 slaves.[4] The population, therefore, may be said to have ranged between 200,000 and 300,000, the latter figure being surpassed before the ravages of the plague in the beginning of the Peloponnesian War.

Our only information on Athenian domestic grain production comes from the late fourth century. An Eleusinian inscription of 329 B.C. allows Attic production to be calculated at 368,850 medimns. But of this total, only 28,500 medimns were wheat, the rest barley, a ratio of less than one to ten. While this may have been a bad year, Gomme estimates the top rate of production at 410,000 medimns.[5] Tod places it at 450,000.[6] On the basis of Beloch's estimate of an average annual per capita consumption of six medimns, at the most 75,000 people could be supported from the domestic crop. With a population range of 200,000 to 300,000, imports of one to one and a half million medimns would be required, or two to three times the domestic crop. Home production must have been too insufficient to feed even the agrarian population. As late as 170 B.C., when the population of Attica was probably much smaller than in the classical era, Athenian ambassadors at Rome claimed that Athens "supported even the farmers on imported grain."[7]

  [2] G. B. Grundy, *Thucydides and the History of his Age,* second edition (Oxford: 1948), Volume 1, p. 90.

  [3] A. F. V. Jardé, *Lés ceréales dans l'antiquité Grecque* (Paris: 1925), p. 184.

  [4] A. W. Gomme, *The Population of Athens in the Fifth and Fourth Centuries B.C.* (Oxford: B. Blackwell, 1933), p. 26.

  [5] Ibid., pp. 28–33.

  [6] *Cambridge Ancient History* (Cambridge: At the University Press, 1927–1939), Volume 5, p. 13.

  [7] Livy, XLIII, 6.

Yet the dependence on foreign grain was even greater than this statistical guess indicates. While the population as a whole needed imports for a large part of its food, the citizenry depended on them almost entirely. Our figures referred to the totals for wheat and barley. But barley was considered fit only for slaves and metics; a citizen would eat barley only if he were very poor or if famine prevailed. Aristophanes, sneering at the democratic grain distributions, reminds his audience that the gift of five medimns in 424 B.C. was mere barley.[8] A speaker in the *Deipnosophists* says, "We have no interest in . . . barley since the town is full of wheat bread."[9] While wheat was considered the citizens' staple, it constituted no more than one-tenth of the home crop—enough to feed perhaps 8000 or 9000 citizens. For Attica, imports thus quite generally meant wheat imports. A good part of the slaves could probably be fed on home barley; the citizens depended entirely on imports.[10] According to Naum Jasny, wheat "dominated the international grain trade of the classical era almost to the exclusion of the other grains."[11]

This state of affairs is specifically confirmed by a speech of Demosthenes, in which he observes that 400,000 medimns of wheat had been imported from the Pontus in 338, and that the imports from "there" generally equal Athens' total imports from all other sources.[12] The figure, he added, could be checked by a glance at the books of the inspectors at the emporium. This would amount to total wheat imports of 800,000 medimns for that year. Kočevalov, a Russian philologist, argues that the figure of 400,000 referred only to Panticapeum, "the home port," not to Theodosia as well, from which an equal amount was shipped.[13] Accepting these figures, we get total imports of 1,600,000 medimns. Including the home-grown grain crop of 400,000, this would amount to about 2,800,000 medimns—considerably more than the traditionally accepted requirement. Inci-

---

[8] Aristophanes, *Wasps*, 717–718.

[9] Athenaeus, III, 113A.

[10] In the Roman army, barley rations instead of wheat were issued to the troops as a punishment.

[11] Naum Jasny, *The Wheats of Classical Antiquity* (Baltimore: The Johns Hopkins Press, 1944), p. 15.

[12] Demosthenes, *Private Orations*, trans. A. T. Murray (Cambridge: Harvard University Press, 1964), 31–32.

[13] Kočevalov, "Die Einfuhr von Getreide nach Athen," in *Rheinisches Museum*, 31, (1932), pp. 321–323.

dentally, this would raise the ratio of imported to home grown grain to six to one.

But there is no need to stress the point further. There is widespread agreement today that the concern about grain supply dominated Athenian foreign policy. Grundy bluntly asserts that foreign policy *was* food policy.[14] So does Glotz.[15] Francotte, still the authority in the field, declared "la première des questions économiques pour les Grecs était celle du pain."[16]

The question is by what methods was the grain acquired? To what extent could Attica rely on price inducements to ensure supply, or were the actual ways of procurement almost exclusively those of diplomacy and civil and military politics?

Three instances come to mind of powers that largely imported their food supply: the city states of Athens and Rome in antiquity, and Britain since about 1770. In each case—differing according to circumstances—significant consequences followed.

Free-trade England represents the classic instance of reliance for organic raw materials on a world market. In principle, she sacrificed her domestic agriculture after 1846 in the name of the doctrine of comparative costs. For half a century, her wealth and power apparently justified her abnegation of self-sufficiency. But since World War I it has become increasingly evident that the successful functioning of the world market itself depended on Britain's financial, military, or political control of the organization of world trade. Having lost that control, Britain is faced with the treacherous mechanism of an unregulated world market. Accordingly, she is trying to free herself from such a dependence, through long-term arrangements and other instruments of administered trade.

The Roman Empire adopted the other alternative. Rather than rely on the "world grain market" which had been established in the late fourth century B.C. in the eastern Mediterranean, Rome deliberately smashed this market and brought the chief grain-producing territories under her direct control. Sicily was conquered first, in the third century, and throughout Roman history remained her "storehouse." In the year 6 A.D., the emperor assumed the responsi-

---

[14] This is the main theme of Grundy's *Thucydides and the History of his Age,* to which we are indebted for many of the insights of this section.

[15] G. Glotz, *Ancient Greece at Work* (London: 1926), p. 297.

[16] H. Francotte, "Le pain à bon marché et le pain gratuit dans les cités grecques," in *Mélanges Nicole* (Geneva: 1905), p. 135.

bility for feeding the city of Rome; he filled this obligation through the tributes levied in kind on the provinces. Besides Sicily, Josephus tells us, Egypt sent enough grain to feed Rome for four months and Africa enough for eight months;[17] this probably amounted to 2,900,000 and 5,800,000 modii respectively.[18] Since the emperor's responsibilities extended far beyond feeding the city of Rome—the army and the imperial household also had to be fed—methods of administered trade were employed. Rostovtzeff, in listing what he deems to be proof of extensive capitalistic activity in the Roman Empire, is compelled to admit the primacy of administered trade:

> It must be admitted . . . that the largest consumer was the imperial *annona* and that most of the merchants, who frequently were at the same time shipowners and owners of storehouses, worked on behalf of the emperor, that is to say, on behalf of the population of the city of Rome and the army. . . . The imperial *annona* was the chief moving force in the interprovincial trade, buying and transporting large masses of corn, oil, wine, meat, fish, lumber, hides, metals, and clothes for the needs of the armies on the Rhine, Danube, and Euphrates, and some of these articles for the needs of the capital.[19]

Athens never achieved the imperial splendor of Rome. During a memorable half-century, hers was a successful thalassocracy which directly ruled the trade routes and controlled, by direct political means, the sources of supply in the Eastern seas. When her strategic hold was lost, she turned to a complex of administrative methods to secure her food supply. Those methods were eminently suited to taking advantage of the market elements now introduced by coastal states into the grain trade of the Hellenic world without subjecting Attica's supply to the control of those states.

II. THE ADMINISTRATION OF TRADE

But let us begin at the beginning.
The Solonic embargo on the export of grain is the first instance of

---

[17] Josephus, *Jewish Wars*, II, 383, 386.

[18] M. Charlesworth, *Trade-Routes and Commerce of the Roman Empire* (Cambridge: 1926), p. 144.

[19] Rostovtzeff, *Social and Economic History of the Roman Empire* (Oxford: Clarendon Press, 1926), pp. 148–149.

grain supply being brought within the realm of public policy; it never left it.

One meeting of the Athenian Assembly in each prytany—a tenth part of the year—was called the "sovereign" Assembly; in this meeting, according to Aristotle,

> the people have to ratify the continuance of the magistrates in office, if they are performing their duties properly, and *to consider the supply of grain* and the defence of the country.[20] (K.P.'s italics)

Grain supply, national defence, and the continuing supervision of the magistrates, in other words, are the three subjects which must be considered, at least once in every prytany, by the Assembly. Grain supply is prominent on a list of subjects the prospective statesman must master, according to Xenophon; the others are state revenues and expenditures, war, home defence, and the silver mines.[21]

The Solonic embargo was never repealed. Rather it was reinforced. Legislation was designed, in a general way, to draw the greatest possible amount of grain to Athens and prevent the movement of grain away from Athens. No Athenian resident was permitted to transport grain anywhere except to Athens; the "severest penalties" were prescribed for violation.[22] No sea-loan could be made on any ship or cargo unless it was ensured that a return cargo of grain, or certain other legally specified commodities, would be brought to Athens.[23] We may assume that timber and other supplies for shipbuilding figured prominently on the list, although only grain is mentioned in the sources. Since, as we have said above, the petty *emporos* could hardly put to sea without the help of a sea-loan, this regulation must have been of great importance.

As can be inferred from these passages, the organization of grain imports was an instance of administered trade. The safety of the trade routes, the terms of trade—including price, to a considerable extent—the sources of goods were mostly fixed by treaty or other diplomatic arrangements, usually through personal privileges as a counterpart of trade preferences, the actual trading taking place, as a rule, in a port of trade. The extent to which this involved the administration of trade is suggested by a revealing passage in Aris-

---

[20] Aristotle, *Constitution of Athens*, XLIII.
[21] Xenophon, *Memorabilia*, III, 6.
[22] Demosthenes, *Private Orations*, XXXIV, 37.
[23] Ibid., XXXV, 50; LVI, 6.

totle's *Rhetoric*. Pointing out the matters a statesman must be conversant with, he sums up succinctly the administrative features of
Attica's food procurement methods.

> . . . in regard to food, he [the statesman] should know what amount of
> expenditure is sufficient to support the State; what kind of food is
> produced at home or can be imported; and what exports and imports
> are necessary, in order that contracts and agreements may be made with
> those who can furnish them.[24]

The great grain producers listed by Theophrastus were Assyria,
Egypt, Libya, Pontus, Thrace, and Sicily. But that was by the end of
the fourth century; in earlier times, the power of Persia blocked
Athenian access to the southeast, as well as to Egypt and Libya in the
south, although Athens appears to have drawn some grain from the
latter; the rise of Syracuse, in the west, along with the rivalry of
the Peloponnesus, checked Athenian influence in Sicily for a long
time. Thrace and the Black Sea region—particularly Crimea's *hinterland*, situated on both shores of the so-called Cimmerian Bosporus—
thus served as the chief granary of Athens in the classical period.

III. GRAIN FROM THE NORTH AND EAST

Peisistratus was the first to make a sustained effort to extend Athenian power towards the northeast, Thrace, and the Black Sea region. He regained Sigeum, on the southern shore of the entrance to
the Hellespont, and supported Miltiades in occupying the northern
shore, the Thracian Chersonese. The grain of this region may have
been partly paid for by the black-figured Attic vases and Athenian
gold and bronzework dating from this period, which have been
found there in numbers. The trade was made possible by the establishment of a "stable equilibrium" among the Scythian tribes at
about this time.[25] Persian expansion into Europe, during the last two
decades of the sixth century, must have cut off this trade, which was
resumed, however, on a grand scale after the Persian defeat at
Salamis.

It seems doubtful whether Greek trade with the Black Sea region

---

[24] Aristotle, *Rhetoric*, I, 4, 11, 1360a12.
[25] E. H. Minns, *Scythians and Greeks* (Cambridge: 1913), p. 442.

was of any account before the seventh century. The early colonies were mere farmers' settlements, not trading stations. A number of such settlements, mostly under Milesian auspices, were established—first on the south shore of the Black Sea, then on its north shore. But not until the fifth century were these brought under Athenian influence or control. In this development, Attica's need for grain was the sole mover.

Up to the middle of the fifth century, the products of the Black Sea were not, as a rule, carried all the way to Greece by ship. The sea route was the cheapest route, but it was often too risky, too arduous, and too slow to be practicable. The powerful and treacherous currents of the Thracian Bosporus were greatly feared, as indeed, they are even today. Polybius' description of them has become famous.[26] This was particularly true before the striking progress in navigation and shipbuilding which resulted from the Persian Wars.[27] The early seafarers never braved the open sea if it was at all possible to go along the coast; they were also in mortal fear of turning a cape, and preferred, if practicable, to portage their tiny boats or transload to an overland route. The early Pontic traders avoided turning the cape that guarded the Thracian Bosporus. Instead of sailing into and across the Sea of Marmora (the Propontis of the ancients) and emerging by the Dardanelles, they landed their goods on the west coast of the Black Sea at Odessos, Mesembria, or Apollonia. From there, they had them carried overland by the natives to the Hebrus Valley, thence rafting them down river to the emporium of Ainos, on the Aegean outlet of the river.[28] This city, although situated in the most barren part of Thrace, was one of the wealthiest in that region,[29] occupying, in regard to the Black Sea trade, a position as strategic as that of Byzantium.[30] The rivalry of Ainos, the port of trade of the land route, and Byzantium, the port of trade of the sea route, will disclose in concrete terms the military and political conditions of the grain trade.

[26] Polybius, IV, 43.

[27] *Cambridge Ancient History*, Volume 5, p. 19.

[28] S. Casson, *Macedonia, Thrace and Illyia* (Oxford: 1926), p. 255. According to Casson this same route was used for local trade in modern times until the building of a railroad early in the twentieth century.

[29] Casson, *Macedonia*, p. 90; cf. J.M.F. May, *Ainos, Its History and Coinage, 474–341 B.C.* (London: 1950), *passim*.

[30] "Because of the peculiar currents of the Bosporus, every ship going through that strait must stop at Byzantium." Polybius, IV, 43.

Byzantium, the Istanbul of our day, ran neck and neck with
Ainos in the fifth century B.C. in their race for primacy. Settled in the
middle of the seventh century, less than 20 years after the city of
Calchedon on the opposite side of the straits, Byzantium, like
Calchedon, remained an unimportant agricultural settlement for the
next two centuries. She was better off than Calchedon only because
of her superior fisheries.[31] Both were founded by colonists from
Megara. Calchedon, as noted, was settled somewhat earlier than
Byzantium, because of the greater fertility of her soil; Byzantium's
fisheries were apparently not utilized until somewhat later.
Herodotus, writing in the middle of the fifth century, when Byzantium's trading advantage was already evident, ridiculed the Cal-
cedonians for their blindness in settling on the wrong side of the
straits.[32] But this only proves how unimportant the route from the
Pontus had been when the city was settled; for the perfect location of
Byzantium could not possibly have been overlooked if, in the early
seventh century, trade had moved through the straits, since the
currents force every ship that comes from the Black Sea to halt in the
Bosporus. Certainly, some Propontic grain reached the Aegean Sea:
Herodotus describes Xerxes watching grain ships pass through the
Hellespont on their way to Aegina and the Peloponnese.[33] Herodotus
even tells that, when Miletus exiled its tyrant, Histiaeus, he sailed to
Byzantium with eight triremes and seized every ship coming from
the Pontus itself.[34] No mention is made of Athens receiving Crimean
grain at that time.

Byzantium fell before the Persian advance into Europe in 512
B.C., and the population fled to the Black Sea port of Mesembria; the
city was burned,[35] and it was not resettled until its recapture from
the Persians in 479.[36] During more than a lifetime, Persian influence
and control extended through most of Thrace; Ainos and the other
Greek cities of the Chersonese began to issue coins on the Persian
standard.[37] Greece must have been now cut off from her Black Sea
grain supply, and even from the Propontis.

[31] Minns, *Scythians and Greeks*, p. 439; cf. Strabo, VII, 6, 2.

[32] Herodotus, *The Persian Wars*, IV, 144.

[33] Ibid., VII, 147.

[34] Ibid., VI, 5 and 26.

[35] Ibid., VI, 33.

[36] Thucydides, *The Peloponnesian War*, I, 94.

[37] A. B. West, "Coins from the Thracian Coast," in *Numismatic Notes and*

In 479 B.C., the year of the Persian retreat from Europe, we find Ainos' swinging toward the height of her glory and wealth, which can be traced through her coins and through the Athenian tribute lists. In 474 she began to strike tetradrachms that, for beauty and workmanship, are not surpassed by those of any other Greek city.[38] She was assessed an annual tribute of 12 talents from 454 to 450 B.C. as a member of the Confederacy of Delos.

But Ainos' wealth and greatness were short-lived; by the third quarter of the fifth century, she had been reduced to poverty and relative obscurity. Her tribute assessment was reduced to 10 talents between 445 and 440 B.C. In the next two years it dropped to only four talents; Ainos paid no tribute whatsoever from 437 onward.[39] From this time on, the city was in a reduced condition.[40]

Byzantium's rise was as meteoric as was the fall of Ainos. In 452, the first year she appears on the tribute lists, she paid nothing. Five years later, she was assessed four talents, 3000 drachmae, which was increased to 15 talents in 443, 18 in 436, and 21 talents 4320 drachmae in 425.[41]

The simultaneous decline of Ainos and rise of Byzantium were rooted in a single event: the substitution of the new sea route for the traditional land route. The impelling factor was the creation of a native Thracian empire that wiped out the overland route, although the improvement in navigation and shipbuilding must have contributed to the process. But the military event was dominant. Between the years 480 and 460 B.C., Teres, the chief of the Odrysians, a Thracian tribe, created an empire extending from Abdera in the Aegean to the mouth of the Danube on the Black Sea,[42] and including as its subjects the Thracian tribes, the formidable Getae,[43] and "the other hordes" around the Danube bordering on Scythia.[44] Under his successors, Sitalces and Seuthes, the empire was consolidated and

Monographs, v. XL. Cf. also M. L. Strack, Die antiken Munzen Nordgriechenlands, who emphasized the Persian influence.

[38] C. T. Seltmann, Greek Coins (London: 1933), p. 145. Cf. also West, "Coins from the Thracian Coast," p. 146.

[39] Seltmann, Greek Coins, p. 141.

[40] West, "Coins from the Thracian Coast," p. 150.

[41] H. Merle, Geschichte der Staedte Byzantion und Kalchedon, p. 19.

[42] Thucydides, The Peloponnesian War, II, 97.

[43] Their savagery remained a problem during the Roman Empire; Strabo, VII, 3, 13.

[44] Thucydides, The Peloponnesian War, II, 96.

made into a great and wealthy power. In 431, two years after Teres'
death, the Athenians sought an alliance with Sitalces, and
Thucydides observed that his kingdom was

> very powerful and in revenue and general prosperity exceeded all the
> nations of Europe which lie between the Ionian Sea and the Euxine; in
> the size and strength of their army being second only, though far
> inferior, to the Scythians. For if the Scythians were united, there is no
> nation which could compare with them . . .[45]

The rise of this empire left the all-sea route as the only alternative, and consequently impoverished Ainos. "The establishment of
the Odrysian kingdom athwart the trade routes that provided the
wealth of Ainos would bring about its virtual extinction," according
to Casson's study on the history and archaeology of this region.[46]
Since the raids of the savage Getae cut off the trade of Apollonia as
late as Strabo's time,[47] we may assume similar interferences at that
earlier date. The archaeologist and the numismatist agree that the
growth of the Odrysian empire made an end to overland trade. So
close was this negative correlation that, at the end of the century,
around 412 B.C., Ainos enjoyed a temporary resurgence of wealth
"such as she had not known for thirty years"[48]—as the result of a
struggle for supremacy among the Odrysian princes. After the death
of Seuthes I, a local prince who had ruled the territory from the
Hebrus River to the Sea of Marmora was exiled, and this territory
became severed from the Odrysian empire. This turn of events once
more opened up the land route to the Black Sea for Ainos, and she
enjoyed a thirty-year prosperity which was brought to an end when
the empire was once again consolidated under Cotys.[49] Correspondingly, we find Byzantium's tribute reduced in 414 to 15 talents from
its highest level of almost 22 talents in 425.

The same events that destroyed Ainos' trade route also cut
Byzantium off from the *hinterland*. Other Thracian tribes, most notably the Astae, began a series of raids that continued for several

[45] Ibid., II, 97.

[46] Casson, *Macedonia*, p. 201; cf. also West, "Coins from the Thracian Coast,"
pp. 57, 147, 150.

[47] Strabo, VII, 3, 13.

[48] West, "Coins from the Thracian Coast," p. 121.

[49] Ibid., pp. 123–124.

centuries. These raids made settled agriculture impossible;[50] the city was thus forced literally to the water's edge and, by necessity, had to make her living from the sea. Byzantium did not miss her opportunity: almost overnight, she was deliberately converted into an *emporium*. Not the gradual growth of economic forces, but a political cataclysm led to the establishment of this trading place. A mutilated description of this transformation has been preserved for us in the pseudo-Aristotelian *Oeconomica*,[51] which will be discussed below when we consider the problem of the port of trade.

Byzantium was recaptured from the Persians by the Hellenic fleet under the command of the Spartan, Pausanias, in 479, and the city was resettled.[52] But some two years later, when Pausanias showed Persian sympathies, he was expelled from the entire area by an Athenian fleet under the command of Cimon.[53] Pausanias' dealings with the Persian emperor were imperiling the Black Sea grain supply.

The next 20 years saw the establishment of the Confederacy of Delos and its conversion into an Athenian empire. By 454, when the treasury of the League was moved from Delos to Athens, the league included perhaps 260 cities, grouped in five divisions: the Thracian, Hellespontine, Ionian, Carian, and the insular. The Thracian district ranged from Methone in the west to Ainos; the Hellespontine included the Chersonese and the Greek cities on the shores of the Propontis and the Black Sea.[54] During this period, the Athenians unsuccessfully attempted to gain control of Thrace in the north and Egypt in the south. They captured Eion, at the mouth of the Strymon River, in 476, but an attempt at colonization was thwarted by the Thracian tribes. They also tried, without success, to seize the city of Doriscus, on the northern side of the mouth of the Hebrus River (opposite Ainos, which is on the south side). The Athenians did secure the seas around Thrace: in 474, for example, they captured the island of Scyros, on the route to western Thrace, and Thasos, with its gold mines, off the Thracian coast, was a member of the League. The Egyptian expedition, intended to outflank Persia, ended in disaster in 455/4.

[50] Polybius, IV, 45.
[51] Pseudo-Aristotle, *Oeconomica*, II, 1346b, 13–26.
[52] Thucydides, *The Peloponnesian War*, I, 94.
[53] Ibid., I, 130–131.
[54] J. B. Bury, *History of Greece* (London: Macmillan, 1913), p. 325, n. 4.

IV.   THE ATHENIAN THALASSOCRACY

As the power of Persia blocked Athenian ambitions in the south, the growth of the Odrysian empire prevented Athenian expansion to the north into Thrace. Accordingly, the middle of the century saw an important shift in Athenian foreign policy. Pericles made Athenian endeavors to veer from the north, south, and west of the Mediterranean and concentrate in the direction of the Black Sea, which was now imperiled.[55]

The immediate danger was to the trade route itself. The Odrysian empire was moving towards the Propontis; control of Byzantium and Sestos would have meant control of the trade going through both ends of the Sea. Officials had been sent to Byzantium, among other cities, in 465 to collect the tribute and to "represent Athens' interests,"[56] and special officials, called "warders of the Hellespont," were stationed at Sestos to control passing ships.[57] Byzantium governs the exit from the Bosporus, while Sestos, the "corn chest of the Piraeus,"[58] guards the exit from the Hellespont. Therefore, Pericles personally led an expedition to the Thracian Chersonese; he established a cleruchy with 1000 men and built a wall across the isthmus, between the Aegean and the Propontis, that protected the isthmus against Thracian incursions.[59] Of all his expeditions, writes Plutarch, this one "was held in most loving remembrance, since it proved the salvation of the Hellenes who dwelt there."[60]

Pericles was determined to protect the trade route from Greek as well as barbarian enemies. From the Hellespont, grain was not carried directly to the Piraeus, since that would have entailed turning the sinister cape of Sunium at the southern tip of Attica. (This was at a time when Pericles was "admired and celebrated even amongst foreigners" for having circumnavigated the Peloponnesus.)[61] Instead, the goods of the Hellespont were landed at Histiaea, on the northern tip of Euboea. From there they were carried to the Euboean Sea and shipped to Oropus, on the northern shore of Attica, thence overland

---

[55] Plutarch, *Pericles*, XX, 2–3.
[56] G. Glotz, *Histoire Grecque* (Paris: 1925), Volume 1, p. 191.
[57] A. E. Zimmern, *The Greek Commonwealth* (Oxford: 1931), 363.
[58] Aristotle, *Rhetoric*, III, 10, 7, 1411a13.
[59] Plutarch, *Pericles*, XIX, 1.
[60] Ibid.
[61] Ibid., XIX, 2.

to Athens via Decelea.[62] The Euboean revolt in 447/6 thus created a danger to the Athenian supply route fully as great as the Odrysian expansion. Pericles promptly attacked the island with 50 ships and 5000 hoplites and brought it to heel. The island was treated leniently, with the exception of Histiaea. Its citizens were removed as a body, and Athenians were settled in their place, because they had dared to interfere with Athenian shipping. As Plutarch puts it, Pericles treated "them, and them only, thus inexorably, because they had taken an Attic ship captive and slain its crew."[63] Pericles' wisdom in recognizing this threat and dealing with it was borne out by Athenian experience in the Peloponnesian War. When the Spartans captured Decelea in 413, grain had to be carried by sea past Sunium, "at great cost."[64]

In 448/7 or thereabouts, a cleruchy with 2000 or more was established also on the isle of Lemnos, and about five years later, one of perhaps 1000 men on Imbros, the island commanding the approach to the Hellespont from the Aegean. Pericles brought the Greek cities of the Black Sea region under the sway of Athens.[65] In 437/6, he led a "large and splendidly equipped armament" into the Black Sea, where

> he effected what the Greek cities desired, and dealt with them humanely, while to the neighboring nations of Barbarians with their kings and dynasts he displayed the magnitude of his forces and the fearless courage with which they sailed whithersoever they pleased and brought the whole sea under their own control.[66]

The Spartocid dynasty in the Crimea, which was to remain friendly to Athens for at least a century, was established in 438/7 with Athenian aid, along with the setting up of an Athenian cleruchy at nearby Nymphaeum.[67] The Spartocid kingdom of Crimean Bosporus had as its capital Panticapeum, and later included Theodosia, the two principal ports of trade for the Crimean and Scythian grain. For unknown reasons, Athens was unable to gain a foothold in Olbia, a key city on

---

[62] Grundy, *Thucydides*, Volume 1, p. 79.

[63] Plutarch, *Pericles*, XXIII, 2.

[64] Thucydides, *The Peloponnesian War*, VII, 28.

[65] Rostovtzeff, "The Bosporan Kingdom," in *Cambridge Ancient History*, Volume 8, p. 564.

[66] Plutarch, *Pericles*, XX, 1.

[67] Rostovtzeff, "The Bosporan Kingdom," pp. 564–565.

the northwestern shore; the grain had, therefore, to move right across the Black Sea and then along the southwestern shore on its way to the Bosporan straits.[68] Athenian colonists were established at Sinope, commanding that route, as well as either side of Sinope, at Astacus and Amisus.[69]

Thus Athenian military control of the grain trade was complete. To ensure her supremacy, Athens forbade any but Athenian ships, i.e., ships carrying grain to Athens, from entering the Black Sea; the prohibition did not stop short of including the Athenian "allies."[70] Byzantium was the focal point of the system; other states could buy grain at Byzantium only by special permission of Athens. One such grant has been preserved for us, in the form of a decree dated 426/5 relating to Methone, a Macedonian city that was a member of the Athenian League. Methone undertook to provide a body of soldiers for a current Athenian war in Thrace; in return, she was granted permission to buy, each year, a specified amount of grain in Byzantium. For each purchase, written notice had to be given to the Athenian officials at Byzantium, and no Methonian ship was allowed to proceed past Byzantium.[71]

In the nature of things, under such conditions grain would be bought and sold at proclaimed equivalencies; the persistence, for several centuries, of the belief that the just price for wheat was five drachmas per medimn,[72] in the face of what appears a secular rise in prices, probably had its roots in such treaty prices. We should also note, at this point, the persistence of a two to one ratio of wheat to barley prices, from the fourth to the second centuries, despite the violent fluctuations in the price of grain in general.[73] The modernizing notion that a grain market, once established, could have secured the same degree of stability of prices, appears unrealistic.

Thus grain moves along a specific trade route, guarded by Athenian colonies and naval power, in accordance with Athenian foreign policy. The grain was bought at the great emporium of Panticapeum;

[68] Ibid., p. 565.

[69] Ibid., p. 564.

[70] Wilamowitz-Moellendorff, *Griechisches Lesebuch*, II/2, p. 249.

[71] See also J. Hasebroek, *Trade and Politics in Ancient Greece*, trans. L. M. Fraser and D. C. Macgregor (London: G. Bell and Sons, 1933), p. 143.

[72] H. Francotte, "Le pain à bon marché," pp. 140–141.

[73] Cf. Jardé, *Céréales*, pp. 182–183; and F. Heichelheim, *Wirtschaftliche Schwankungen der Zeit von Alexander bis Augustus* (Jena: 1930), pp. 51–52, 57–59.

Rostovtzeff infers a sort of *oikos* trade on the part of the Greek lords and tyrants of that region, in which they sold both the products of their own feudal estates and, to an even greater extent, the grain purchased from the Scythian tribes of the interior.[74] Herodotus tells, not without amazement, that the Scythians grow grain "not for their own use but for sale."[75] In the middle of the fourth century, the Bosporan kingdom opened another emporium, Theodosia, which, by virtue of its superior harbor facilities, soon supplanted Panticapeum.[76] These emporia could not have differed much in their organization from the early European factories and ports of trade as we find them established on the Pepper, Tooth, Gold, and Slave Coasts of West Africa. From Panticapeum, the grain crossed the Black Sea and moved along the southern shore to Byzantium, where some of it was resold to various Greek states. The bulk was shipped to the great emporium of the Piraeus, where two-thirds—a fourth-century regulation that may have existed even earlier—had to be carried on to Athens.[77] That the Greek states of the mainland did, in fact, buy much of their food in the Athenian emporium of the Piraeus is evident from the importance generally ascribed to Pericles' decree forbidding the Megarians from entering the Athenian market—the immediate cause of the Peloponnesian War. While Thucydides demonstrates that this was more a deliberate provocation than an underlying cause, Aristophanes' picture of the starving Megarian peasant in the *Acharnians* cannot have been altogether off the truth. Artistophanes, of course, gives this as *the* cause of the war in order to denounce what he regarded as its triviality. The Old Oligarch also explains the crucial role of Athenian sea power in maintaining her empire:

> . . . since there is no state in existence which does not depend upon imports and exports, and these she will forfeit if she does not lend a willing ear to those who are masters by sea.[78]

Athens' defeat by Sparta in the Peloponnesian War temporarily destroyed her hold over the grain trade. One of the instruments of the Spartan strategy was, in fact, an attack on the enemy's supply

[74] Rostovtzeff, "The Bosporan Kingdom," p. 569.
[75] Herodotus, *The Persian Wars*, IV, 17.
[76] Demosthenes, *Private Orations*, XX, 33.
[77] Aristotle, *Constitution of Athens*, II.
[78] Psuedo-Xenophon ("The Old Oligarch") *Constitution of the Athenians*, II.

route. Agis, besieging Athens in 409, saw "great numbers of grain-ships sailing in to Piraeus," and decided that Athens could not be defeated unless her grain supply was cut off. He therefore sent the son of the Byzantine *proxenos* at Sparta to Byzantium in an effort to win that city, as well as Calchedon, over from Athens.[79] This occurred after the Spartan capture of Decelea—halfway between Oropus and Athens—had closed the land route from Euboea. The Spartans also attempted to cut off grain shipments from Egypt. Eventually, Athens lost her fleet, and the war, in 405.

V. DEVELOPMENTS IN THE FOURTH CENTURY

As soon as Athenian naval supremacy was recovered after the Peloponnesian War in 394, a commercial treaty was signed between Athens and Satyrus, the ruler of the Bosporan kingdom.[80] But the administered trade of the fourth century differed much from that of the fifth as to the degree of Athenian control. In the fifth century, Athens administered the trade almost single-handedly, since the Bosporan cities were under her rule. In the fourth century, the Pontic trade was administered as treaty trade between great powers. Athens ruled the seas only from the Thracian Bosporus westward, while the now powerful kingdom of the Cimmerian Bosporus maintained dominance over the Black Sea.[81] The Bosporan kings were chieftain traders whose wealth derived from the grain trade which they appropriated; Athens in turn needed the Bosporan grain. In the same way, after Alexander's death, when Egypt, under Ptolemy Philadelphus ruled the Aegean, we find close diplomatic relations between the Bosporus and Egypt.[82]

Details of this administered trade during the reign of the greatest of the Bosporan kings, Leucon (circa 388 to 348 B.C.) have been preserved in several speeches of Demosthenes. Leucon, "who controls the trade," granted priority of lading to any merchant carrying grain to Athens, and exempted such merchants from the customs

[79] Xenophon, *Hellenica*, I, 1, 35–36.
[80] Rostovtzeff, "The Bosporan Kingdom," p. 567.
[81] Ibid., p. 506–507.
[82] Rostovtzeff, "Greek Sightseers in Egypt," p. 14.

dues of a thirtieth.[83] These rights traditionally applied to Panticapeum, the port of trade for grain. But Leucon also opened another *emporium*, as Demosthenes himself calls it, at Theodosia, and applied the same privileges there.[84] Theodosia had been an important emporium in earlier times, before Scythian incursions put an end to this role. Leucon's conquests restored Theodosia as an emporium.[85] In return, Athens conferred citizenship on Leucon, exempting him from all civic obligations, and crowned him with a golden wreath at the Panathenaic festival. The decree giving him these rights and honors was set out in stone in triplicate; one copy was set up in the Piraeus, one at Panticapeum, and one in the temple of Zeus at the entrance to the Black Sea.[86] In 347, the year following Leucon's death, his sons, Spartocus II and Paerisades I, who succeeded him, sent emissaries to Athens to announce their father's death and their intention to continue his policies; the Athenians set up a decree in their honor in the Piraeus (also honoring a third brother who did not share in the rule).[87] Paerisades became the ruler in 334/3, and an Athenian orator credits him with a renewal of the privileges.[88]

While Athens was the most favored nation under this treaty trade, she did not enjoy the same monopoly that she had in the preceding century. A decree in honor of Leucon passed by Arcadia in 369 B.C. suggests that she, too, received some privilege. And in 350, Mytilene, on the island of Lesbos, received permission from Leucon to buy 100,000 medimns of grain at an export duty of only $1\frac{1}{9}\%$; on exports above that amount, a duty of $1\frac{2}{3}\%$ was charged, in itself a saving of half the normal export tax.[89]

King Leucon also made gifts of grain to Athens. Demosthenes says that the gift in 357 was so large that the *sitones* (a tamkarum-type official appointed to purchase grain on governmental account during emergencies) had a surplus of 15 talents left for the treasury after disposing of the grain.[90] This should mean one of two things: either

---

[83] Demosthenes, *Private Orations*, XX, 31–32.

[84] Ibid., 33.

[85] Minns, *Scythians and Greeks*, p. 574.

[86] Demosthenes, *Private Orations*, XX, 36.

[87] Minns, *Scythians and Greeks*, p. 571. Cf. also Hasebroek, *Trade and Politics*, p. 114.

[88] Demosthenes, *Private Orations*, XXXIV, 36.

[89] Minns, *Scythians and Greeks*, p. 576.

[90] Demosthenes, *Private Orations*, XX, 33.

the grain was an outright gift and was distributed on some conventional basis to the citizenry, the remainder being sold for the benefit of the treasury; or else Leucon sold the grain to Athens at much less than the normal price, the 15 talents being the difference between the cost and the resale price. The first alternative seems more likely in this case. Strabo, in writing of Theodosia's superiority over Panticapeum, remarks that Leucon once sent 2,100,000 medimns—a very large amount—to Athens from Theodosia.[91] This may refer to the same gift or to another, or it may simply represent the total of a year's shipments to Athens.

The example of Mytilene shows that the administered trade between Athens and the Crimea was exceptional. Hasebroek perceived that "all the so-called commercial treaties which have come down to us from pre-Hellenistic times are concerned not with commercial advantages, but with the supply of grain and other indispensable commodities, including materials for defence and for shipbuilding."[92] Grain supplies were almost universally secured through treaties, which were generally concerned with the right to buy goods in a certain port or ports and with obtaining advantages in transportation; full or partial exemption from duties; safety from seizure; and priority in lading—i.e., the conditions of the Athens–Bosporus trade.[93]

Athens was only partially successful in her efforts to retain control of the western half of the Pontic route. In 387, a treaty with Clazomenae, on the Asia Minor coast, granted that city permission to buy grain in certain specified cities.[94] But other former dependencies, notably Byzantium herself, asserted their independence from time to time by seizing grain ships, either expropriating the grain or forcing the ships to pay duty. Thus, during a Spartan war with Athens, in 387/6, the Spartan general, with more than 80 ships under his command, prevented the ships from the Black Sea from sailing to Athens.[95] One of the first steps taken by Philip of Macedon, Alexander's father, making a bid for an Aegean empire, was to reach out for a stranglehold on Athenian grain supply. According to Demosthenes, King Philip

[91] Strabo, VII, 4, 6.
[92] Hasebroek, *Trade and Politics,* p. 111.
[93] Ibid., pp. 126–127.
[94] Francotte, "Le pain à bon marché," p. 136.
[95] Xenophon, *Hellenica,* V, 1, 28.

observing that we consume more imported grain than any other nation
. . . advanced towards Thrace, and the first thing he did was to claim the
help of the Byzantines as his allies in a war against you.[96]

Athens had increasing difficulty in keeping Byzantium within her
sphere of influence. About 360, she found herself compelled to convoy her grain ships because the Byzantines were "again" forcing
them to put into Byzantium and unload their cargo there.[97] Instances
of the seizure of grain ships by Byzantium, Calchedon, Cyzicus,
Chios, Cos, Rhodes, and Macedonia are recorded between 362 and
338.[98] Two years later, Alexander succeeded his father to the throne;
as soon as his great campaigns in the east were launched, the grain
supply of the Black Sea was diverted for the use of his armies, and
Athenian trade was practically at an end. It can hardly be mere chance
that, over the next years, Attica saw her worst famine since Solonic
times.

More than anything else, the political genius of Pericles was
responsible for the organization of Athenian grain trade with the
Black Sea. He was a master of *Realpolitik;* he was governed by the
principle of limiting Athenian policy to the attainable. Control over
the route to the Black Sea and the surrounding countries was within
the scope of Athenian power; hence he sought to channel Athenian
efforts in this direction and to restrict them in others. Plutarch, following upon his description of Pericles' expedition to the Black Sea,
offers an analysis full of rare insight:

> But in other matters he did not accede to the vain impulses of the
> citizens, nor was he swept along with the tide when they were eager,
> from a sense of their great power and good fortune, to lay hands again
> upon Egypt and molest the realms of the King (i.e., of Persia) which lay
> along the sea. Many also were possessed already with that inordinate
> and inauspicious passion for Sicily which was afterwards kindled into
> flame by such orators as Alcibiades. And some there were who actually
> dreamed of Tuscany and Carthage. . . .
>
> But Pericles was ever trying to restrain this extravagance of theirs, to lop
> off their expansive meddlesomeness and to divert the greatest part of
> their forces to the guarding and securing of what they already had won.

[96] Demosthenes, *Private Orations,* XVIII, 87.
[97] Ibid., L, 17.
[98] Rostovtzeff, "The Bosporan Kingdom," p. 574.

. . . That he was right in seeking to confine the power of the Athenians within lesser Greece, was amply proved by what came to pass.[99]

Pericles, in short, developed the Black Sea grain supply as an alternative to the Egyptian and the Sicilian, which were blocked by the powers of Persia and Syracuse, respectively. Athens had made a tremendous effort to wrest power over Egypt from Persia a few years earlier. The attempt proved abortive, and very nearly ended in total disaster. Pericles eventually resisted all further attempts to renew the attack on Egypt.

VI. EGYPT

Athens' interest in Egypt was prompted at least in part by a desire to tap Egypt's vast grain production. Thus, a Libyan pretender to the throne of Egypt sent a gift of 40,000 medimns of wheat to Athens in 445 B.C. in the hope of winning her support.[100] Some 20 years later, the Egyptian king, Amasis, sent Athens a large quantity of barley during a famine, in exchange for an alliance against Persia;[101] a gift that Aristophanes ridiculed because only barley was sent, instead of wheat. Grain clearly was the means of persuading Athens to take a hand in Egyptian–Persian relations.

It is difficult to assess the extent to which Athens received grain from Egypt during this period; the evidence is inconclusive. There may have been a trickle of trade between Greece and Egypt from the third millennium until about the tenth century, when the convulsions attendant upon the breakdown of Mycenaean civilization stopped it altogether. Trade moved from Egypt along the Syrian and Palestinian coast, either by land or by sea, then to Cyprus, and thence to Greece.[102] After a 300-year lapse, trade was resumed in the seventh century, maybe because of increased mastery of the sea, since it was now possible to sail from Egypt directly to Rhodes and

[99] Plutarch, *Pericles*, XX, 2; XXII, 1.

[100] Ibid., XXXVII, 3. Cf. also Dominique Mallet, *Les Rapports des Grecs avec l'Egypte* (Le Caire: 1922), p. 47.

[101] Scholiast to Aristophanes, *Wasps*, 716, referred to by Dominique Mallet, *Les premiers etablissements des Grecs dans l'Égypte*, p. 283.

[102] Harry R. H. Hall, *The Ancient History of the Near East*, ninth edition (London: Methuen, 1936), pp. 144, 161.

Crete, and thence to the Greek settlements in Asia Minor.[103] Miletus took the lead in this phase of the trade, carried on exclusively through the port of trade of Naucratis, which had apparently been founded as a Greek city in the sixth century by the Egyptian king, Amasis.[104] There is no mention of Athens in connection with Naucratis in this early period.

Although most writers assume that grain was one of the principal exports from Naucratis,[105] a list of Egyptian exports to Greece through that port of trade during the seventh and sixth centuries does not mention grain.[106] On the other hand, Egyptian myths recorded by Diodorus (an unreliable source) say that some of the ancient kings of Athens were Egyptian. One in particular, Erechtheus, "through his racial connection with Egypt, brought from there to Athens a great supply of grain" during a famine and thereby became king.[107]

While gift trade of an occasional character is on record in the fifth century, it is hard to determine how much trade of a more regular sort did occur. Certainly the Persian conquest of Egypt must have had some disturbing effect. However much wheat Athens did or did not obtain from Egypt, she certainly did not control the trade. Sparta apparently drew some grain from Egypt, too, since, during the Peloponnesian War, Athens attacked the Spartan island of Cythera, off the southern tip of Laconia, where "the merchant vessels coming from Egypt and Lybia commonly put in."[108] At the same time, Athenian imports from Egypt are mentioned about 408 B.C. Andocides persuaded Cyprus to lift the embargo on grain exports to Athens. Fourteen ships were about to enter the Piraeus, with more on their way.[109] Since the coasting route from Egypt to Cyprus was still popular, perhaps more popular than the direct sea route,[110] we may reasonably assume that this shipment originated in Egypt.

---

[103] Ibid.

[104] Herodotus, *The Persian Wars*, II, 178–179.

[105] E.g., Grundy, *Thucydides*, Volume 1, p. 64, n. 1.

[106] Prinz, *Funde aus Naucratis*, pp. 111–12. The administered character of this trade is made evident by Prinz's remark that the pottery and other finds show that the same wares always go to the same place, without exception (p. 144).

[107] Diodorus, I, 29, 1.

[108] Thucydides, *The Peloponnesian War*, IV, 53, 3.

[109] Andocides, II, 21.

[110] Grundy, *Thucydides*, Volume 1, p. 327.

Athenian grain imports from Egypt seem to have increased in the late fifth century, as Andocides' speech shows. Thus Rostovtzeff points to "the prevalence of Athenian influences in Naucratis in the late fifth and fourth centuries," shown by the pottery and coinage finds.[111] In the middle of the fourth century, the Athenians passed a decree in honor of a Naucratis citizen, Theogenes, a man "kindly disposed toward the Athenian people, who does whatever good he can to those who come to him on both public business and privately."[112] We may assume that the "public business" included the purchase of grain.

VII. SYRACUSE

The third great source of grain—the island of Sicily—lay just outside the orbit of Athenian power. The position of Athens was tantalizing. The size of the Sicilian grain crop can be gauged by the offer made by Geló, tyrant of Syracuse, to supply grain "for the whole Grecian army" for the duration of the Persian War, on condition that he be made commander-in-chief of either the Greek army or the Greek fleet.[113] While there is no positive evidence of Sicilian wheat exports to Greece before the fifth century, we cannot doubt that there was, in fact, significant trade; the western colonies could have paid for their imports from continental Greece in no other way.[114] While the volume of the trade during the fifth century cannot be accurately judged, it was of a regular character.[115] The Peloponnesus was the main customer.

Athens was barred from this source by Corinth, which sat astride the trade route. Her strategic site, together with her colonies in the Adriatic, gave her dominance over trade with the west.[116] The Athenian break with Corinth about 460, at the time of the expedition to Egypt, can have been meant only as an attempt to press for the

[111] Rostovtzeff, *Social and Economic History of the Hellenistic World* (Oxford: Clarendon Press, 1926), Volume 1, p. 89.
[112] II² 206, referred to by Smith, *Naukratis*, p. 64.
[113] Herodotus, *The Persian Wars*, VII, 158–160.
[114] T. J. Dunbabin, *The Western Greeks* (Oxford: 1948), p. 214.
[115] Ibid., p. 216.
[116] Ibid., p. 227.

mastery of all overseas sources of grain.[117] Athens first attacked Corinth indirectly, by seizing Aegina, destroying the commerce of Megara, and bringing Boeotia to heel, so as to gain a footing in the Corinthian Gulf. But ultimately, securing imports from the west depended upon at least partial control of the Sicilian and southern Italian ports of trade themselves. "Nothing less than the success of the Syracusan expedition could have achieved it."[118] Thus the Athenians intervened on behalf of the Leontines in their local war with Syracuse,

> professedly on the ground of relationship, but in reality because they did not wish the Peloponnesians to obtain corn from Sicily. Moreover they wanted to try what prospect they had of getting the affairs of Sicily into their hands.[119]

It was this threat to the food supplies of the Peloponnesus that brought Athens into conflict with Sparta. The Athenian pressure towards the Corinthian isthmus was clearly recognized as a peril to Sparta and her allies; Sparta and Corinth were thus drawn together by the common danger. The Peloponnesian War was the outcome of the Athenian aim of controlling the western grain supply.

We have concentrated on the grain trade, both on account of its crucial importance to Attica and because the bulk of the evidence on Greek trade naturally refers to it. Historians recognize today that grain imports ruled Athenian foreign policy and largely determined the course of its history. While this has been recognized as a fact, economic historians have failed to give full weight to it as the force shaping the organization of that trade. It was administered trade, carried on through ports of trade and treaties, closely adjusted to naval policy. No other means would have met the circumstances. It is the only form of trade that can be fitted in with a use of maritime power strictly applied to the insurance of definite routes and certain supplies of vital import.

---

[117] Ibid., p. 215, Grundy, *op. cit.*, vol. I, pp. 185–187.
[118] Dunbabin, *The Western Greeks*, p. 215.
[119] Thucydides, *The Peloponnesian War*, III, 86.

☞ 15 ☞

The Growth of Market Trade

I. ADMINISTERED TRADE

Nothing could be more definite than the administered character of the grain trade of classical antiquity. We have concentrated on this branch of trade because of its crucial importance to Attica; yet it is almost equally certain that not only grain trade but trade in general was administered in that period.

Let us quote the Old Oligarch's forceful words:

> As to wealth, the Athenians are exceptionally placed with regard to Greeks and barbarians alike in their ability to hold it. For given that some state or other is rich in timber for shipbuilding, when shall they dispose of it except by persuading the rulers of the sea? Or suppose the wealth of some state or other to consist of iron, or maybe of bronze, or of hemp, where shall they dispose of it except by permission of the supreme maritime power? Yet these are the very things, you see, I need for my ships. Timber I must have from one, from another iron, from a third bronze, from another hemp, from a fifth wax, etc.[1]

In other words, naval stores, essential for the fleet upon which Athenian power in turn depended, were objects of tightly controlled, administered trade. As with grain, Athens maintained a tight monopoly on the trade in timber, iron, bronze, hemp, wax, and the like; no state could buy these without Athenian permission, wherever Athenian power ruled. And this Athenian policy was mirrored in

---

[1] Pseudo-Xenophon ("The Old Oligarch"), *The Constitution of the Athenians*, II.

identical regulations in areas outside Athenian naval control. For, adds the Old Oligarch, "such as are our rivals will not allow people to carry these things to any other parts than where they themselves command the sea."[2]

Athenian dependence on imports of timber was particularly great, since Attica, like most of Greece proper, was largely deforested by the classical period. Macedonia and Thrace (and partly Thessaly) were the major source of supply, along with northern Asia Minor. The importance of the Thracian–Macedonian supply, as early as the late sixth century, is suggested in the famous story of the Persian protest against Darius' gift of a Thracian city to the Ionian tyrant, Histiaeus. The Persian general, Magabazus, reproached the emperor:

> What mad thing is this that you have done, sire, to let a Greek, a wise man and a shrewd, get hold of a town in Thrace, a place too where there is abundance of timber fit for shipbuilding, and oars in plenty, and mines of silver. . . . [3]

Control of the timber supply figured prominently in the Peloponnesian War. The Spartan capture of Amphipolis, at the mouth of the Strymon river, "caused great alarm" at Athens, in large part because of its importance as a source of timber for shipbuilding.[4] When the Spartans failed to conduct their campaign in accordance with the desires of the Macedonian king, Perdiccas, who had temporarily allied himself with Sparta, Perdiccas concluded a treaty with Athens in which he agreed (among other things) not to permit the export of wood for oars anywhere except to Athens.[5] Similarly, the Greek cities of Chalcidice signed a treaty with Amyntas of Macedonia in 389, establishing conditions for the export of pitch and timber; and there are several instances of individuals (perhaps acting in an official or semiofficial capacity) being formally granted the privilege of cutting and exporting wood without paying any duty. A stele, dated about 350, records joint decrees of Athens and of the Cean cities of Carthaea, Coresus, and Iulis, granting Athens a monopoly on Cean reddle (red ochre), vital as a pigment and drug. According to the decree, reddle could be exported only in Athenian bottoms, the transport

---

[2] Ibid, II.

[3] Herodotus, *The Persian Wars*, V, 23.

[4] Thucydides, *The Peloponnesian War*, IV, 108.

[5] H. Michell, *The Economics of Ancient Greece* (Cambridge: At the University Press, 1940), pp. 261–262.

charge (paid by the producers) being fixed at one obol per talent.[6] All of these regulations are reminiscent of the organization of the grain trade. We can hardly assume that the other staples mentioned by the "Old Oligarch" were obtained in any other way.

One trade staple of great importance remains—slaves. These were supplied entirely from external sources, the most important being prisoners of war. From the fifth century until the battle of Mantinea in 223, however, the general rule was to sell only the non-Greek and nonfree segment of the population, the main source of slaves thus being captured "barbarians."

The disposal of prisoners of war raises tactical problems of the greatest magnitude (as does the problem of booty disposal in general): there are both physical problems involved in storing and moving the booty, and financial ones in evaluating it. Thus slave trade, at least in its first stage, could hardly have been other than administered trade. At the same time, its administration provided a major impetus to the growth of ports of trade and markets. In the fifth century, the enslaved captives were transported to a nearby port, where they were sold.[7] In the early fourth century, the Spartan mercenary general, King Agesilaus, seems to have developed the technique of auctioning on the spot—thus shifting the logistic burden to the slave merchants.[8] This method is closely linked to a shift in the methods of army provisioning; instead of foraging through the countryside, or depending on markets provided by the cities in the area, the army is accompanied by hosts of sutlers who sell directly to the general or, with his permission and at settled prices, to his soldiers.

Certainly there was trade in articles other than staple products; modern historians—and the Athenians themselves—love to dwell on the wonderfully wide range of goods available in Athens. One such list, compiled through literary references, includes Chalcidian swords and cups, Corinthian bronzes, Milesian woollens, Argive weapons, garlic from Megara, game and fowl from Boeotia, cheese and pork from Syracuse, raisins and figs from Rhodes, acorns and almonds from Paphlagonia, mustard from Cyprus, cardamon from Miletus, onions from Samothrace, marjoram from Tenedos, wine

[6] M. N. Tod, ed., *Greek Historical Inscriptions* (Oxford: Clarendon Press, 1933), Volume 2, pp. 183–185.

[7] Thucydides, *The Peloponnesian War,* IV, 108.

[8] Xenophon, *Agesilaus,* I, 18.

from Attica, Chios, Cnidus, and Thasos, trumpets from Etruria, chariots from Sicily, luxurious chairs from Thessaly, bedsteads from Miletus, carpets and pillows from Carthage, incense from Syria, hunting dogs from Epirus.[9] And all or most of these must have been available in Athens, to judge by the boasts of Xenophon, Isocrates, and others. Imposing as this list certainly is, apart from foodstuffs, these articles are luxury goods or objets d'art. While their availability added color and excitement to the life of the wealthy and contributed to the cosmopolitan atmosphere of Athens, we can hardly assume an extensive volume of trade in mustard or chariots or pillows. Here, too, the Old Oligarch is suggestive; trade in luxuries, he suggests with a sneer, is one of the accompanying advantages of thalassocracy. In his mind, these goods merely contribute to weakening the moral fiber of Athens.

> If one may descend to more trifling particulars, it is to this same lordship of the sea that the Athenians owe the discovery in the first place, of many of the luxuries of life through intercourse with other countries. Thus it is the choice things of Sicily and Italy, of Cyprus and Egypt and Lydia, Pontus, or the Peloponnesus, or wheresoever else it be, are all swept, as it were, into one center, and all owing, as I say, to their maritime empire.[10]

Trade in luxuries, in short, is an interesting but minor by-product of the administered trade in staple goods. Such a relationship existed during the first two centuries of the Roman empire; cargo ships organized through the imperial *annona* were permitted to utilize extra cargo space for private trade.

II. THE INTRODUCTION OF MARKET ELEMENTS

Our history of the grain trade in Chapter 13 carried us down to the last quarter of the fourth century; for almost two centuries, the grain trade was administered, nonmarket trade. Yet there is no doubt of the existence of an international grain market in the eastern Mediterranean in the last quarter of the fourth century (and enduring in substantially unaltered form until the systematization of the imperial

[9] Michell, *Economics of Ancient Greece,* pp. 233–234.
[10] "Old Oligarch," *Constitution of the Athenians,* II.

annona under Augustus). Already in 324 B.C., grain supplies moved throughout the eastern Mediterranean in response to the movements of relative prices, and price tended toward uniformity in the entire area. Paradoxical this development certainly was; but in no sense does it vitiate our argument. Far from being the result of the evolution of the Attican organization of trade, it was its complete antithesis. This high point in market development in classical antiquity was the product, in fact, neither of Athens nor of the Greek states at all, but of the superplanners of Ptolemaic Egypt, who adapted Greek marketing methods to the traditional redistributive techniques of the Pharaohs. And it provoked not cooperation, but the most violent opposition on the part of Athens and the Greek states—so much so, in fact, that the organizing genius behind the development, Cleomenes of Naucratis, has remained vilified and despised as few other men in ancient history, down to our own day.

Cleomenes, of course, did not create the "world" market from a vacuum; there were certain anticipations of his market development throughout the fourth century, when the Athenian hold on the grain trade was weakened. Thus, for example, Xenophon, writing perhaps after 385, remarks that the *emporoi* love grain so intensely that

> on receiving reports that it is abundant anywhere, merchants will voyage in quest of it; they will cross the Aegean, the Euxine, the Sicilian sea; and when they have got as much as possible, they stow it in the very ships in which they sail themselves. And when they want money, they don't throw the corn away anywhere at haphazard, but they carry it to the place where they hear that corn is most valued and the people prize it most highly, and deliver it to them there.[11]

This passage indicates the growth of certain market elements in the fourth century, but hardly the existence of anything in the nature of a market system. The tendencies toward economic "rationality" in the distribution of grain are at best incipient. For example, the emphasis is on the means of procuring grain: merchants rush to any spot reputed to have a surplus of grain, *not* to that spot where grain prices are low! There is, in fact, no mention of *price* in any technical sense; rather, the context suggests a certain novelty in the idea that a merchant might himself decide where to sell his grain, instead of acting in accordance with imperial directions. Hence the attempt at

[11] Xenophon, *Oeconomicus*, XX, 27–28.

an explanation: "They don't throw the corn away anywhere at haphazard, but they carry it to the place where they hear that corn is most valued and the people prize it most highly." The passage was written, we may presume, shortly before the construction of the second Athenian confederacy and before the resumption of close relations between Athens and the Bosporan kingdoms; Athenian control of the grain trade, in short, was at a low ebb at the moment.

But whatever the circumstances, nothing could have been more irrational than attempts to base grain movements on relative price movements. Our knowledge of prices for this period (indeed, for all of antiquity, and for modern times until quite recently) is sadly poor; the data are so limited that it is impossible to construct any sort of indices, indeed to make any but the crudest comparisons of price movements. Paradoxically, it is this inadequacy of the data for most purposes that provides an impressive argument against the existence of any sort of market organization outside the strict confines of the *polis*. We should expect a market organization of trade to produce some degree of uniformity of prices and regularity in their movements. But what makes the price data so difficult to use for most purposes is precisely the lack of any pattern whatsoever. According to Jardé, the authority on the subject, "la règle est la continuelle variation des prix"—continual variation for any one area, between the different months of any one year, between the years themselves, and similarly between different areas.[12] These variations, moreover, are random, showing no pattern between areas for any one period of time or between different periods of time for one or more areas. The movements of grain prices, in fact, can be correlated only with political events, prices fluctuating in accordance with the opening and closing of the trade routes.[13] Riezler, in fact, insists that there is no justification for speaking of a "world price" or of a "world market" for the Mediterranean, but only of "world commerce."[14] The degree of variation is suggested by the following table of Athenian wheat prices constructed by Jardé:[15]

[12] A. Jardé, Les céreales dans l'antiquité Grecque (Paris: 1952), p. 164. (The fact that death prevented Jardé from adding his projected volume on grain distribution is one of the great tragedies of modern scholarship.)

[13] Ibid., p. 166.

[14] K. Riezler, Über Finanzen und Monopole in alten Griechenland (Puttkammer und Mühlbrech, 1907), p. 55.

[15] Jardé, Les céreales, p. 179.

393 B.C.	3 drachmas per medimn
"beginning of the	
fourth century"	6 drachmas per medimn
340-330	9 drachmas per medimn
About 330	5 drachmas per medimn
330/329	5 drachmas per medimn
329/28	6 drachmas per medimn
329/28	10 drachmas per medimn

The evidence is incisive and is confirmed by two added facts: the persistence over two centuries of a wheat–barley price ratio of two to one, regardless of the variations in their respective prices;[16] and the persistence and strength of the view, throughout the Greek world, that the fair and proper price for wheat was five drachmas per medimn, anything over six drachmas being regarded as a public calamity.[17] Since barley and wheat were generally consumed by different groups, and partly produced in different regions, the persistence (with minor exceptions) of a two to one ratio in their prices is all the more striking. We remain ignorant of the precise mechanism involved, although the secular permanence of the ratio is suggestive of the barley–silver equivalence of Sumeria and Babylonia. The negative inference is clear; a price-making market could never have produced such uniformities over time when the conditions of both production and consumption in regard to the two cereals were different. Nor should we regard the preference for five drachma wheat as mere sentimentality or prejudice. Rather, it appears as a normative principle of great effectiveness: we find a definite tendency, even in the Hellenistic period, to return to this price. Such stability and uniformity should not surprise us; the real problem might more accurately be how to explain the fluctuations that did occur.

Perhaps the first question to be asked of the price data is: to what place they specifically refer. When Jardé, for example, quotes grain prices at Athens, it is not clear whether he refers to the price in Athens proper, i.e., in the *agora*, or to the price in the port of trade or emporium, in the Piraeus. The distinction is not simply one between wholesale and retail trade, for we frequently find the retail price lower than the wholesale. This should not really be surprising to an age like ours, accustomed (if not resigned) to dual pricing systems for

---

[16] Ibid., p. 182.
[17] Ibid., p. 140. Cf. also E. H. Minns, *Scythians and Greeks* (Cambridge: 1913), p. 575.

internal and international trade. The institutional separation, not simply of internal and external trade and traders, but of their sites and prices as well, is central to this whole problem.

Grain moving into Athens as a result of Athenian control of the grain trade did not enter the city indiscriminately or directly. Goods acquired from overseas were brought to the emporium located in the harbor of Athens, the Piraeus: the separation of the emporium from the rest of Athens in every sense was symbolized by the boundary stones that surrounded it and separated it from the Piraeus proper, which legally and institutionally (although not administratively) was a part of Athens. The physical location of the emporium was, in fact, a real problem for the Greeks. Aristotle believed that its institutional separation should be reinforced geographically; he implicitly rebuked Athens for locating her emporium within the city limits proper:

> . . . even now we see many countries and cities possessing seaports and harbors conveniently situated with regard to the city, so as not to form part of the same town and yet not be too far off, but commanded by walls and other defense work. It is manifest that if any advantage does result through the communication of the city with the port, the state will possess this advantage, and if there is any harmful result it is easy to guard against it by means of laws regulating which persons are not and which persons are to have intercourse with one another.[18]

Locating their emporium where they did, on the east side of the harbor of Cantharus, must have only slightly complicated matters for the Athenian, however. A greater complication stemmed from the fact that the Athenian emporium served the entire Aegean, not merely Athens—a development Aristotle frowned upon, "for the state ought to engage in commerce for its own interest, but not for the interest of the foreigner." Such an emporium is necessary, since a city must import what is not found within its borders and export its own surpluses; this is a legitimate purpose. But "people that throw open their market to the world do so for the sake of revenue, but a state that is not to take part in that sort of profit-making need not possess an emporium." These profits, it must be remembered, are largely the revenues derived from excise on imports and exports, harbor dues, and the like—"fiscalism" in its purest form. The main

[18] Aristotle, *Politics*, VII, 6 (1327a).

problem, it is clear, is the legal and administrative one of regulating the emporium.

Within the emporium itself, transactions were centered on a long pier, known as the *deigma,* extending into the harbor in about the center of the emporium. The *emporoi* displayed their wares, in the form of samples, on the *deigma;* the Greek term for *sample* was itself a derivation of *deigma.* Here the moneychangers, the *trapezites,* sat at their tables, changing and testing money, accepting deposits for payment, and greatly facilitating transactions. Polyaenus describes an enemy attack on Athens during which the attackers leap ashore on the *deigma,* seize the money on the bankers' tables, and sail away.[19] Xenophon depicts an even more dramatic scene in which the attackers leap ashore, seize merchants and shipowners, and carry them off.[20]

Besides the *deigma,* where the transactions are concluded, sales of goods to be carried into Attica proper, and sales to other foreigners to be carried abroad once again, the emporium contains its own *agora,* in the northern tip. We have found no explicit literary reference to this *agora,* but its unquestioned existence implies that those whose business took them to the emporium could be provisioned there, without the need to enter the city proper. This purpose seems evident from the usual presence of such food markets within the African ports of trade of the sixteenth to eighteenth centuries. Without question, there were lodging houses within the emporium to accommodate overnight travelers, although many may have preferred to remain aboard ship. Xenophon, who seems to be proposing the conversion of the entire Piraeus into a vast emporium in his *Ways and Means,* argues the advantages of constructing hotels and places of amusement in order to attract more metics and foreigners. Those who were in the emporium temporarily had thus no occasion to enter Athens; those who were there permanently were metics, hence subject to Athenian law.

One major reservation seriously modified the degree and extent of Athenian control over the emporium: the predominance of the import interest of Athens, as well as of most other Greek cities. Athens wanted cheap grain and she would attempt to keep prices low; but above all, she *needed* grain. There could be no conflict

---

[19] Polyaenus, *Stratagems of War.*
[20] Xenophon, *Hellenica,* V, 1.

between these two interests during the Periclean age. "For given that some state or other is rich in timber for shipbuilding, where shall they dispose of it except by persuading the ruler of the sea?" Interestingly enough, scanty and spotty as our price data are for the fourth century, we have none whatsoever for the fifth century. While no proof is possible we may infer that proclaimed equivalencies were maintained in the emporium during this period; since grain could be sold nowhere but at the Piraeus or Byzantium, excessive prices could not have been a problem. The empire acted as a monopoly of grain purchases.

But the problem must have taken on a different complexion after the fall of the Athenian empire. Then, Athenian control of the Bosporan grain supply would rest not on direct military control of the seaways, but on financial advantages offered to those willing to sell grain to Athens as a result of Athenian diplomacy. Admittedly, Athenian naval power won these concessions from the Black Sea monarchs; but, as the frequent seizures of grain ships demonstrate, this power was far from absolute. Thus, the remission of customs dues to merchants lading for Athens was merely relative, particularly since Leucon also gave remissions, though lesser ones, to other states, for example, to Mytilene about 350 B.C.[21] Should Athens attempt to keep prices too far below those in other cities, she would court the possibility of losing her grain supply altogether, since merchants would then simply avoid Athens.[22]

At the same time, high prices would amount to a public calamity, because of the central place of grain in the diet. The delicacy of the Athenian position could hardly have been greater. This should not be regarded as an exceptional situation, however; Western medieval cities were in substantially the same position with respect to foreign trade, as were many of the North American colonies in the seventeenth century.

A variety of techniques were used in order to overcome the difficulty; all of them involved a distinction between emporium prices and *agora* prices. Perhaps the most successful and interesting of these devices has come down to us from the early Hellenistic period (and to our knowledge it was not used in that form at Athens);

[21] Tod, *Greek Inscriptions*, Volume 2, pp. 185–186.
[22] See Chapter 13, pp. 194–195.

its logic, however, reveals much of the Athenian situation. The city of Lagina bought its entire grain requirements from private merchants at prevailing prices and resold the grain to its citizens at the "just price" of five drachmas per medimn. A revolving fund was established for that purpose by a special assessment (*liturgy*) of the wealthy, which was then invested so as to produce an annual income. Thus, the citizens were always provided with cheap grain, while the merchants, on whom Lagina depended for their performance, had no complaint. Francotte describes identical arrangements in five other Greek cities of Asia Minor.[23] Tarn reports on what seem to be similar arrangements in another group of cities.[24]

Athens, however, was not willing to give up all control over price; her technique, therefore, was only partly to insulate the *agora* price from external fluctuations and partly to link the *agora* price to the external price. Two-thirds of the grain arriving in the emporium had to be brought into the city; this was a specific charge on the ten "Supervisors of the Emporium," whose general obligation was to "superintend the Mart."[25] Middlemen were excluded by a law forbidding anyone to buy more than 50 measures of grain at one time;[26] cornering the market, or similar practices, were thereby avoided. The agora price was further held close to the price in the emporium by the grain commissioners (*sitophylakes*) who were to

> see to it that the unprepared corn in the market is offered for sale at reasonable prices, and secondly . . . that the millers sell barley meal at a price proportionate to that of barley, and that the bakers sell their loaves at a price proportionate to that of wheat, and of such weight as the Commissioners may appoint; for the law requires them to fix standard weight.[27]

At the time of Aristotle's writing, there were 20 *sitophylakes* for the city and 15 for the Piraeus; at an earlier date there had been five for each. So strict was the supervision that on occasion *sitophylakes* were put to death for failure to enforce the laws.[28]

[23] H. Francotte, "Le pain gratuit et le pain à bon marché dans les cités grecques," in *Mélanges Nicole* (Geneva: 1905), pp. 143–144.

[24] W. W. Tarn, *Hellenistic Civilization*, second edition (London: E. Arnold and Co., 1930), p. 99.

[25] Aristotle, *Constitution of Athens*, 51.

[26] Lysias, "Against the Corn Dealers," XXII, 6.

[27] Aristotle, *Constitution of Athens*, 51.

[28] Lysias, "Against the Corn Dealers," XXII, 8.

Our picture, so far, is nonetheless one of competitive price determination in the emporium: Lysias, in his oration denouncing the retailers' profiteering, presents a picture of short supply there pushing up prices in the *agora*.[29] This is supported by other sources; a later orator, for example, describes how seizures of grain ships by Byzantium, Calchedon, and Cyzicus caused a grain shortage in the emporium, with consequent high prices.[30] But such a description should not be pushed too far. At a certain point we find the correlation between supply and price snapping: instead of the price rising steadily as supply drops, we find the reverse—the price suddenly drops. It is at this critical point that the mechanism of state control came fully into operation. Athens could link its *agora* to the emporium so long as the emporium price fluctuated within certain limits; to abandon itself completely to the vagaries of the external prices would have been suicidal.

In such a crisis, the delicacy of the situation must have been heightened. For how were the Athenians to deal with foreigners, who were now more vital than ever. The method must remain partially obscure to the modern rationalistic mind. The solution was neither force (which was not available) nor even an appeal to the self-interest of the merchant (couched, perhaps, in references to his long-run interests in creating customer good will rather than short-run profits). The appeal, rather, was to his pride, his ego, his desire for status and prestige. The magistrates persuaded (or tried to persuade) the merchants to sell their grain at the conventional price of five drachmas per medimn, regardless of how high the prevailing price was in the emporium; in return, the grateful city would pass a decree in praise of the merchant, perhaps grant him some special honor, or post the decree in the emporium of Byzantium. Thus, two alien litigants suing to recover a sea-loan remind the jury that a few years earlier they had sold 10,000 medimns of corn at five drachmas per medimn when the prevailing price was 16 drachmas.[31] A merchant from Salamis in Cyprus, Heracleides, was honored by a decree for selling 3000 medimns at five drachmas in 330/329.[32] Still others sold

[29] Ibid., XXII, 16.

[30] Demosthenes, *Private Orations*, L, 6.

[31] Ibid., XXXIV, 39.

[32] G. W. Botsford and E. G. Sihler, eds., *Hellenic Civilization* (New York: Columbia University Press, 1915), p. 588.

quantities of 10,000, 12,000, and 40,000 medimns, respectively, at the same price during this famine.[33]

Not only were the merchants prevailed upon to sell at the "just price"; it has also been suggested that some of the largest gifts of grain to Athens from foreign states were actually sales by these states at the five-drachma price. Leucon, the ruler of the Bosporan kingdom, gave many such gifts, presumably at times of grain shortage; one, in 356, was so generous that, in some way which is unexplained, the Athenian treasury—taking over the retail sale of such grain—made a profit of 15 talents.[34] Leucon was greatly extolled for these gifts and granted honorary citizenship. Perhaps the largest gift received by Athens was 100,000 medimns, given by Cyrene between 330 and 326 B.C.; Tod believes that this grain was sold at the normal price, and was not an outright gift.[35] The Athenian decree in honor of Leucon's sons suggests the same possibility, since on their succession, Spartocus and Paerisades promptly informed Athens of their intention to continue their father's favorable policies. They also raised the question of a debt owed to Bosporus by Athens; in Tod's opinion, this was a *state* debt, not one owed by private individuals.[36] Such a public debt may very well have been for state purchase of grain from Leucon.

We do not know precisely what inducements or pressures were brought to bear on the merchants to sell at the conventional price; but we have the same difficulty in understanding clearly how the Athenian citizens reacted to the *liturgies* imposed on them. Yet this technique of influencing grain prices was, in principle, merely an extension of the *liturgy* system to the alien and the metic. Besides selling at the lower price, the merchants were even induced to contribute money to the city to finance grain purchases; that grain, we may assume, was resold to the citizen at the five-drachma price. Thus, the same two clients of Demosthenes, who sold grain at five drachmas when the emporium price was 16, on another occasion contributed a talent to the city for grain purchases; Heracleides, the merchant from Salamis, contributed 3000 drachmas in 328/7.

Athens was by no means exceptional in this regard; Francotte

[33] *Cambridge Ancient History,* Volume 6, p. 449.
[34] Demosthenes, *Private Orations,* XX, 33.
[35] Tod, *Greek Inscriptions,* Volume 2, p. 274.
[36] Ibid., p. 197.

ascribes similar techniques to the cities of Ephesus, Ilion, Parion, Astypalaea, Oripe, and Priene.[37] In a general way, as Jardé points out, *all* the Athenian techniques of controlling prices and supply are to be found in *all* the Greek cities.

These techniques proved increasingly inadequate, however, as the fourth century progressed, probably because of the continuing disruption of traditional trade routes that attended the growth of Macedonian power. Thus, a new figure appears on the scene for the first time, in 328—the *sitones,* a *tamkarum*-like figure (actually a board of three officials) appointed to purchase grain on government account during a period of famine. Demosthenes was chairman of the board, and himself contributed one talent to its funds. The grain was resold to the citizenry at five drachmas per medimn.[38]

The net result of these policies, therefore, was to tie the *agora* price to the emporium price, so long as the latter remained within reasonable limits, but to sever the connection completely whenever the emporium price rose to a threatening level. Francotte could hardly be more emphatic in insisting on the sharp institutional distinction between the internal and external grain markets; he is inclined to believe that the *agora* price was almost always fixed by the *sitophylakes.* Jardé seems also to suggest some comparable distinction. These policies clearly involved a large element of continuity from the redistributive past of Athens.

III.   THE EMERGENCE OF THE MARKET

The famine of 330–326 brought about more than some new Athenian techniques for maintaining low internal prices. It marked the turning point in the history of the grain trade, for it was in connection with this famine that the eastern Mediterranean grain market was first organized. Rostovtzeff calls this event the beginning of "a new period" in the history of the grain trade,[39] but even he underestimates its importance. Having assumed the existence of a grain market all along, he tends to think of this event in terms of a

[37] Francotte, "Le pain," p. 142.

[38] Ibid., p. 149. Cf. also *Cambridge Ancient History,* Volume 6, p. 449.

[39] M. Rostovtzeff, "The Bosporan Kingdoms," in *Cambridge Ancient History,* Volume 8, p. 575.

triumph for laissez-faire principles: "after Alexander, it [the grain trade] became free, once and for all."

The outbreak of the famine by itself offered dramatic evidence of the inadequacy of the existing organization of the grain trade; the growth of Macedon under Alexander had disrupted any pretences Athens might still have had at controlling the sources and trade routes. It seems clear that, although the famine affected almost the entire Greek world, it was not due to any crop failure within Greece. Rostovtzeff, in fact, suggests that there was no shortage in the grain-producing countries either; the problem was entirely an organizational one.

> There was plenty of grain in the market and in most cases plenty of money to buy it. The problem was how to distribute and regularize the supply, and how to stabilize the price. Athens, the great corn-exchange of antiquity, was unequal to the task, and her successors, Alexandria, Rhodes, Miletus, and Ephesus, required time to discover the appropriate methods.[40]

Such a view is supported by Jardé's belief that the famine did not continue throughout the entire five-year span, but rather was intermittent, with wide variations of supplies from year to year. For example, a decree of the year 328 speaks of the famine of the *preceding years*, thus implying relatively normal supplies at the moment.[41] The main immediate cause, actually, was the loss of part or all of the Bosporan supply to Alexander's army.[42] The growth of a new and hostile power spelled the end of Athenian control—or even influence—over grain supply.

The need for complete reorganization of the grain trade must have been self-evident. The prospects, moreover, were favorable. For the "new power" was unlike those of the recent past. Alexander was no mere conqueror; he envisaged a unification of east and west, an integration of all parts of his empire. Trade played no small part in his scheme of things; the scale on which the new city in Egypt, named after him, was planned and built makes it clear that Alexandria was intended by her founder to serve as both a cultural and a commercial center for the western half of the empire. Alexander,

---

[40] M. Rostovtzeff, *Social and Economic History of the Hellenistic World* (Oxford: Clarendon Press, 1926), Volume 1, pp. 168–169.

[41] Jardé, *Les céreales*, p. 47.

[42] *Cambridge Ancient History*, Volume 8, p. 575.

with his deep insight into Greek politics and economics, must have known the comprehensive importance of grain for Greece: whoever controlled the grain trade controlled Greek livelihood, and hence controlled the political fate of the Greeks. The location of Alexandria at the mouth of the Nile, the main artery of the fabulously wealthy grain producer, Egypt, could not have been accidental; why start afresh when such emporia as the Piraeus, Rhodes, and Corinth already existed? Centralization of the grain trade must therefore have been one of Alexander's objects; and so we find the same man— Cleomenes of Naucratis—responsible both for the creation of a centralized grain market and for the building of Alexandria. It would be a mistake, however, to assume that Alexandria was built solely for commerical purposes. Groningen has argued persuasively that, had trade been his sole objective, Alexander would more likely have developed Naucratis as his chief entrepôt. Both the choice of the site and the scale of the city, he insists, suggest the primacy of political and strategic considerations.[43]

The combined vilification and neglect of Cleomenes of Naucratis on the part of most scholars is one of the truly puzzling chapters in classical historiography. For Cleomenes was surely one of the greatest and most influential men of the Alexandrian period. At the same time, this neglect of Cleomenes explains why the decisiveness and importance of his organization of an eastern Mediterranean grain market in this period has generally been missed, since Cleomenes dominated both the event and the few surviving contemporary reports of it. For the past two centuries, historians, with a few notable exceptions, have concentrated so completely on Cleomenes' alleged venality and extortion that they have ignored his achievements; even those like Rostovtzeff, who acknowledge his greatness, feel constrained to make apologies for him. His reputation for evil deeds is as incorrect as it is irrelevant; if historical perspective means anything at all, it is that individual motives and personalities are quite unimportant compared with institutional changes. The incident of the cherry tree is, after all, no longer of burning interest to historians of the American revolution.

The defamation of Cleomenes' character rests on two main pieces of evidence, with support coming from several minor

---

[43] B. A. van Groningen, "Sur le fondation d'Alexandrie," in *Raccolita di Scritti in Onore di Giacomo Lumbroso*, pp. 200–218.

episodes. The one is his apparent role as an extortionist and racketeer in the great famine of the 320s, the other a letter quoted by Arrian from Alexander to Cleomenes offering to "pardon any offenses you may have committed" as well as remission of any future sins on compliance with certain requests. Arrian himself refers to Cleomenes as a "bad man," who had "committed many acts of injustice in Egypt."[44] The minor evidence concerns several incidents related in the second book of the pseudo-Aristotelian *Oeconomica*.

The first charge touches on our central problem of the creation of the "world" grain market, for this was accomplished in connection with the famine. Because establishment of the grain market was regarded as a serious threat to Athenian independence, Cleomenes was defamed by the Athenian writers. The episode will be discussed in detail below.

The second—Alexander's implicit rebuke, together with Arrian's unequivocal denunciation—has generally been regarded as the most convincing piece of evidence against Cleomenes. The letter, though, is now regarded as a forgery. Mahaffy was perhaps the first historian to point out that it could not be genuine, since in it Alexander commands Cleomenes to build two chapels in honor of his friend Hephaestion, one of them in Alexandria, the other on the island of Pharos, "where the tower is situated." But the famous Pharos lighthouse was not built before the reign of Ptolemy II, at least forty years after the letter was supposedly written.[45] W. W. Tarn, who is an extreme critic of Cleomenes, also rejects the letter's authenticity, but on stylistic grounds; he suggests that Arrian was "taken in" by the forgery but was nevertheless uncomfortable about it, since he feels moved to add a rather peculiar running commentary on the letter.[46] Tarn also rejects the letter, on the grounds that Alexander never would have forgiven a man as evil as Cleomenes.

The origin of the forgery is fairly obvious; Ptolemy Soter himself was responsible for blackening Cleomenes' name, in order to justify his assassination. In the struggle for power after Alexander's death, Egypt was one of the prizes. While the rule of Egypt was given to Ptolemy, Perdiccas insisted that Cleomenes remain as his assistant,

[44] Arrian, *Anabasis*, VII, 23, 6–8.

[45] J. Mahaffy, *The Ptolemaic Dynasty* (London: Methuen and Co., 1899), p. 23, note 1.

[46] W. W. Tarn, *Alexander the Great* (Cambridge: At the University Press, 1948), Volume 2, pp. 303–304.

in order to keep a check on Ptolemy's power; Perdiccas was still trying to keep the empire intact. Ptolemy soon broke with Perdiccas and allied himself with Antipater; he thereupon killed Cleomenes because of his close relationship to Perdiccas.[47] Tarn, Bevan, and Mahaffy are agreed that Ptolemy proceeded to malign Cleomenes, since the latter's claim to rule was at least as legitimate as Ptolemy's.

For the rest—the minor incidents of the *Oeconomica*—we need not concern ourselves in detail; we tend to agree with Mahaffy's dictum (as one of the few consistent defenders of Cleomenes) that none of the stories "show an oppression of the poor, but rather of the financiers and priests. From what we know of them and their doings we shall be slow to condemn Cleomenes upon their complaints."[48] We might merely add that the incidents have very close parallels in the *Oeconomica* itself;[49] Cleomenes' actions, therefore, appear typical of his time. His attack on the priests and local rulers, moreover, was one of the prerequisites of that superbly effective and efficient planning of the Ptolemies, which would not have been possible given the degree of autonomy enjoyed by the priests and nomarchs (local governors) at the time of the conquest.

It seems very likely, then, that together with his murderer and successor Cleomenes deserves a large part of the credit for the development of the economic system, credit usually given to the second Ptolemy, Philadelphus. Rostovtzeff, for example, decries the tendency to "underestimate the achievements" of both Cleomenes and Ptolemy Soter, although he feels that Philadelphus inherited his main problems from them.[50] Ulrich Wilcken definitely sees "certain connections between the economic tendencies of the Ptolemies and of . . . Cleomenes."[51] While the thesis cannot be proven with certainty, since almost all the documentary evidence dates from

[47] E. Bevan, *History of Egypt*, Volume 4, pp. 17, 22; Mahaffy.

[48] Mahaffy, *Ptolemaic Dynasty*, p. 27.

[49] Compare the incidents involving the Egyptian priests and temples, II, 1352a, 23–28 and 1352b, 20–25, with Chabrias' advice to the Egyptian king Taus, II, 1350b, 33–36. Wilcken has pointed out the almost exact parallel between the measures of Chabrias and the taxes listed on the famous stele of Naukratis, *Zeitschrift für Ägyptische Sprache*, Volume 38, p. 133. Compare also Cleomenes' ruse with the mercenaries with the ruse of his contemporary, Memnon, tyrant of Lampsacus, *Oeconomica II*, 1351b, 11–18.

[50] Rostovtzeff, *Hellenistic World*, p. 262.

[51] U. Wilcken, *Alexander the Great* (New York: Norton, 1967).

Philadelphus, there can be little doubt that this is so. Cleomenes was the satrap of Egypt until Alexander's death[52] and, in addition, was in charge of the finances of Lybia, Cyrenaica, and Marmorica.[53] His activities included raising a fleet and a mercenary army, the financial reorganization of Egypt, the reorganization of the grain trade, and the building of Alexandria.

We know little or nothing of the details of Cleomenes' financial administration except its fabulous success. When Ptolemy Soter took over the rule of Egypt from Cleomenes, he found the staggering sum of 8000 talents in the treasury.[54] This treasury accumulation, incidentally, provides the clearest insight into the scholars' unreasonable prejudice against Cleomenes. Tarn, following a long tradition, accuses Cleomenes of appropriating that sum for himself:

> The guilt of the worst offender (of the Alexandrian period) Cleomenes, is corroborated from better sources. . . . He amassed 8000 talents by his misdeeds; a fantastic sum at a time when the richest man in Greece was perhaps worth 160 talents. . . ."[55]

Yet the only reference to that sum in all the ancient sources is Diodorus' explicit statement that Ptolemy found 8000 talents *"in the treasury"* when he took over from Cleomenes.[56] That 8000 talents was a very large sum is, of course, true; but what it proves is not Cleomenes' "guilt," but his effectiveness as financier and administrator, particularly since there is no evidence to show any oppression of the Egyptian population. For all we know, Ptolemy's haste to kill

[52] Tarn vigorously denies the title of satrap to Cleomenes, arguing that "Alexander had never had a satrap of Egypt, and he certainly would not have appointed a Greek financier from Naukratis to such a very important post"; he concedes that Cleomenes was the de facto governor (*Alexander the Great,* Volume 2, p. 303 and note 1). His argument rests on two main points: that Arrian says merely that Cleomenes was appointed by Alexander "to govern this satrapy" (*Anabasis,* III, 5) and that only Pausanias, unreliable for precise details, expressly calls him satrap (I, 6, 3). But Arrain is notoriously biased against Cleomenes; Tarn, moreover, has overlooked the most important sources on Cleomenes' actual activities; the pseudo-Aristotelian *Oeconomica,* II, which specifically calls him "satrap of Egypt" (1352a16), and Demosthenes' *Private Oration* LVI (against Dionysodorus), 7, which refers to him as "the former satrap of Egypt." Whether or not Cleomenes held the title is of course completely beside the point, since the fact of his rule and of his absolute power is unquestioned.

[53] Arrian, *Anabasis,* III, 5.

[54] Diodorus, XVIII, 14, 1.

[55] Tarn, *Alexander the Great,* Volume 1, p. 129.

[56] *Cambridge Ancient History,* Volume 6, p. 427.

Cleomenes and blacken his reputation may have been prompted by the affection in which he was held by the populace.

Cleomenes' responsibility for the construction of Alexandria is impressive proof, both of his own abilities and of the high regard Alexander had for him. Pseudo-Callisthenes calls him Alexander's chief adviser at the city's founding, while Justin refers to him as the man "who had built Alexandria"; the pseudo-Aristotelian *Oeconomica*, in a passage apparently antedating the naming of the city, reports that "King Alexander had given Cleomenes command to establish a town near the island of Pharus, and to transfer thither the emporium hitherto held at Canopus."[57] And Cleomenes' name is particularly connected with the founding of Alexandria in the "Romance," local traditions written some three or four centuries later.[58] The importance Alexander attached to the founding of this city is suggested by the fact (or legend) that he himself marked out the plan of the city;[59] the role he planned for it is suggested by the report of the augurs he consulted in the legendary account of its foundation:

> O king, begin the building of the city, for it will be great and renowned and abounding in revenues, and all the ends of the earth will bring articles of trade to it. Many countries will be fed by it, but it will not be dependent on any country for sustenance, and everything manufactured in it will be esteemed by the world, and they will carry it to remote lands.[60]

Cultural and political capital of the western half of the empire (if not of the entire empire), principal emporium of the Mediterranean—these are the roles Alexander clearly planned for his city in Egypt. Who but a man of the greatest ability and integrity could be entrusted with so great a responsibility? That Cleomenes was such a man, that he was, indeed, one of Alexander's closest advisers and confidants, is confirmed by one last, impressive piece of evidence. In his eloquent description of Alexander's last moments, Arrian—the man who stigmatized Cleomenes—tells that Cleomenes was one of the three men who acted as intermediaries with the gods in a last

---

[57] Pseudo-Callisthenes, I, 30; Justin, XIII, 4; *Oeconomica*, II, 1352a, 29ff. Cf. also Julius Valerius, I, 25.

[58] Bevan, *History of Egypt*, p. 17. Note also that the *Oeconomica*, II, written probably in the third century, refers to him as "Alexandrian."

[59] Arrian, *Anabasis*, III, 1.

[60] Pseudo-Callisthenes, I, 33.

attempt to save the emperor's life, while another chosen four kept an all-night vigil at his deathbed.[61] These seven men, out of all the emperor's followers, were picked to be with him in his last moments. No more powerful proof of Cleomenes' stature can be offered.

Let us return, therefore, to our main subject, the creation of a "world" grain market in the eastern Mediterranean. The story, while simple in its basic structure, must be pieced together from confusing and cryptic sources; its tentative and hypothetical character cannot be sufficiently stressed. It might be useful, therefore, to quote these sources at this point before proceeding to the analysis of the event. The first two are from the *Oeconomica*, II;[62] the third from the oration against Dionysodorus.

> At a time when the price of grain in Egypt was ten drachmas [a measure], Cleomenes sent for the growers[63] and asked them at what price

---

[61] Arrian, *Anabasis*, VII, 26.

[62] A brief explanation on the extensive use we shall make of this frequently maligned work may be in order. The *Oeconomica*, II is one of the most difficult and obscure sources for the study of Greek economics—but at the same time one of the most fertile. Its obscurity stems both from the character of the original work and the condition of the surviving manuscript. The book consists primarily of a compendium of anecdotes, mostly tinged with scandal, describing the various ways in which cities and individuals solved their financial difficulties. The authorship is uncertain, although it probably was composed by one or more of Aristotle's pupils who followed a suggestion in the *Politics* I, 11, 1259a, 2–4. The edition which survives, however, seems to be a greatly abbreviated version by a later editor, which omits some stories, cuts others, and runs still others together. The text itself is so mutilated as to make many words and even a number of passages unintelligible. Its use is therefore fraught with difficulties, even for the expert classical scholar. It is this very obscurity of the text, however, which justifies our own use of it, since the classicist is himself thrown onto the realm of rather free interpretation. Our study claims to be in no sense definitive, only suggestive; it employs the published Forster and Loeb Library translations and the critical exegeses of van Groningen, Riezler, Wilcken, Schlegel, and Schneider.

While it is fashionable to dismiss the *Oeconomica*, II as both trivial and bad economics, this view has never been shared by the best historians. Rostovtzeff has referred to "the remarkable scholar" who wrote the *Oeconomica*, which he calls "one of the most interesting products of Greek speculative thought combined with practical sagacity. . . . It is unique of its kind and therefore merits the attention and study that modern students of Greek economics are devoting to it" (*Social and Economic History of the Hellenistic World*, p. 74). August Boeckh used the *Oeconomica*, II perhaps more than any other single literary source in his classic work, *The Public Economy of Athens* (London: J. Murray, 1828).

[63] We prefer the rendering of this word as "growers" by the Loeb translator to that of "dealers" of the Forster translation as being closer to the probable economic

they would contract to supply him with their produce. On their quoting him a price lower than what they were charging the merchants, he offered them the full price they were accustomed to receive from others; and taking over the entire supply, sold it at a fixed rate of thirty-two drachmas (for the same measure).[64]

While Cleomenes of Alexandria was governor of Egypt, at a time when there was some scarcity in the land, but elsewhere a grievous famine, he forbade the export of grain. On the local governors representing that if there were no export of grain they would be unable to pay in the taxes, he allowed the export, but laid a heavy duty on the corn. By this means he obtained a large amount of duty from a small amount of export, and at the same time deprived the officials of their excuse.[65]

All these men . . . were underlings and confederates of Cleomenes, the former ruler of Egypt, who from the time he received the government did no small harm to your state, or rather to the rest of the Greeks as well, by buying up grain for resale and fixing its price, and in this he had these men as his confederates. Some of them would despatch the stuff from Egypt, others would sail in charge of the shipments, while still others would remain here in Athens and dispose of the consignments. Then those who remained here would send letters to those abroad advising them of the prevailing prices, so that if grain were dear in your market, they might bring it here, and if the price should fall, they might put in to some other port. This was the chief reason why the price of grain advanced; it was due to such letters and conspiracies. Well then, when these men despatched their ship from Athens, they left the price of grain here pretty high. . . . Afterwards, however, . . . when the ships from Sicily had arrived, and the prices of grain here were falling, and their ship had reached Egypt, the defendant straightway sent a man to Rhodes to inform his partner, Parmeniscus, of the state of things here, well knowing that his ship would be forced to touch at Rhodes. The outcome was that Parmeniscus discharged his cargo of grain at Rhodes and sold it there. . . . [66]

The two anecdotes from the *Oeconomica*, II should be read together as part of one story;[67] they describe the creation of the grain market

structure; Mahaffy, Tarn, Gernet, and Andreades translate it "growers"; Westermann concurs with the Forster translation. There seems little evidence for the existence of a class of native grain dealers in this period.

[64] *Oeconomica*, II, 1352b, 15–20.

[65] Ibid., 1352a, 16–23.

[66] Demosthenes, *Private Orations*, LVI (against Dionysodorous), 7–10.

[67] The authority for our so doing is B. A. van Groningen, "De Cleomene Naucratita," *Mnemosyne*, 1925. (Groningen later reversed his earlier judgment.)

from the Egyptian (or supply) side, while the Demosthenes passage describes the operation of the market as a whole. The precise dating of the *Oeconomica* incidents is open to question; Riezler dates them between 330 and 328 B.C., Groningen after 328, and Rostovtzeff 332–331 B.C.;[68] in any event, they occurred at some point during the great famine in the Greek world that we discussed in some detail above. The pseudo-Demosthenes text describes the operation at a slightly later date. The allusion to Cleomenes as the "former" ruler fixes the speech as after 323 B.C., the year of his death; the incident described in the speech took place either one or two years before the speech was made.[69] The speech, therefore, is evidence that Cleomenes' organization survived his death.

Egypt, according to the *Oeconomica* text, was affected by the general famine that was attacking the Greek world, but to a very much lesser extent; the ten-drachma price of grain mentioned in the one paragraph was unusually high, and must refer to the famine mentioned in the other paragraph. The difficulty in interpreting the incident is heightened by our uncertainty about the internal economic organization of Egypt in this period; we do not know whether ten drachmas was an internal or external, retail or wholesale, price. Certainly the bulk of the Egyptian population grew its own food at this period directly from the soil, either from their own holdings or from distributions in kind on large estates. While there is no evidence of the existence of any extensive trade in food, or of any numerous body of native traders,[70] markets did exist,[71] and the city population may have been provisioned from them; state power was probably too weak, in this rather anarchic period, to maintain any extensive redistributive structure. Traders were largely Greek, Syrian, or Phoenician; Rostovtzeff speaks of the growth of a native retailing class under Philadelphus as an innovation closely connected with the Ptolemaic reorganization of the economy.

This relative scarcity in Egypt, coming at a time of extreme

[68] Riezler, *Über Finanzen und Monopole*, p. 31, B. A. van Groningen, ed., *Aristotle, Le second livre de l'Economique*, p. 190; Rostovtzeff, *Hellenistic World*, p. 172.

[69] Demosthenes, *Private Orations*, LVI, 4, 5. Cf. the introduction in the Loeb edition, Volume 6, p. 193.

[70] Cf. A. Erman, *Life in Ancient Egypt*, p. 494; N. Flinders-Petrie, *Social Life in Ancient Egypt*, p. 20; Hartmann, *L'agriculture dans l'ancienne Egypte*, pp. 143–146; Dykmans, *Histoire économique et sosiale de l'ancienne Egypt*, Volume 2, p. 248.

[71] Herodotus, *The Persian Wars*, II, 35.

famine in Greece, must have threatened the supply available for internal sale, since the Greek traders (probably buying largely from great landowners) must have offered terms that made export sales much more profitable than local sales. Cleomenes therefore placed a firm embargo on all grain exports and then proceeded to take over the entire supply, calling in the growers and offering them the full price even though they were willing to take less. While the foreign middlemen were thus wiped out, the Egyptian farmers—as even Tarn admits—could not have been harmed, and probably they benefited.

The texts say nothing on this point, but we can reasonably assume that Cleomenes proceeded to reorganize internal distribution completely, under state control. Certainly the Ptolemies retained the state monopoly of the grain trade, and their magnificent centralized organization of the supply of all staples (with credit-transfers and checks drawn in kind on state warehouses), while also using private retailers, undoubtedly proceeded on lines anticipated by Cleomenes.

After reorganizing the internal supply, Cleomenes permitted the resumption of exports through a governmental monopoly, selling at a fixed price of 32 drachmas, certainly exceptionally high. This level suggests another inference, that Cleomenes reduced the internal price of grain substantially, subsidizing the operation by the export profits. This governmental monopoly created a minor administrative problem: the provincial governors, or nomarchs, complained that the absence of private trade in grain made it impossible for them to remit the taxes for which they were liable. Cleomenes thereupon permitted the resumption of private trade on a limited scale, taxing the merchants who participated in the operation. "By this means he obtained a large amount of duty from a small amount of export, and at the same time deprived the officials of their excuse."

How long the price remained fixed at 32 drachmas is a matter of conjecture; certainly it was substantially below that level at the time of the pseudo-Demosthenes speech. Indeed, the speech makes no allusion to such a price, although it accuses Cleomenes of raising the price of grain throughout all of Greece. We may reasonably assume, therefore, that the fixed price obtained for only a brief period, until Cleomenes' export organization had been fully established.

The organization was as simple as it was effective; it brought into being a price-making market under strict administrative surveillance. The participants were divided into four main categories:

some remained in Egypt, in charge of the actual export of grain; some sailed with the cargos; a third group was stationed in Rhodes, which was used as the seat of the operation; while the fourth group was stationed in the various Greek ports to handle the consignments and keep the Rhodian agents informed of price movements. Grain thus was shipped from Egypt to Rhodes, which was kept continually informed of the most recent prices in all Greek cities buying from the syndicate; the grain was then transshipped from Rhodes to those cities where prices, at last report, were highest, or else was sold at Rhodes. Under these conditions, the price at Rhodes would tend to reflect the average of prices in the Greek cities, i.e., the Rhodian price would tend to be a "world" market price, the various local prices tending to differ by the amount of transport charges. These are *no more than tendencies,* it should be noted. Thus, in the case at hand, a shipment intended for the Piraeus was sold at Rhodes when the arrival of a convoy of Sicilian grain at the Piraeus depressed prices there.

The success of this superbly conceived market organization may be measured by the strength and violence of the Athenian reaction to it, which had so great a part in establishing revulsion against Cleomenes through the ages. Boeckh, for example, refers to him as "this notorious extortioner in the grain trade." No charge could inflame an Athenian audience more than that of raising grain prices or diminishing supplies, and later generations have tended to share the feeling. But apart from the brief 32-drachma episode, the charge that Cleomenes forced grain prices to rise is naive and uncritical. The charge to that effect in the pseudo-Demosthenes speech cannot be taken at face value, for the speech itself proves the opposite.

> . . . if grain were dear in your market, they might bring it here, and if the price should fall, they might put in to some other port. *This was the chief reason why the price of grain advanced.* . . . (K. P.'s italics)

Diversion of supplies from areas of abundance to areas of scarcity, where price reflected relative scarcity or abundance, can only have had the effect of lowering the *average* price throughout Greece. Certainly it would tend to reverse a downward price movement in a surplus area, but it would, at the same time, lower the price in a scarcity area. For the first time, the prices in the various Greek cities were closely related to one another on a consistent basis; we can speak here of a true market price for the eastern Mediterranean, with supplies being moved according to price ratios. Maybe the net effect on Athens proper was a certain increase in prices, since Athenian political influence had previously brought Athens a larger share of supplies than her size alone warranted, but this was certainly not true for Greece as a whole. Prices did rise, compared with preceding years, but the major cause was the loss of the Bosporan supply. To the extent that the Greek food problem in this period resulted from faulty distribution rather than absolute shortage, as Rostovtzeff asserts, Cleomenes' scheme provided a solution; supplies now moved rationally in accord with actual need, and not erratically in accord with political influence or military power.

But this explains precisely why the Athenians reacted so violently. The fact that, in the long run, prices would be lower and supplies more regular under such a market organization could not—and did not—blind them to the fact that, in the long run, they would, as Lord Keynes once put it, all be dead—and dead as a *result* of that long-run mechanism. For them, relying on a market mechanism for their provisioning appeared incompatible with surviving as a political entity. It was not simply a matter of dependence on an "autonomous" mechanism, which would have been bad enough. Just as the world market of the nineteenth century depended on British military, financial, and political supremacy, and collapsed with the end of British power, so this market rested on Egyptian power and administrative genius. Suppliers moved in accordance with price ratios as a result of administrative decisions that took the prices into account, *not* as the "automatic" response of large numbers of profit-seeking entrepeneurs. Egypt dominated this market trade, just as Athens had dominated the administered trade of the preceding century. Indeed, the degree of rationality must have depended closely on the degree of administrative control, largely because of the communications problem. All the will in the world could not have moved supplies "rationally" without information about prices on which to base the movements. Under primitive conditions of transport and communication, only an elaborate organization was able to supply that information. Otherwise the price information, on which sellers acted, would frequently be out-of-date; conditions might be reversed before the seller acted. The pseudo-Demosthenes speech is evidence that Cleomenes' organization survived his death, by a few years at least. The Ptolemies retained the monopoly of the grain trade introduced by Cleomenes, and we find cordial diplomatic relations between

Egypt and the Bosporan kingdoms during Philadelphus' reign,[72] so we may safely assume that the market organization continued in some form in the next century.

The Athenians did more than react verbally, however, and the form of their reaction shows the nature of the problem. In the year 325/4—at the most five years after Cleomenes' operation began—we find Athens decreeing the establishment of a colony in the Adriatic (its precise location is still questioned) "in order that for all time the people may have a market and a source of corn-supply of their own."[73] Once again, in a last, desperate move, Athens turned westward for her corn supply. The decree makes its urgency clear. A fleet was established to maintain permanent protection against the Etruscan pirates; the colony was thus to be strengthened by a naval base. To hasten the execution of the decree, three gold crowns worth 500, 300, and 200 drachmas, respectively, were to be awarded to the first three trierarchs whose ships were ready to sail. A fine of 10,000 drachmas, sacred to Athena, was proclaimed for any magistrate or citizen who failed to fulfill any duties imposed by the decree; and while the council could vote any needed additions to the decree, it was forbidden to invalidate any of its clauses.

No more eloquent testimony to the complete antithesis between the two methods of provisioning can be imagined. Clearly, the Athenian resistance was doomed to failure. But the blow came, unexpectedly, from a new quarter: the force that was to doom for good any and all Athenian prospects of independence and power came out of the west, to which Athens now was looking. Rome was on the move, and in a few centuries was to shatter both the new market organization and the Greek attempts at administered trade. Rome assured her own food supply by bringing all the sources of supply—Sicily, Libya, Egypt, the Crimea, and Asia Minor— under her military and political control. The Athenian dream was realized in the power that was to transmit Hellenic civilization, in a much reduced form, to the modern age.

[72] M. Rostovtzeff, "Greek Sightseers in Egypt," *Journal of Egyptian Archaeology,* 14, 1928.

[73] Cf. Hasebroek, *Trade and Politics in Ancient Greece,* p. 107. Details are from Tod, *Greek Inscriptions,* Volume 2, pp. 284–289. Cf. also *Cambridge Ancient History,* Volume 6, p. 449; G. Glotz, *Histoire Grecque,* Volume 4, p. 211.

⊂≣ 16 ⊂≣

Money, Banking, and Finance

The ancient Greeks provide the first instance, to our knowledge, of the linking of trade and money uses with market elements. Yet to their mind, no natural affinity existed among these three members of the modern triad. They were familiar with trade—mainly gift trade and administered trade—and with the primitive money uses of payment and standard; even with specific market crowds, if you will, such as the welcome event of pirate crews harmlessly revealing themselves as exchange-eager foreigners whose display of goods before the king's house made them into an ad hoc supply crowd; domestically, local markets seem to have had the purpose of catering to the poor. But all these elements did not seem to belong together. For as long as reciprocity and redistribution prevail, trade, money, and markets do not form an institutional whole. Indeed, money and markets were hardly discernible, even separately.

I. MONEY

Neither the concept of money nor that of markets can be said to have existed. Rather, like trade itself, with which familiarity was far greater, each seemed to belong to different worlds of discourse, namely, *mores* and *devices*. As to *mores,* sharing and mutuality are of the very stuff of communal relationships. In regard to economic matters, ethics is no more than the intelligent manner of discussing reciprocative and redistributive attitudes. And yet, inextricably linked

253

with custom and morality, technique is the way, not merely of thinking about doing things, but actually of doing them. The Greek mind naturally moved on these two levels. Their alleged "ethical" approach to economics is a misunderstanding. It would be truer to call it anthropological, since its argument followed from a reasoned view of *mores*, supplemented by a description of *devices*. Although they did not overlook the connection to the modern mind, it is amazing how little they made of it.

Both Herodotus, in the fifth century, and (much more so) Aristotle, in the fourth, were already conscious of the connection between certain money uses and commercial trade. Yet the market mechanism entirely escaped them. Herodotus, without any discussion, went so far as to link the origin of coins with that of retailing. But he thought of coins as an ingenious device on which the Lydians had hit by virtue of their wealth of gold and their playfulness of mind, for both of which they were famed; as to the market habit, he clearly did not know what to make of it. As a problem of *mores*, it fell into the category of native customs (like sexual freedom or religious superstitions) which are sometimes too controversial to allow of even an unambiguous definition. In any event, he thought it significant enough to let his hero, the King of Kings (and a great man on all counts), Cyrus the Persian, make a memorable slip in regard to the market habit of his Greek adversaries. As to the common use of gold, Herodotus tells us only of Mount Tmolus near the capital, which sent river gold down its slopes; of the actual retailing of food in the market place of Sarids, he tells us nothing. Obviously, the term *kapelike* was self-explanatory. But for his explicit mention of the minting of coins, we might have confidently assumed from his account that gold dust was the common means of exchange in the market, as it was, for instance, in seventeenth-century Whydah on the Guinea Coast, or in the West Indies trade as late as the first quarter of the nineteenth century. But coins are an altogether different matter. Gold dust and food markets, linked through the persons of female marketers, are often found together, yet nowhere, to our knowledge, did the presence of gold dust lead to the introduction of gold coins; on the contrary, both the Whydahsians and the Ashantee and, up to the 1870s, most of the Sudan rejected the use of coins, especially if they were of gold. Even silver was demonetized, foreign silver coin being melted down and turned into ornaments; from Abyssinia to the Niger, the Maria Theresa dollar was the only exception. Instead, where gold dust was employed in the market, as in southwest China, eastern India, or the Guinea coast, it was linked with the use of cowrie money, never with the minting of gold coins. On the other hand, Herodotus appears to connect the premarital prostitution of young girls with the use of gold dust in the market. Precisely the same complex of *mores* is on record in the western Sudan of the early nineteenth century, and if our reading of Nadel's *Black Byzantium* is right, even in Nigerian Nupe of our days.

We will give Herodotus' account in toto. It shows how the *mores*-cum-devices pattern of early society still wholly absorbed the distinctive economic elements of coins and retailing:

> Lydia, unlike most other countries, scarcely offers any wonders for the historian to describe, except the gold-dust which is washed down from the range of Tmolus. It has, however, one structure of enormous size, only inferior to the monuments of Egypt and Babylon. This is the tomb of Alyattes, the father of Croesus, the base of which is formed of immense blocks of stone, the rest being a vast mound of earth. It was raised by the joint labour of the tradesmen, handicraftsmen, and courtesans of Sardis, and had at the top five stone pillars, which remained to my day, with inscriptions out on them, showing how much of the work was done by each class of workpeople. It appeared on measurement that the portion of the courtesans was the largest. The daughters of the common people in Lydia, one and all, pursue this traffic, wishing to collect money for their portions. They continue the practice till they marry; and are wont to contract themselves in marriage.[1]

Of the gold sand of Tmolus, we hear later on that it flows right across the market place of Sardis, the cradle of *kapelike*. Immediately following upon this, the dual innovations of retailing in markets and striking coins from elektron (a natural mixture of gold and silver) are mentioned, followed by a list of other devices and gadgets with whose invention the Lydians were credited.

> The Lydians have very nearly the same customs as the Greeks, with the exception that these last do not bring up their girls in the same way. So far as we have any knowledge they were the first nation to introduce the use of gold and silver coin and the first who sold goods by retail. They claim also the invention of all the games which are common to them with the Greeks. These they declare that they invented about the time

---

[1] Herodotus, *The Persian Wars*, I, 93.

when they colonized Tyrrhenia, an event of which they give the following account. In the days of Atys the son of Manes, there was great scarcity through the whole land of Lydia. For some time the Lydians bore the affliction patiently, but finding that it did not pass away, they set to work to devise remedies for the evil. Various expedients were discovered by various persons; dice, and knucklebones, and ball, and all such games were invented, except draughts the invention of which they do not claim as theirs. The plan adopted against the famine was to engage in games one day so entirely as not to feel any craving for food, and the next day to eat and abstain from games.[2]

While some Lydians employed the device of coined money to buy food in retail, at another occasion Lydians had been engaged in thinking up a series of devices as an alternative to the consumption of food. No people except the ancient Greeks could ever have been credited with the superlative deliberateness in the use of one's mind that this anecdote suggests. Yet the manner in which Herodotus centers his story on the inventiveness of the Lydians offers proof that he was not yet conversant with the category of the economic.

A century later, Aristotle returned to the identical theme of the origin of coins and *kapelike*. Although he treats his subject on the philosophical level, on looking more closely, we will perceive that his approach is still in terms of *mores* and devices. The Peloponnesian War left Attica impoverished; *metic* ways and *metic* occupations were spreading into the eastern Mediterranean. New forms of trade, in which men intended to make money and did so, were no longer infrequent among the well-born and respectable in Attica; local markets had been established in innumerable cities and had their share in men's normal environment. Yet there was still little to indicate that new order of things so familiar to us today, in which the market would become the universal organizer of trade and profit be recognized as a legitimate aim of activity.

In effect, in Aristotle's analysis of commercial trade, its origin, and its mechanism, there is still no mention of markets.[3] Trade was mainly organized through political means, and money was made by a clever use of the chances of war and politics, including booty, fines, bribes, confiscations, sequestrations, and the rest; the *agora* was a place for humble hucksters. Aristotle even failed to fall back on

[2] Ibid., I, 94.
[3] The remarks on Aristotle which follow are based on *Ethics*, V, and *Politics*, I.

Herodotus and his Lydians for the factual connection between small coins and retailing food. He may have doubted the authenticity of the source, although Herodotus was actually putting on record a most valuable item of the economic history of antiquity. Although Aristotle's interest centered on *kapelike,* he hardly mentioned the *agora* but spoke only of trade and, quite incidentally, of money. He consistently did this in such a manner as to leave no room for gain or profit made on exchange. He insisted that the human animal is originally self-sufficient, and trade is hence only the natural way of restoring self-sufficiency, when the aboriginal families, having become too populous, split up and settled apart. The ensuing barter aims to return to the state of self-sufficiency, not at any gain or profit. Custom or law sets the rate of the exchange in such a way that the natural friendliness, which prevails among the members of a community, is maintained. This requires that they reciprocate in the exchange of their produce or services, at a set rate proportionate to their relative status in the community. Operationally, the requirement is fulfilled if no gain is made on exchange and no obligations for either party ensue. Hence Aristotle's insistence, first, that only such amounts as happen to be needed, be bartered; second, that the exchange be in kind; third, that it should be performed *pari passu,* i.e., excluding credit.

Money serves as a device to ascertain the right amount of the goods to be exchanged. Goods bartered at equivalents are actually reckoned in terms of either one or another of the goods exchanged; whether the operation is carried out *pari passu* or not makes no difference. The standard is, in every case, the unit in which the other good is physically reckoned. Much can be said for a literal interpretation of the Old Testament phrase to "reckon" units of the commodity A "with" units of the commodity B. In bartering staples for staples, for instance, exchanging a shipload of corn for jars of oil or wine stacked in the gates, the procedure might have been to count the amount of the grain by the basketload dumped into the stores of the gates, simultaneously releasing units of wine or oil from the gates, in exchange. Such a procedure would save much of the time and effort that would be taken up by measuring the amount of staples contained in the bottoms or the gates, making sure at the same time that at all stages the partners could stop the procedure without owing anything to each other. Coined money units, then, are a device that should make it easier to employ units as a standard.

Convention enters only insofar as the standard may be conveniently selected. In all this there is a striking absence of any mention of the employment of coins in the market, of the special function of small denominations in food markets, of the limited circulation of local money, of the role played by arbitrary convention in setting the rates of local money in terms of money employed in foreign trade, or any other feature of market dealings.

Hence the spectacular failure of Plato or Aristotle to master conceptually what we would call the elements of the economic phenomena. To them, these did not present themselves in that character.

II. COINAGE

The fundamental distinction in Greek money uses was the distinction between local and external money; the dichotomy was of the sharpest. Silver coins of small denomination and, particularly after the fourth century, bronze coins, were used for local trade or the *agora,* while silver coins of larger denomination, such as the stater, were used in external trade.[4]

But the distinction was not simply one of coin size. One might naturally expect to find coins of larger denomination used in foreign trade. The point is that the large coins used in external trade circulated almost entirely at their bullion value.[5] The contrary was true of the local coinages (*nomisma epichorion*). While the value of a small local coin might be its metallic content, this was not the significant factor; what gave the coin its value was the authority of the issuing city.

> . . . if a piece of metal received the stamp which indicated that it was issued as a drachma by the governing body of a city, it was immaterial, for the purposes of trade in that city, what the metal value was; and in some place plated coins were struck simultaneously with those of good metal, while in many there is evidence to be found in the coins them-

----

[4] Cf. J. G. Milne, *Greek and Roman Coins* (London: Methuen and Co., 1939), pp. 23, 107–108. P. Gardner, *A History of Ancient Coinage, 700–300 B.C.* (Oxford: Clarendon Press, 1918), p. 41.

[5] Gardner, *Ancient Coinage,* pp. 3, 56–57.

selves that the mint-masters paid little regard to the weight of the coins they issued.[6]

Bronze coins were usually token money; their use began in Athens around 400 B.C. but spread very rapidly throughout the Greek world. The fact that plated and genuine coins circulated side by side at the same value is convincing evidence that local coinages were essentially token coins whose value was fixed by state authority. Cities that did not have a supply of raw metal frequently struck their coins on old coins that were used as blanks, the old type being defaced by hammering or melting.[7] The Greek cities of Asia Minor did not even bother to restamp, but placed a secondary stamp on a coin, thus altering its value. This method was used at Byzantium for a long period.[8] In the absence of markets, Gresham's Law is by no means a universal phenomenon.

Much more light is shed by several anecdotes in the pseudo-Aristotelian *Oeconomica*, II on the ease with which new coinages were introduced, old ones recalled or altered in value; the incidents cover a wide range of time and territory. The first marks an important episode in the early history of Athenian coinage. It bears out the suggestion that the intriguing (but obscure) story of Athenian coins may hold the key to the roles of both the early aristocracy and the *tyrannis*. The *Oeconomica*, II relates the story of a coinage change instituted by Hippias, Peisistratus' son and successor, who

> declared the coinage current among the Athenians to be unacceptable, and fixing a price for it, ordered it to be brought to him. But after there had been a meeting to consider the striking of a new denomination, he re-issued the same silver.[9]

The story has been variously interpreted. Seltman suggests that the text contrasts the recall of *coins* with the reissue of the same *silver*.[10]

---

[6] Ibid., pp. 2–3.

[7] Milne, *Greek and Roman Coins*, pp. 36–37.

[8] Ibid., p. 75.

[9] Pseudo-Aristotle, *Oeconomica*, II, 1347a, 8ff.

[10] C. T. Seltman, *Athens, Its History and Coinage* (Cambridge: At the University Press, 1924), pp. 77–78; cf. Gardner, *Ancient Coinage*, p. 159; B. V. Head, *Historia Numorum* (Oxford: Clarendon Press, 1887), pp. 369–370: A. R. Burns, *Money and Monetary Policy in Early Times* (New York: Knopf, 1927), p. 363.

The incident, in his view, refers to the supplanting of the old Eupatrid coinage by the newer owl issues of the Peisistratids. It is expressly stated that revaluation was considered at a meeting, probably
of the assembly, and rejected.[11] What happened, it seems, was that
the old coins were recalled at a slight discount, melted down, and
then restruck and issued at face value. The incident would then mark
no less than the liquidation of the monetary legacy of semifeudal
anarchy.

The ease with which a token currency could be substituted for a
precious metal is illustrated by a story concerning the Asia Minor
coast town of Clazomenae.[12] The city being unable to pay a troop of
mercenary soldiers their pay of 20 talents, the money was advanced
by the mercenary generals, and the city paid annual interest of four
talents to the generals:

> But finding that they did not reduce the principal and that they were
> continually spending money to no purpose, they struck an iron coinage
> to represent a sum of twenty talents of silver, and then distributing it
> among the richest citizens in proportion to their wealth they received in
> exchange an equivalent sum of silver. Thus, the individual citizens had
> money to disburse for their daily needs and the state was freed from
> debt. They then paid them interest out of their revenues and continually
> divided it up and distributed it in proper proportions, and called in the
> iron coinage.[13]

Rather than pay annual interest of four talents without any
prospects of repayment, the city, in short, resorted to a forced loan
from its wealthy citizens to repay the entire loan owed to the generals. To make advancing the taxes an honorific duty of the rich was of
the essence of the liturgy, which was called *proeisphora*. It was here
made relatively painless and costless through the expedient of issuing new iron coins to the lenders, in proportion to their loan to the
state and at the same value as the borrowed coins. The lenders thus
suffered no loss of income. The iron coins were retired, probably
over a five-year period, by allocating the sum which had formerly
been paid in interest to the generals, i.e., four talents of the iron

---

[11] The extant coins lend no support to Head's assumption that the light Euboic
standard was here substituted for the heavy.

[12] Dated about 360 B.C. by van Groningen, and 387 B.C. by Riezler.

[13] Pseudo-Aristotle, *Oeconomica*, II, 1348b, 23 ff.

coins were replaced each year by the traditional silver coins.[14] To assume with Riezler and Burns that the iron coins would depreciate in value because the supply of money was thereby increased is to take too much for granted. If the silver was paid to the mercenary generals—any other assumption is dubious—there need not have been any increase in the domestic money supply. In any event, to postulate that an increase in the supply of coins would, as a matter of course, bring about a depreciation in their value is to make the anachronistic assumption of a market system in which prices fluctuate freely in response to shifting demand.

Our own view[15] that the iron coins circulated *at their face value* is strongly supported by two other incidents of a comparable sort, one earlier, one more or less contemporary. The earlier case concerns an issue of tin coinage by Dionysius of Syracuse about 400 B.C.

> And when he was in need of money he struck a coinage of tin, and calling an assembly together he spoke at great length in favor of the money which had been coined; and they, even against their will, decreed that everyone should regard any of it that he accepted as silver and not as tin.[16]

This closely parallels the Clazomenae episode; its authenticity cannot be doubted.[17] The discussion in the assembly probably referred to the relation of the nominal value of this coinage to its metallic content. According to Pollux its nominal value was four times the metallic content.[18]

---

[14] Cf. the commentaries of van Groningen and Riezler, *ad locum*, and A. R. Burns, *Money in Early Times*, p. 375.

[15] Held also by van Groningen.

[16] Pseudo-Aristotle, *Oeconomica*, II, 1349a, 33 ff.

[17] The passage affords an explanation for the otherwise puzzling fact that the series of Syracusan silver tetradrachms breaks off at this date. While no tin coins as such have been found, this provides no negative evidence, since tin oxidizes rapidly in the earth. A debased imitation of the silver decadrachm dating from this period has been found, however; the coin is bronze, but was originally washed over with tin, hence may be the coinage referred to. Nor is it an inferior imitation; rather, it was struck by "the great monetary artist" who then had charge of the Syracusan mint. Dionysius' reign is considered by numismatists to be "the most brilliant and prolific period" of Syracusan coinage. A. J. Evans, "The finance and coinage of the elder Dionysius," in E. A. Freeman, *History of Sicily*, Volume 4, pp. 230–238; cf. van Groningen and Riezler, *ad locum*.

[18] Pollux, VIII, 79.

On the way in which the circulation of emergency token coinage was assured, more light is thrown by a story about the Athenian general Timotheus; it is from the same period as the Clazomenae episode.

> Timotheus, the Athenian, when he was at war with the Olynthians, and in need of money, struck a bronze coinage and distributed it to the soldiers. When they protested, he told them that the merchants and retailers would all sell their goods on the same terms as before. He then told the merchants, if they received any bronze money, to use it again to buy the commodities sent in for sale from the country and anything which was brought in as plunder, and said that if they brought him any bronze money which they had left over, they should receive silver for it.[19]

That the story is true cannot be doubted.[20] The details are provided by Polyaenus, who offers parallels and repeats the *Oeconomica*, II. In this version, Timotheus

> mixed the Macedonian money with the Cyprian brass, and from thence struck a new coin, of the value of five drachmae, one fourth of which consisted of silver, and the rest was an alloy of brass.[21]

Polyaenus tells of a similar expedient by Timotheus on another occasion, when the Athenian army was short of money. The general persuaded the sutlers to accept what our translation calls his "drafts" in lieu of currency, pledging eventual redemption in coin.[22] Regling has suggested that these were pieces of pottery bearing Timotheus' personal seal; they functioned, therefore, very much as a token coinage. Polyaenus has still another case, this time involving the Macedonian general Perdiccas who,

> when his coffers were very low, struck a coin of brass mixed with tin, with which he paid his army. The money, bearing the royal impression, the sutlers took as currency: and it bore no value beyond the king's domain, he took it again in payment for corn and the products of the country.[23]

Oeconomica, II provides us also with an example of the restriking

---

[19] Pseudo-Aristotle, *Oeconomica*, II, 1350a, 24 ff.
[20] Cf. Riezler and van Groningen, *ad locum*.
[21] Polyaenus, *Strategems*, III, 10, 14.
[22] Ibid., III, 10, 1.
[23] Ibid., IV, 10, 2.

or countermarking of coins. Dionysius, when a loan from his citizenry came due, ordered them to turn in their coins.

> When the money had been brought, he re-issued it again after stamping it afresh so that each drachma had the value of two drachmae, and paid back the original debt and the money which they brought him on this occasion.[24]

While none of the extant Syracusan coins show signs of countermarking at double the value, the substance of the passage is borne out by Pollux's reference to a reduction of the Syracusan talent from 24 to 12 drachmas, which probably occurred during Dionysius' reign.[25] This is a mere conjecture on our part; but Polyaenus mentions that the very same device was used by the Bosporan king, Leucon, who called in all coins, restruck them at double the value, and reissued coins of the same total value as turned in, thus keeping half for himself.[26]

The details of these stories are less important than the picture they present. To the modern mind it is a most surprising one. For there is complete absence of any indication of currency depreciation or price inflation, of "good" coins being forced out of circulation by "bad" ones—indeed, there is hardly any hint of opposition or unrest caused by what we would think of as audacious manipulations. The worst violator of modern monetary morality, Dionysius, appears, in the perspective of history, as "a sober and temperate tyrant"[27] whose reign marks the "most brilliant and prolific period of Syracusan coinage."[28] He was a "drastic and ingenious financier" whose policies saved Syracuse from destruction at the hand of Carthage.[29]

The explanation is, of course, simple. The nonmarket, integrated economies of these communities were held together and run by redistributive and reciprocative methods. An elaborate network of social and territorial divisions made business arrangements workable, which were initiated by the magistrates and enabled them to

---

[24] Pseudo-Aristotle, *Oeconomica*, II, 1349b, 28 ff.
[25] Pollux, IX, 87; cf. Gardner, *Ancient Coinage*, pp. 414–415, and Evans, "Finance of Dionysius," p. 238.
[26] Polyaeus, *Strategems*, VI, 9, 1.
[27] Freeman, *History of Sicily*, Volume 4, p. 5.
[28] Ibid., p. 234.
[29] Burns, *Money in Early Times*, p. 368.

deal smoothly with what we would regard as highly complex ventures of public finance.

III.   LOCAL AND EXTERNAL COINAGE

The distinction between local and external coins, vital to an understanding of Greek money uses, should not be overdone. Such a dichotomy was not uniquely Greek. It is reflected in such diverse sources as the Talmud and the relatively modern practices of the west African coast. What is remarkable in the Greek experience is the degree to which the traditional separation of local and external coinage was overcome. While in some west African cases food could be bought only with cowries, never with gold, this was not true for Athens, or Greece in general. The two types of coins, the local and the foreign, while institutionally separate, were nevertheless interchangeable. Nor was this interchangeability limited to the relationship between the internal and the external coinage of one city; the external coinages of any two cities were interchangeable, as, perhaps, were their local coinages.

To provide such capacity of being interchangeable was, perhaps, the major contribution of that Greek economic innovation, the trapezite banker.[30] He was an occupational appendage of the use of coins in early times. Like small copper coins, the trapezite banker did not appear much before 400 B.C.; to our knowledge, both made their appearance in Athens but spread throughout the Greek world with utmost rapidity, both coins and moneychangers being facts of public, not of private, life. Seated at his table in the *agora*, the trapezite banker made it a simple matter to change large silver staters or tetradrachms into small copper obols or half-obols. And, seated at their tables on the *deigma*, another group made it a simple matter to change foreign coins into Athenian coins, and Athenian into foreign. Xenophon was thus able to proclaim that everyone wants to sell at the Peiraeus, because from there the foreigners can take home money

---

[30] We follow Westermann's usage of the dual Greek–English term here, so as clearly to distinguish the primitive operations of the Greek *trapezites* from the elaborate operations of the modern banker. We are much indebted to the insights provided by Westermann in his "Warehousing and Trapezite Banking," *Journal of Economic and Business History*, Vol. 3, No. 1.

rather than only merchandise. Moneychanging formed part of the services provided by port of trade authorities.

Testing and changing coins were certainly the original official functions of the Greek banker; the word *trapeza* meant the bench at which he sat and changed coins, as our own term, derived from the Italian, refers to the *bench* at which the medieval moneychanger sat. While the trapezite bankers took on other functions, testing and changing remained major activities and were often made an express state monopoly during the Hellenistic period. These other banking functions facilitated the growth of money uses and their linkage to trade; we must be careful, however, not to exaggerate their level or their importance.

A most useful function performed by the trapezite bankers, particularly in the troubled period after the beginning of the fourth century, was that of acting as depositories for money, valuable articles, and treasure, as well as legal documents. Keeping coins or treasure in the unprotected Greek house must have entailed some danger during the social strife of this period, hence they were frequently deposited with bankers. However, a good many coin hoards that have been found in recent years come from private houses.

A deposit, when made, was largely for safekeeping, and it is unlikely that interest was paid—unless by the depositor. Certainly, the deposits were not used by the banker unless the depositor authorized such use; in that case, the banker acted primarily as an agent for the depositor in making loans. A deposit remained the property of the depositor and did not merge in general funds; even when changing coins, the banker would place the coins in bags and seal them, nor could he make any use of them. That bankers did make loans is certain; but this was either on order of the depositor or from the banker's own funds. Certainly bankers could not have regularly made loans on security of real property, since the bankers were almost without exception slaves, freedmen, or at best, aliens—and only a citizen could own landed property. Foreclosure, therefore, would be impossible, as was recognized by the banker, Phormion, when he leased the bank from his former master, Pasion. Pasion, a former slave who had been granted citizenship by a grateful Athens, had lent 50 talents on the security of real property, of which 11 talents were bank funds, the rest his private funds. Since his former slave, Phormion, could not foreclose, Pasion continued to hold the mortgages on the 11 talents after he leased the bank, while the bank remained indebted to Pasion.[31] And in Isocrates' *Trapeziticus*, in which Pasion, depicted as a scoundrel, is alleged to have defaulted on a seven-talent deposit because he had lent it out, this action is evidently treated as an illegal and underhand matter that Pasion must keep close. Thus, Pasion is pictured as pleading with the depositor "to forgive him and to keep his misfortune secret, in order that he, as receiver of deposits, might not be shown to have been culpable in such matters."[32]

When a banker made a loan, therefore, he did not *create credit.* Yet apart from the use of credit instruments, such as bills of exchange, it is credit creation that is the essence of the modern bank loan. The Greek banker either lent his own capital or placed deposits that had been authorized for such use—in which case the loan had to be recorded as made from a specific depositor's coins. In general, the scale must have been very small. We should not be misled by the extent of Pasion's operations. They were notoriously exceptional; no other bank approached Pasion's in scope. And even Pasion was also a pawnbroker, lending money on the security of bronze vessels, and even lending blankets, bedding, silverware, and goblets to a distinguished citizen entertaining foreign rulers.[33] How important bank loans were is hard to judge; it is significant, however, that the orations of Demosthenes show no single case of a sea-loan advanced by a banker, and sea-loans were the most important type of lending operation.[34]

Apart from testing and changing coins, the most important banking function appears to have been facilitating payments. One of the reasons why only *in rem* transactions were known to antiquity was the impossibility of securing a deferred payment, in the purely operational sense of making sure that the money to be paid over would be equivalent to the stipulated sum. It was possible to deposit

[31] Demosthenes, *Private Orations,* trans. A. T. Murray (Cambridge: Harvard University Press, 1964), XXXVI, 5–6; cf. also, Westermann, "Warehousing and Trapezite Banking."

[32] Isocrates, *Trapeziticus,* XVII, 18.

[33] Demosthenes, *Private Orations,* XLIX, 21, LIII, 9.

[34] Two qualifications may seem to be needed. In one instance, a banker, Heracleides, lends 30 minas on the security of a ship in the harbor; this is not a sea-loan in the strict sense, however. (Dem., XXXIII, 7.) In another instance, it is alleged that Pasion had made a sea-loan to a servant of the general, Timotheus; Pasion argues, however, that he had actually advanced money to Timotheus to pay the freight bill on a gift of timber to Timotheus from the Macedonian king. (Dem. XLIX, 26.)

a sum of money with a banker for the purpose of making a payment at some later time to a third party. This did not involve either a transfer of credit, as in payment by check, or a credit transfer through a bookkeeping transaction by the bank—the *giro* transfer that played so important a part in medieval European trade and finance. In Greece—as in the early European deposit banks—the identical coins that were deposited were transferred to the payee. We have one completey documented case. A merchant from Heracles, Lycon, before leaving Athens on a business trip, deposited 16 minas and 40 drachmas in Pasion's bank, to be paid to his partner, Cephisiades of Scyrus, on the latter's return. The deposit was made in the presence of two citizens, who were also to introduce Cephisiades to Pasion. Pasion recorded the identity of the depositor and the amount and the directions for payment, as well as the names of those who will identify the payee. The speaker observed that this is the common procedure.[35] Five months after the deposit, Cephisiades is introduced to Pasion and the payment made. No credit is created or extended in this transaction, yet such a facility must have greatly aided the development of transactions covering a period of time. The fact that the bank made payments only in the presence of witnesses facilitated payment even when no time interval was involved: this was a means of insuring publicity to the transaction as well as convenience.[36]

Pasion played a part in another instance in which payment over a wide distance was facilitated. A young man from the Bosporan kingdom, who had been sent to Athens by his father to trade and study, arranged to get money out of the kingdom by using Pasion's credit. Stratocles, a merchant about to sail for the Bosporus, left a large sum of money with the youth in return for a letter to the youth's father directing him to pay the merchant an equivalent amount on his arrival. This arrangement was possible because Pasion guaranteed payment of the principal and accrued interest on Stratocles' return to Athens, should the youth's father default.[37] The merchant's advantage lay in avoiding the risks of traveling with a large sum of gold: by leaving his money in Athens, he could arrange to be reimbursed at his point of arrival. This is obviously a primitive arrange-

---

[35] Demosthenes, *Private Orations*, LII, 3 ff.

[36] Ibid., XXX, 23; XXXVIII, 12; XLVIII, 51, 57, 64.

[37] Isocrates, *Trapeziticus*, XVII, 35–37.

ment in which the banker acted merely as guarantor; it is not a credit transaction. Also, such transactions were occasional and accidental. Thus, when the youth's father, the prime minister of the kingdom, sent him to Athens to study, he provided him with grain ships to provide money on his arrival in Athens. Were bills of exchange or letters of credit regular affairs, we could not imagine so cumbersome an operation to finance a boy's college education! The letter of credit is no different from the way in which Cicero financed his son's education in Athens through his friend Atticus several centuries later.

Bank payment and transfers remained a manipulation of specific coins right down through the Hellenistic period. In Ptolemaic Egypt, where Greek banking methods reached their highest pinnacle, no *giro* transfers of money ever existed—but *giro* transfers of grain and other staples were made through the state banks on a very elaborate scale.[38] No more powerful evidence of the superiority of administrative methods, compared with the primitive level of the money uses of the time, could be adduced.

Perhaps the most convincing evidence of the absence of any sort of credit mechanism based on banking is the collection of devices used by earlier statesmen "for the replenishment of the treasury." The *Oeconomica*, II is intended in the first place as a manual of public finance, not as a scandal sheet; the anecdotes related "seemed to us by no means lacking in utility, being capable from time to time of application by others to the business they themselves have in hand."[39] Its originality of conception is as striking as that of the *Ways and Means* of Xenophon, which first developed the idea that wealth might be a product of peace as well as of war. The *Oeconomica*, II puts forward the novel idea of a balanced household, i.e., the proposition that state or individual expenditures should be kept within the limits of revenue; this idea, the author stresses, should receive "more than cursory attention."[40]

If bank loans played any sort of role in the credit system of this period, we would expect some mention of state loans from bankers in a discussion of emergency finance methods. Municipal and state loans, after all, were the foundation on which European banking

---

[38] Westermann, "Warehousing and Trapezite Banking," p. 49.
[39] Pseudo-Aristotle, *Oeconomica*, II, 1346a, 30.
[40] Ibid., 1346a, 15 ff.

developed from the late medieval period on. Yet in the 41 groups of anecdotes—more than 60 stories in all—there is not a single incident in which a state or ruler solves financial difficulties by borrowing from a banker. The devious and tortuous methods actually used prove conclusively the lack of any sort of developed system of credit.

Some of the more interesting expedients will suffice. The coinage incidents, which have been discussed above, were partly or wholly revenue-producing devices. They were supplemented by a host of other techniques, frequently involving some sort of forced loan to the state by either a special group or by the citizenry at large; interest on such loans was generally paid by the state. Thus, the city of Clazomenae, when "suffering from a dearth of grain and scarcity of funds," ordered all citizens who had stores of olive oil, an abundant crop in that region, to lend them to the state at interest. The city then hired ships and sent the oil to the emporia from which it bought its grain, apparently pledging the oil as security against the purchase price of the grain.[41]

On a similar occasion, the city of Heraclea financed a war with the help of a forced loan made in kind. The city was about to send an expedition of 40 triremes but lacked sufficient funds to pay the fleet. They therefore "bought up all the merchants' stock of corn and oil and wine and other marketable commodities, agreeing to pay at a future date"—obviously a forced loan, although the merchants were apparently not unwilling, since they "had disposed of their cargos without breaking bulk." Heraclea sent the commodities along with the fleet under the charge of public officials. The sailors were paid two weeks in advance (instead of for the entire expedition), and purchased their needs from the public officials in charge of the food and supplies.

> In this way, the money was collected before the leaders again paid their men; so that the same payment sufficed until the expedition returned home.[42]

That is, the men were paid again with the money they had spent on provisions, this circular process being repeated for the duration of the campaign.

The city of Ephesus, perhaps because the reconstruction of the

[41] Ibid., 1348b, 17 ff.
[42] Ibid., 1347b, 2 ff.

temple of Artemis had impoverished the city, passed a sumptuary law forbidding women to wear gold ornaments and ordering them to lend the gold to the State; the city also inscribed on a temple pillar the names of citizens who gave the city a fixed sum.[43] Dionysius of Syracuse raised funds, about 399 B.C., through a very similar expedient: first he ordered all gold ornaments to be brought to the temple of Demeter and appropriated them as a loan from the goddess. After a period of time, more gold apparently having been accumulated, he permitted the women to wear gold jewelry on dedication of a specified sum to the temple.[44] The use of sumptuary laws as a financial expedient was general throughout antiquity, as witness the story of the golden calf in *Exodus* 35. Similar measures in Rome are related by Livy and Strabo. Borrowing from temple treasuries was, of course, the oldest and most usual method of meeting financial emergencies, the most famous cases being Attica's use of Athena's treasure.

An interesting story, dated sometime between 361 and 348, involves the use of market elements to make use of a forced loan. The city of Mende, needing funds during the Olynthian War, ordered its citizens to sell all their slaves in excess of one male and one female on behalf of the state.[45] It is probable that the slaves were delivered to the state, which itself arranged the sale, although this is not vital to the understanding of the story. In any case, the success of the device presupposes the existence of a fairly well developed slave market.

In fact, a small group of incidents in the *Oeconomica,* II point to the ways in which the market institution could be used to solve a financial difficulty. One is tempted to conclude that one of the main reasons why the Greeks could afford to rely on highly imperfect markets to provision their cities was the ease with which the *agora* could at any time be transformed into a redistributive mechanism.

On one occasion, when its grain market was not being supplied and the city was financially impoverished, Byzantium seized the grain ships in the Black Sea, detaining the merchants and forcing them to sell their grain to the citizens in retail quantities. When, after a time, the merchants protested against their detention, the city raised grain prices by 10%, paying the proceeds to the merchants

---

[43] Ibid., 1349a, 9 ff.
[44] Ibid., 1349a, 15 ff.
[45] Ibid., 1350a, 12 ff.

as an indemnity.[46] The novelty of this procedure lay not in seizing the grain ships, a fairly common occurrence, but rather in forcing the merchants to remain. Normally, the city would have bought the seized cargos at a fixed priced; lacking the funds, it was retailing the grain and paying the merchants piecemeal as the money was received.

Anticipating an attack at the end of the fifth century, the city of Lampsacus raised prices in the *agora* by 50%, the state receiving the difference between the former and the new prices. "The price of barley meal being the four drachmas for a medimn, they instructed the retailers to sell it at six drachmas. Oil, which was at three drachmas for a *chous*, was to be sold at four drachmas and a half, and wine and other commodities at a proportionate increase. In this way the retailer got the original price, while the State took the addition and filled its treasury."[47] A similar proposal was made to the Athenians at a later date: an otherwise obscure figure named Pythocles suggested that the state buy all the lead from the Laurium mines at the conventional price of two drachmas and resell the lead at a fixed price of six drachmas.[48]

The Hellespontian city of Selymbria anticipated Cleomenes' grain export monopoly by a generation. Since the city had abundant stores of grain, it ordered all citizens to deliver their stocks in excess of a year's supply to the state, at a fixed price. This grain was exported at a fixed price yielding the state appropriate revenue.[49]

Use of market methods as a means of supplying financial needs seems to have become more prevalent during the fourth century. Thus, the Athenian general, Timotheus, met his budget, during the siege of Samos in 366/5 B.C., by confiscating the produce of the country and selling it to the Samians themselves.[50] This sophisticated device seems to earn the admiration of the author of the *Oeconomica*, II; in effect, Timotheus may have had to create a market in order to do so. The story has several nonmilitary parallels in the *Oceonomica*, II. Thus, when the Naxian tyrant, Lygdamis, found difficulty in selling, except at very low prices, the confiscated property of a group he had exiled, he sold the property to the exiles themselves.[51]

[46] Ibid., 1346b, 30 ff.
[47] Ibid., 1347a, 32 ff.
[48] Ibid., 1353a, 15 ff.
[49] Ibid., 1348b, 33 ff.
[50] Ibid., 1350b, 5 ff. (cf. also Polyaenus, XXX, 10, 9).
[51] Ibid., 1349b, 1 ff.

The story recalls Herodotus' remarks on the Athenians' unwilling-
ness to buy the Peisistratids' property on their expulsion from
Athens, for fear of their future return and retaliation. Unable to raise
a loan from the Syracusans, Dionysius sold his palace furnishings
and then confiscated them from the purchasers—a reverse twist to
Lygdamis' technique.[52] Antimenes of Rhodes, an aide of Alexander
in charge of the state roads around Babylonia, transformed the redistributive structure of the area into market elements. Making use of a
law requiring the satraps to keep the royal storehouses along the
roads filled, he sold stores from the magazines to any army or any
other body of men passing through the country.[53] This is an interesting marriage of Rhodian marketing and eastern redistributive
methods. Somewhat earlier in the century, the Athenian general,
Iphicrates, transplanted Athenian insights to Thrace. Having married the daughter of the Thracian king, Cotys, Iphicrates helped the
consolidation of Cotys' power after the beginning of his reign. According to the *Oeconomica*, II, Iphicrates suggested that Cotys

> order each of his subjects to sow for him a piece of land bearing 4½
> bushels. A large quantity of grain was thus gathered, for the price of
> which, when brought to the emporia on the coast, the king obtained as
> much money as he wanted.[54]

Here again we see a close fusion of redistributive and market elements. Probably the main innovation was that the Thracian king
organized the sale of the grain himself, rather than relying on passive
sale to Greek and Phoenician merchants.

---

[52] Ibid., 1346b, 7 ff.
[53] Ibid., 1353a, 24 ff.
[54] Ibid., 1351a, 18 ff.

17

"Capitalism" in Antiquity

Economic life in antiquity reached its height under Hellenism in the eastern, and under the Roman Empire in the western Mediterranean. The Hellenistic period is counted from the conquest of Asia by Alexander the Great about 332 B.C., while the flowering of the Roman Empire falls into the first two centuries A.D. These five centuries are the high period of ancient "capitalism." However, it was also the height of noncapitalist economic activity. From the point of view of the forms of integration, it should be said that both exchange and redistributive forms reach their highest ancient development, either one or the other alternatingly dominant, according to the region envisaged.

In the eastern Mediterranean, trade shifts toward the southeast, with Alexandria, Antioch, and Seleucia as its centers, while the island of Rhodes and later, to a minor extent, Delos are the great entrepots of maritime trade. Attica is now off the great sea lanes, and the Piraeus loses its importance.

But while international trade, especially the grain, slave, and luxury trade, develops on an unprecedented scale, supported by a strong upsurge of banking activities—mainly Rhodian and Delian— at the same time Ptolemaic Egypt produces, under Macedonian Greek rule, the most complete system of a marketless, centrally planned economy the world has ever seen. Ptolemaic Egypt was regarded by contemporaries as a country of fabulous wealth whose civilization

273

surpassed its contemporaries in almost every respect. This should be
noted in order to understand the superlative prestige of Egyptian
ways, including their business methods during this period. We
might, in contrast, sum up the Greek contribution to human
economy by saying that the Greeks almost singlehandedly developed
both types of economy—the market and exchange type as well as the
planning and redistributive type—to their highest form reached up
till then. Both influenced Roman development, which followed first
in the wake of the Greek trading and coined money practices used in
local markets, together with banking and bookkeeping as practiced
by the Greeks of Southern Italy. Later the Ptolemaic techniques of a
refined redistribution based on storage and accountancy "in kind,"
influenced the methods employed by the Roman Empire in reorganizing their administration and finance.

Incidentally, Hellenism shows a combination of planning and
marketing that has puzzled the marketing intellect unduly.
Cleomenes of Naukratis was not only the organizer of the Egyptian
grain export monopoly, and most probably of a domestic governmental monopoly of the grain trade as well, but he was also the
organizer of the "world" corn market, and thus of the most important
market institution of the ancient world. But who other than the
greatest supplier of grain could have possessed the means of achiev-
ing so enormous a task, and how, except through a farsighted and
assiduously pursued effort to set up world information agencies and
shipping service with the help of the state, could it have been carried
into effect? (By the time Lloyd's list was first published by private
merchants, Cromwell had passed the Navigation Acts and the British
navy had gained the policing of the seven seas.)

In the eastern Mediterranean, this combination of domestic
planning and governmental trade with an increasingly free trading
activity in the foreign field continued to dominate. It is primarily in
regard to this development that Michael Rostovtzeff has queried
whether we are not witnessing a development which, but for political intervention, would have developed into the type of industrial
capitalism we are familiar with. Indeed, perhaps except for the forcible destruction and brutal spoliation of the East by Roman armies
and proconsuls, the East would have altogether avoided the great
recession of the early centuries of our era, which engulfed the Roman
Empire. Even so, the recession did not affect the East with anything
like the same strength that it did the West, and in Byzantium the

Eastern Roman Empire survived by a thousand years the fate of Western Rome.

Be that as it may, in the ancient West trade and market methods never reached the same level as in the East. The overall story of Rome reveals a high pitch of speculative business and a seemingly high development of exchange techniques toward the end of the Republic, followed by a general reversion to redistribution, economy in kind, and an eclipse of markets.

Here we meet one of the most important problems of the study of antiquity: the problem of the factors responsible for the decline of the Roman Empire. According to Rostovtzeff, this is identical with the problem of the character of capitalism in antiquity. As he sees it, under Hellenism and the first period of the Empire, ancient capitalism was about to flower into modern industrial capitalism when the decline of the Empire bore the economy down in disaster. This implies that ancient capitalism was broadly of the same character as modern capitalism, and that the decline of the Roman Empire was the factor that interrupted this development. Rostovtzeff argues that the actual cause of that decline, and therefore also of the recession of capitalism, was of a general order not attributable to any single cause, but that if any one single cause was to be emphasized, it should be the overdose of planning which, with its accompanying bureaucracy and all round restraint, debilitated both the Empire and its nascent capitalism.[1]

Max Weber, on the contrary, insisted that capitalism in Greece and Rome was altogether different in character from its modern counterpart—it was grounded "primarily in politics," not in economics. That is why political reform under the Empire — peace and rational government — spelled ruin to this essentially non-productive type of capitalism, based on booty, slave labor, and the private exploitation of such governmental functions as taxation and public works. (Weber had in mind here three main revenue sources of equestrian capitalism: tax fanning, contracting for public works, and lease of public domains.) As to the decline of the Roman Empire — a later and essentially different development — it was inherent in the coastal character of Roman civilization, the defense of which

---

[1] M. Rostovtzeff, *Social and Economic History of the Hellenistic World, op. cit.,* vol. II, Ch. VIII, esp. pp. 1301 ff.; and *A History of the Ancient World* (Oxford: Clarendon Press, 1926), Volume I, Chapters 2, 24, 25. See also Rostovtzeff's review of J. Hasebroek in *Zeitschrift für die Gesammte Staatswissenschaft,* 92 (1932).

eventually compelled the Empire to spread into vast continental areas, a development which, especially in its economic aspects, was incompatible with the Empire's slim coastal foundations.[2]

For Rostovtzeff, the problem of ancient capitalism and the decline of the Roman Empire are actually one and the same. To Weber they are essentially distinct and separate. For Weber, the rise of the Empire was the cause of the downfall of ancient capitalism, while, of course, the Empire was called into being, inter alia, in order to remedy the grave ills inherent in ancient capitalism. This capitalism, again, he envisages as being essentially different from modern. It was primarily based on the political exploitation both of conquered peoples and of the peoples of the mother country itself. While peace and rational administration are a powerful assistance to the modern type or capitalism, the ancient type could not survive such a reform of the state. For Weber, the problem stated by Rostovtzeff does not logically arise. Ancient capitalism did not tend in the direction of modern capitalism, consequently it is hardly justified to query what caused it not to develop that way. As to the decline of the Roman Empire, Weber adduces reasons inherent in the geographical and strategic structure of the Empire that would first induce its economy to be based on slave labor and slave wars and eventually force it off its original foundations into a blind alley where neither its economic nor its strategic problems could be satisfactorily resolved.

Actually, the whole discussion suffers from vagueness of terms. The elusive "capitalism" is nothing more than markets. Weber means that economic activities were carried on through the redistributive methods of conquest, seizure, and capture of men and lands offering slaves, serfs, treasure, the exploitation of public utilities, and public services by private individuals. Such public utilities and services are tax collecting, building and contracting, and administration of public domains. All this happens either through redistributive methods utilized by private individuals, with the help of a private bureaucracy of slaves, or through redistributive methods of a central administration with the help of public bureaucracy. In either case, market methods are not in evidence. Economic activity — trade and money uses — is not channeled through organized markets to any considerable extent in the ancient world.

[2] Max Weber, "Die sozialen Gründe des Untergangs der antiken Kultur," *Gesansmelte Aufsätze zur Sozial-and Wirtschaftsgeschichte* (Tübingen: 1924). See also *Wirtschaft und Gesellschaft* (Tübingen: 1922), Chapter 8; and *General Economic History*, esp. pp. 331 ff.

Subject Index

STUDIES IN SOCIAL DISCONTINUITY

Under the Consulting Editorship of:

CHARLES TILLY
University of Michigan

EDWARD SHORTER
University of Toronto

David Levine. Family Formations in an Age of Nascent Capitalism

Dirk Hoerder. Crowd Action in Revolutionary Massachusetts, 1765-1780

Charles P. Cell. Revolution at Work: Mobilization Campaigns in China

Frederic L. Pryor. The Origins of the Economy: A Comparative Study of Distribution in Primitive and Peasant Economies

Harry W. Pearson. The Livelihood of Man by Karl Polanyi

In preparation

Richard Maxwell Brown and Don E. Fehrenbacher (Eds.). Tradition, Conflict, and Modernization: Perspectives on the American Revolution

Juan Guillermo Espinosa and Andrew S. Zimbalist. Economic Democracy: Workers' Participation in Chilean Industry, 1970-1973

Randolph Trumbach. The Rise of the Egalitarian Family: Aristocratic Kinship and Domestic Relations in Eighteenth-Century England

A 7
B 8
C 9
D 0
E 1
F 2
G 3
H 4
I 5
J 6